THE JOURNAL OF ELIZABETH BENNIS

Rosemary Raughter

The Journal of Elizabeth Bennis
1749-1779

the columba press

First published in 2007 by
the columba press
55A Spruce Avenue, Stillorgan Industrial Park,
Blackrock, Co Dublin

Cover by Bill Bolger
Origination by The Columba Press
Printed in Ireland by ColourBooks Ltd, Dublin

ISBN 978 1 85607 566 4

Table of Contents

Acknowledgements

In the course of preparing Elizabeth Bennis's journal for publication, I have received assistance from a number of colleagues, friends and institutions. However, I am particularly indebted to two people, without whose co-operation this book in its present form would have been impossible. Shortly after I began editing the Philadelphia journal, I was contacted by Barbara Parshley. Barbara, a descendant of Elizabeth Bennis, notified me of the existence of the Willamette volume, provided me with a copy and with access to other family papers, and located the portrait of Elizabeth which appears on the jacket of this book. Her interest and empathy have been an inspiration, and her generosity in sharing her discoveries has greatly added to my understanding of her redoubtable ancestor. My second benefactor has been Dudley Levistone Cooney. Since my first contact with Dudley – coincidentally, on the 250th anniversary, almost to the minute, of Elizabeth's first encounter with Methodism – he has been an unfailing source of practical help, expert advice and moral support. He has promoted the publication of Elizabeth's journal since it first came to light, has offered invaluable guidance throughout and, as the leading historian of Irish Methodism, has been able to set Elizabeth Bennis in the context of an emerging and vibrant religious movement.

I am grateful to the Women's History Association of Ireland and to the Wesley Historical Society of Ireland: grants from these two bodies made possible the photocopying of the Philadelphia journal. My thanks to St George's United Methodist Church, Philadelphia and to its administrator, Brian McCloskey, to Willamette University, Oregon and to Ford Schmidt, Head of Reference Services in the Mark O. Hatfield Library there, to the National Library of Ireland and to the Wesley Historical Library, Belfast. Winterthur Museum and Country Estate, Winterthur, Delaware, kindly gave permission for the use of Elizabeth's portrait, and Susan Newton of Winterthur's Photo Services division was a helpful and courteous contact. Donal Moore, Waterford City Archivist, responded generously to my queries about Elizabeth's Waterford connections, while Noreen Ellerker, Archivist of St Mary's Cathedral, Limerick, provided information on some of those mentioned in the journal. Conferences of the Women's History Association of Ireland, the Historians of Women Religious of Britain and Ireland and the Mission History Society have provided valuable opportunities for discussion and debate, and the 2005 Conference of the Wesley Historical Society in York, which focused on the role of women in Methodism, opened up a number of fruitful lines of enquiry.

An extremely informative and enjoyable morning was spent in the company of Liam Irwin, who was my guide on a walking tour of eighteenth-century Limerick and brought alive for me the world which was Elizabeth's. Professor Nial Osborough provided information on the law relating to debtors in eighteenth-century Ireland, while Catherine Cox directed me to sources on the perceived association between madness and Methodism. Ken Rouse, another Bennis descendant, discussed with me his researches into family history. Phil Kilroy generously undertook to read and comment on a first draft of my biographical essay, and our conversations have been a most pleasurable part of this project. She and Margaret MacCurtain have been both friends and mentors, and their expertise and example have enhanced my understanding of early modern and women's history, and of the spirituality which was at the very core of Elizabeth's existence. Caitriona Crowe, Mary Cullen, Rosemary Cullen Owens, Marie Hammond Callaghan, Leeann Lane, Felix Larkin, John Lenton, Maria Luddy, Deirdre McMahon, Éamon Ó Ciardha, Mary O'Dowd, Jane Ohlmeyer, Charles Wallace Jr and Bernadette Whelan have assisted and encouraged me in ways too various to enumerate, and I am extremely grateful to all of them.

I thank my friends and family for their tolerance of Elizabeth's presence in my life and thoughts over a considerable period. Marie Kavanagh and Roisin Long have endured lengthy expositions on the subject of women and religion in general, and Mrs Bennis in particular. My family has been supportive throughout: in particular, Ruth and Olivia have been a delightful distraction from research and writing. Above all, I owe a debt of gratitude to my husband, John, and my daughter, Emma, who have borne the brunt of my obsession, and have given me the support which has made this and all other journeys possible.

Editorial Note

The main consideration in editing the journal has been to ensure its readability. Standard eighteenth-century contractions have been expanded, spelling standardised, punctuation supplied where necessary and Elizabeth's extravagant use of capitals modified. Where possible, individuals referred to in the text have been identified in the footnotes.

The original text of the three volumes of the journal runs to approximately 250,000 words. In abridging this, I have omitted much repetitive material, without, I hope, compromising the journal's essential purpose – that is, to record the author's ongoing journey of faith. I have retained all references to Elizabeth's involvement in Methodism, to her contacts with John Wesley and other individuals within the movement and to her domestic and family life.

Elizabeth Bennis: Memorable Methodist

Dudley Levistone Cooney

One of the exciting events of the last years in the history of Irish Methodism was the discovery of some Bennis papers in Philadelphia. Long forgotten, they had been found at the back of a cupboard in Historic St George's United Methodist Church and included one large notebook of the journal of Elizabeth Bennis, and the *Recollections* of her American grandson, Henry Bennis. Henry's *Recollections*, written in 1868, record the fact that he then had in his possession three books containing Elizabeth's journal. Sometime after that date the three were dispersed, probably divided among surviving grandchildren, so that only one was lodged in Historic St George's.

This was read by Ms Rosemary Raughter when visiting Philadelphia, who reported the find to me, and we began to negotiate the obtaining of a copy of the document for Ireland. It had never been copied. Eventually the Wesley Historical Society in Ireland and the Women's History Association of Ireland shared the cost of having it digitally photographed by the Athenæum of Philadelphia, from which two facsimiles of the pages were made.

Through the internet, Ms Raughter later located more of the journal in the Library of Willamette University at Salem in Oregon. Through the courtesy of Ms Barbara Parshley, a descendant of Elizabeth, a disc of these pages came to Ireland, and the examination of them made it evident that they were the two volumes which preceded the Philadelphia document. It is thus clear that we have the three volumes which were formerly in the possession of Elizabeth's American grandson Henry. The abrupt end of the third would suggest that there may well have been a fourth, and there is at present no means of knowing anything about it. It is unlikely that Elizabeth stopped writing at the date when the third volume ends, but the fourth was unknown to

Henry, and there is a possibility that it was destroyed by Thomas, Elizabeth's eldest child and Henry's father, because of what it contained about the family misfortunes.

The importance of Elizabeth Bennis's journal lies in the fact that it is the only spiritual journal written by an Irishwoman of evangelical faith known to us. Social journals have been published, giving us some insight into the occupations and amusements of Irish women at the time, but this is quite different. It reveals the faith of the writer and the working of her conscience. Who was she?

The first of the Bennis family to come to Ireland was one Gerard Bennis from Avignon. He was a Huguenot who was driven from his native city by persecution and arrived in Ireland in 1602. He then bought land at Corkamore, which remained in the family for nearly two centuries.[1] The first indication of the family appearing in the Limerick area is to be found in the records of the Diocese of Killaloe. In the year 1633 one Thomas Bennis was vicar of Bunratty and Fynnagh, where the rector was Robert Sibthorpe.[2]

We skip over a century after that to the first quarter of the eighteenth century, when one James Bennis was living in Limerick city. He married Elinor, a daughter of Thomas Mitchell of St Thomas's Island in Co Clare. Frances was their daughter, and they also had a son born in 1720. The son was given his mother's maiden name as a Christian name – Mitchell – and this led to a considerable measure of confusion in future years. Unless the name was written very clearly, typesetters and others were apt to suppose that it was Michael. Elinor's sister, Alice, had married Isaac Patten, with whom she had at least two children, Alice and Elizabeth. In 1745 Mitchell Bennis married his cousin Elizabeth Patten.

In his book *Memorable Women of Irish Methodism* Charles H. Crookshank says that Elizabeth was born in 1725, and that her parents were Presbyterian.[3] She seems to have been blessed with religious influence as a child, for at the age of about thirteen or fourteen she read Joseph Alleine's *Alarm to the Unconverted*. This classic of seventeenth century evangelicalism would seem to have been rather heavy reading for so young a girl, but in the eighteenth century children were generally treated as small adults. Crookshank goes on to comment that at times she was deeply concerned about the state of her soul, at times very happy, and at times rather careless. In other words, she experienced the fluctuations of mood which we would now regard as normal for an adolescent. Crookshank states that her father died when she was eighteen – in 1743 – and that she married at the age of twenty. Since their children were baptised or married in the Church of Ireland, it is evident that Mitchell Bennis belonged to that denomination.

His business was variously described in a variety of Deeds relating to property dealings. Up to 1769 he is described as a 'sadler' with a single 'd' as was the fashion at the time. In that year, according to Ferrar's *Limerick Directory*, he was the Master of the Corporation of Sadlers in the city. For some unknown reason he is not listed among the tradesmen elsewhere in the same volume. His business was prospering, and in 1770 he begins to be described as a gentleman. However, the business got into some difficulty, which we must discuss later, and in 1782 he is again a 'saddler', but this time with the double 'd' more familiar to us. In 1784 the description of his occupation is hardware merchant, and the advertisement of an auction of his effects, after his death and the bankruptcy of the business, calls him an ironmonger.

In fact, he probably dealt in saddlery, hardware and ironmongery throughout his career, the description merely indicating where the largest part of his trade lay at any given moment.

Ferrar's *Directory* lists three other tradesmen by the name of Bennis in Limerick. Richard Bennis was an innkeeper in Little Fish Lane, Jacob Bennis was a peruke-maker in Main Street, and John Bennis was a smith in Mungret Street. But Richard Bennis, not John, was Master of the Corporation of Smiths. There were instances in nineteenth century Dublin of sons and even grandsons being admitted to a trade guild, even though they themselves no longer carried on the trade. It may have been the same in Limerick. Jacob Bennis, the peruke or wig maker, was Master of the Corporation of Surgeon Barbers, but here the connection is obvious. A fourth Bennis, Philip, was Master of the Lodge of Freemasons No 271. Since all would have been descended from the Gerard Bennis who came to Ireland in 1602, and the number of generations in 160 years is unlikely to be more than five, their relationship to each other could not have been more distant than the third or fourth degree of cousinship.

It was on St Patrick's Day, Friday 17 March 1749, that Robert Swindells preached the first Methodist sermon in Limerick city. Elizabeth Bennis had her attention drawn to him by the fact that, on his way to the place where he preached, he had passed her house in Bow Lane (now St Augustine Lane near St Mary's Cathedral) followed by a small mob that hissed and hooted at him. He preached on the King's Parade at the Castle gate. In spite of the hostile reception, he announced his intention of preaching again in the evening.[4] Two of those who heard him that evening left significant marks on the history of Irish Methodism. One was the nineteen year old Thomas Walsh, who became a distinguished Methodist preacher, and who died worn out by his labours ten years later. The other was Elizabeth Bennis.

Having heard a good report of Swindells' morning sermon, she made her way to the Parade that evening to hear him preach from 'Come unto me, all ye that labour and are heavy laden, and I will give you rest.'[5] The feelings which the reading of Alleine's *Alarm to the Unconverted* had produced fourteen or fifteen years before were reawakened, but Swindells was careful also to suggest to his hearers a way of positive response. Not only was the sermon of great help to her, but so was some conversation she later had with the preacher. When, in the following month, Swindells returned to Limerick and proposed to form a Methodist society, she was the first to give her name.

In the Limerick Methodist society she was very quickly accorded a position of leadership. Originally a member of Mrs Beauchamp's 'class' of women, on Mrs Beauchamp's death she somewhat uncertainly took over its leadership. Before long she was the leader of two 'classes' of women.[6] That would have involved her in conducting a meeting of each class once a week to encourage and guide them in their religious experience, exhorting the members and giving them pastoral oversight. Dr Samuel Johnson, who did not favour Methodist ways, said of women preachers:

A woman's preaching is like a dog's walking on his hinder

11

legs. It is not done well; but you are surprised to find it done at all.[7]

Wesley did allow a number of women to preach, but public opinion was against it and in the nineteenth century the Irish Methodist Conference prohibited it. Elizabeth Bennis never 'preached', but between preaching and exhorting the line is so fine as to be imperceptible to many people. Of course, her exhortations were confined to her groups of women. However, she did spread her influence more widely, using her social contacts as opportunities of speaking or writing about her faith. Her extensive correspondence was a source of encouragement to the Methodist preachers at a time when their life was always demanding, and sometimes actually dangerous at the hands of mobs, magistrates, and other hostile individuals.

She is best known for her correspondence with John Wesley, the founder of Methodism, which on occasion reveals her as a woman perhaps too inclined to introversion and self-criticism.[8] She also wrote to him about the problems of the Methodist societies in Limerick and Waterford, and on one occasion at least persuaded the great man to change his plans for the stationing of his preachers. From time to time he seeks her assistance in ensuring that the Limerick preachers remain fervent and diligent.[9] It is clear that in both cities she exerted a strong and beneficial influence. One of those in Waterford who owed his religious awakening to her was John Stretton, who shortly afterwards emigrated to Newfoundland, where he had had business interests for some years. He played a significant role in the early development of Methodism there, and at his own expense built the first Methodist chapel in Harbour Grace

It was when she joined the Methodist society at Limerick that she began to write her journal, a practice encouraged by Wesley among his preachers and the members of the Methodist societies. The word 'society' is still the correct term for a local group of Methodists rather than parish or congregation. It derives from the fact that Wesley organised his societies as a movement within the Established Church, not as a withdrawal from it. They were the largest part of the Evangelical Revival in the eighteenth century, a time when the word 'evangelical' did not have the narrow connotation it acquired in the later decades of the twentieth century. It was Wesley's intention that members should continue to attend the worship of the parish church, and in addition to develop their spirituality in the Methodist meetings.

In contrast to other evangelicals, who were strongly Calvinist, Wesley stressed the new religious experience of his converts as the beginning of a process by which God transformed their lives, making them holy. It was, he believed, the chief purpose of the Methodist societies to spread scriptural holiness through the land.[10] The reaction of the Established Church clergy to this in Ireland varied considerably. Some acknowledged that when their parishioners became Methodists the attendance at Sunday services, and particularly at the sacrament, increased in number and regularity. A few became actively supportive and rather more were quietly approving. Others saw the new movement as a threat to their authority or a rebuke to their inactivity. The best of these contented themselves with hostile sermons, but some went to the point of fomenting mobs to physically attack the Methodists or their property. Over the years the two groups gradually grew apart, but it was not until 1816 that the majority of the Irish Methodists recognised themselves as a separate denomination. A minority clung to the tradition of attending the parish churches until the Disestablishment of the Church of Ireland in 1871.

Elizabeth Bennis's journal must be seen in this context. The early Methodists did not keep journals merely to remind themselves of what they did from day to day. Theirs were spiritual journals. They were intended as a means of measuring progress on the way to holiness, and this is the main reason why the Bennis journal is so introverted. At one point Wesley becomes aware, not from the journal but from her letters, that she was carrying the introversion to extremes, and counsels against it. It is a recurring theme in their correspondence.[11] Possibly the most interesting feature, however, is the way in which her writing moves so rapidly and easily from self-examination into prayer. A comparison with the surviving journals of contemporary English Methodist women shows exactly the same characteristic. It is as though these women were conscious of God looking over their shoulder as they wrote, and they turn to speak to him about what they have written. It is an eighteenth-century counterpart of the practice of the presence of God more often associated with the seventeenth-century French Carmelite, Brother Lawrence.

The entries in the journal were not made daily. Sometimes in fact they were, but more often a number of days intervened between each successive entry. Not surprisingly in something designed to measure spiritual progress, there is a strong element of self criticism. She grieves about the hastiness of her temper with her children, and the sharpness with which she rebukes her servants. However justified may have been the remonstration with them, she cannot avoid the sense that she has gone too far, and deplores the hastiness of her judgement. By far the most dominant note, however, is that of thankfulness. Gratitude is expressed for every good experience, in company and in solitude.

Some entries illustrate a point that is often overlooked. The Methodist movement has been seen as a preaching revival; what is often forgotten is that it was also a sacramental revival. Wesley saw the Holy Communion as the chief, and most effective means of grace, and encouraged all of his people to be as regular as possible at the holy table. Since it was to the Established Church that they were expected to go to receive the sacrament, it has to be admitted that in some areas celebration was far less frequent than Wesley would have wished.

One of the other means of grace developed by the Methodists was the band meeting. This was a gathering of a small number of people for mutual examination and support. There were in fact two sorts of band. One, called simply the band meeting, was where everybody began. The other, called the select band, was rather more advanced.

It must be remembered that this is not the devotion of a cloistered woman. Elizabeth Bennis maintains her spiritual experience against the background of a busy domestic scene, with an increasingly wealthy husband, four growing children to look after, and a small number of servants to manage. Her husband's business gets little mention until he begins to speculate in property, and she begins to be aware that he is contracting debts. Then it is not the fear of poverty that disturbs her, but the loss of integrity.

Elizabeth Bennis's interest in Waterford began in 1768, when her daughter Eleanor married Jonas Bull of that city. He too was a man with a confusing name. In some documents it is recorded as Jonas, and in others as Jones. He was a gold and silversmith and jeweller with a business at Barronstrand Street in Waterford.[12] His first wife died in the March of that year.[13] In those days a couple did not generally fall in love and then get married; a marriage was arranged, and they learned to love each other. It was not uncommon, therefore, for the death of a first spouse to be followed fairly quickly by a second marriage. So it was with Jonas Bull; he was married to Eleanor Bennis within eight months. The report in the newspaper describes her as 'the agreeable Miss Bennis'.[14] The marriage took place in St Mary's Cathedral in Limerick on 3 November 1768.

Twelve years later another daughter married a Waterford man. She had been named Elizabeth after her mother. Her bridegroom was the Rev John Finney, only son of the late Daniel Finney and Jane Roberts. After Daniel's death Jane had married again. Unhappily John Finney died four and a half years later, his death being reported in the *Limerick Chronicle* on 14 April 1785.

There was a third connection with Waterford. Crookshank refers to 'the placing her eldest son in business in the same city.'[15] This was Thomas, who was apprenticed in 1773 to a Robert Tegart to learn the saddlery business.[16] His mother's journal proudly and thankfully records the consistently good reports Thomas earns from his master.

When he comes to write about Elizabeth Bennis, Crookshank says little about the religious interest of her husband, Mitchell. He does tell us, however, that under the influence of his wife he came to share her faith. There is reason to believe that this did not happen until quite late in his life, but he must have given at least tacit support to her. Indeed, one can hardly imagine Elizabeth doing so much without his consent. That such consent is likely appears from a deed executed in 1764. In that year he owned or had leased a property jointly with Charles Harrison, a clockmaker, and John McGregor, a tallow chandler. The three of them granted a lease to seven men, in which the building was thus described:

... the large new house the lower part of which was then made use of as a place of Devotion by the people called Methodists next to and adjoining the large building there erected and intended for a City Court House and the cellars under the same then in the occupation of Philip John Roche of the said City Merchant with all and singular the ways parts parcells and appurtenances thereunto belonging or in any wise appertaining situate lying and being on the west side of the lane leading from Creagh Lane to Quay Lane commonly called Cross Lane in the Parish of the Blessed Virgin Mary Middle Ward and City of Limerick ...[17]

Two years previously Wesley had visited Limerick at the end of May 1762, and had told society members there that if they could find a site on which to build a preaching-house, he would return a month later. They did, and on 30 June he fulfilled his promise. In his journal he wrote:

Wed 30: I rode to Limerick. I had promised to come again, if our brethren found a convenient place to build a preaching-house. One now offered, proper in all respects.

July 3, Sat: I met the society, and inquired what each was willing to subscribe. A considerable sum was subscribed immediately.[18]

It was not uncommon when the Methodist societies built new premises for the actual making of the lease to be delayed for more than a year. This one was signed on 12 July 1764, and was to run for eighty-one years from 29 September 1763. The rent of £20 over and above all taxes was to be paid in half yearly moieties at Ladyday and Michaelmas.

The wording of the lease suggests that the Limerick society was already using the place by the July of 1764, but when Wesley next came to the city in 1765 he seems to suggest that the building took longer. He writes:

I rode to Limerick, and found the preaching-house just finished. I liked it the best of any in the kingdom; being neat, yea elegant, yet not gaudy.[19]

It was probably the case that the Methodists went into occupation before the fittings were finished, and these were completed in the early half of 1765. Assuming that the practice here followed that of the Bristol and Dublin houses, the congregation sat on backless benches, women on one side of the building and men on the other.

An interesting feature of the lease is that it gives the names and social class of the seven trustees of the Limerick Methodist society:

Andrew Peterson	whipmaker
Thomas Mason	clothier
Alexander Palmer	shopkeeper
John Hennessy	joiner
John Podner	wheelwright
Herbert Tomkins	baker
	all of Limerick city
Francis Evans	linen weaver
	of Meelick, Co Clare

Mitchell Bennis apparently was a very successful businessman, and like all successful people felt the need of a better house to match his improved status and circumstances. He moved from Bow Lane, but only just around the corner. The move, described in Elizabeth's journal, was made at the end of August in 1767, and in the following year the journal gives the address as facing Bow Lane. The larger house was in Nicholas Street. In 1752 Mitchell had let a shop and lodgings in Bow Lane to Margaret Seymor, a widow.[20] Nearly twenty years later, in 1771 Philip Bennis, a shoemaker inserted an announcement in the newspaper that he had moved from Baal's Bridge to the corner of Bow Lane, where Michael (sic) Bennis had formerly lived.[21] The 'Michael' is presumably a typesetter's misreading of a poor manuscript, but there is no mention of the Widow Seymor. It is safe to assume that Mitchell owned more than one property there. The house in which he and Elizabeth had lived was occupied by another Bennis – Philip the shoemaker – but whether it had lain vacant for three years, or had been briefly occupied by another tenant, or Philip was tardy about advertising his business, there is at present no way of knowing

In the 1770s Mitchell and his wife Elizabeth were experiencing the period of their greatest prosperity. He was Master of his trade guild, the Corporation of Sadlers; he was better housed than in Bow Lane; he had acquired a number of housing properties in the city and in property deeds he was beginning to describe himself as a gentleman. In 1779 he co-operated actively in the formation of a Limerick corps of Irish Volunteers. The Volunteers had been formed in the previous year to defend the country against a French or Spanish invasion while the British Army was busy fighting the American War of Independence. Such an invasion never came, and the Volunteers developed into a convivial debating society which began to demand the freedom of Irish trade from British restrictions, and moved on to demand reform of the Irish House of Commons. Mitchell was named Major in the Corps. George Geary Bennis, a grandson, suggests that he participated in the Dungannon meeting in 1782, but this was confined to Ulster delegates, and it is more likely to have been the National Volunteer Convention in the Rotunda, Dublin which Mitchell attended.[22]

However, Elizabeth was troubled by her wealth. The evidence is in a letter Wesley wrote to her from Bristol in 1773, his opening paragraph asking her to encourage the Limerick preachers in certain aspects of their duty. Then, responding to a comment in her letter of a fortnight earlier which suggested that she found a certain burden in all the comforts with which she was surrounded, he says:

> I thought you had been in more danger of being hurt by worldly abundance than worldly care. But we cannot stand under either one or the other unless we be endued with power from on high, and that continually from hour to hour, or rather from moment to moment.[23]

Elizabeth Bennis replied:

> Though the Lord has blessed my husband's industry far above our expectation and has given me both the necessaries and conveniences of life, yet with these I feel such a measure of trouble and care and such a mixture of uneasiness as makes me often sick of the enjoyment ... There is one particular evil that cleaves to me and causes me much bitterness of soul – that is, a hastiness of spirit with my children, a fire within, that like lightning suddenly flashes and is ready to

burn up all before it.[24]

To this Wesley responded:

> Some time since, when I heard Brother Bennis had got very rich, I was in fear for you lest the world should again find a way into your heart and damp your noblest affections. I am not sorry that you have not that temptation.[25]

Already, however, there was a worm in the apple. It was in 1770 that Elizabeth's journal first recorded her anxieties about Mitchell's business activities, and she asked some friends to endeavour to persuade him against a project, unspecified, which she feared would bring the family to ruin. Their intervention only made him more determined to go on with the project. This was but one instance of many where the reader wishes that she would be a little more frank about her troubles, but she preferred to cloak them in general terms, or pious language. She was unwontedly candid in September when she referred to two debts, the earlier being of £1,500 and the later of £650. In contemporary values the total of these would be over £160,000 or €200,000.

A clue to the nature of the trouble may be found elsewhere. Their American grandson Henry, in his *Recollections* written in 1868, is not always very accurate as to family history, but there is a ring of truth about one assertion. 'Grandfather making a bad speculation in buying some property, and Father endorsing his notes, both closed business together, and paying all off, Father brought over a few thousand dollars …' 'Father' was Mitchell and Elizabeth's elder son, Thomas.

It is probable that we can locate the property concerned. In 1761 Mitchell bought a number of houses at White Cross in Mungret Lane, which even after he had spent £200 on them were still no better than tenements, and certainly the losses on them were never recouped. There were other properties in Main Street and on the Quay, and a house and demesne at Crevill.[26] It is very likely that these deals rather than his regular trade were the source of Elizabeth's anxieties.

The financial troubles were not the only ones to cause her concern; other problems were coming to Elizabeth's notice. She discovered that the marriage of Eleanor was not as happy as she had hoped. Jonas Bull was proving to be a cruel husband, though there is no indication of the form his cruelty took. In 1774 her younger son, Henry, crossed to England to continue his education at Kingswood School, which Wesley had established at Kingswood, near Bath for the education of the sons of preachers. It took a number of other boys as well, and Elizabeth doubtless thought that going there would be a privilege for her youngest child. The Headmaster was then a preacher named Thomas Simpson, a Scotsman who was dominated by his wife. In 1777 Henry Bennis ran away, and arrived back home in Limerick 'a poor, starved, dejected figure' claiming to have been badly treated. In spite of furious letters from the school, Elizabeth believed Henry, and would not permit him to return to Kingswood.

His view is confirmed by the great biblical scholar and polymath Dr Adam Clarke, who spent some time at Kingswood in 1782 while preparing himself for the ministry. The historian of the school quotes Clarke as many years later writing:

The school was the worst I had ever seen, though the teachers were men of adequate learning. It was perfectly disorganised and in several respects each one did what was right in his own eyes. There was no efficient plan pursued; they mocked at religion, and trampled under foot all the laws. The little children of the preachers suffered great indignities; and it is to be feared, their treatment there gave many of them a rooted enmity against religion for life. The parlour boarders had every kind of respect paid to them, and the others were shamefully neglected. Had this gross mismanagement been know to the Methodist preachers, they would have suffered their sons to die in ignorance, rather than have sent them to a place where there was scarcely any care taken either of their bodies or souls.

Clarke himself was a young man of twenty or twenty-two (the date of his birth is disputed) when he stayed at Kingswood, and strictly speaking he was not a pupil there, but because he had just arrived from Ireland he was compelled to rub himself with Jackson's itch ointment.[27]

By 1784, however, there were signs that Mitchell's business difficulties were coming to a head, for in that year he mortgaged a house on the Quay to Michael Arthur for £200.28. Four years later, in 1788, he died, his death being announced in the *Freeman's Journal* on 15 May. For what happened next we have a number a clues, but no satisfactory account.

In his book *Memorable Women*, C. H. Crookshank says:

Yet it seems that they sustained ... large pecuniary losses, referred to by one of her correspondents as 'disappointments and complicated troubles,' which led to their removal to Waterford. In 1788, Mr Bennis died. He had been one of the kindest and most affectionate of husbands ...[29]

In one respect Crookshank is incorrect: Bennis died in Limerick, and not in Waterford. Otherwise he is evidently relying on Elizabeth's published correspondence, which her son edited to ensure that nobody was embarrassed. Crookshank is quite content to confess ignorance of the nature of the loss. He is probably quite accurate in describing Mitchell's qualities as a husband, for Elizabeth's concerns would appear to have been with his property speculations, and the state of his soul.

Further evidence of the rise and fall of the family fortunes are to be found in three advertisements in the *Limerick Chronicle* relating to Thomas Bennis, elder son of Mitchell and Elizabeth.

The first, in the issue of 14 March 1782, announces that Mr Thomas Bennis is conducting a hardware business 'near the Exchange'.

The second, in the issue of 14 May 1789, a year after the death of his father, announces that Thomas is in business as a saddler 'nearly opposite the Main Guard'.

Finally, four months after that, the third, in the issue of 17 September 1789, announces a bankrupt's auction. It states that the assignees of Mitchell Bennis and Thomas Bennis, ironmongers, would sell their interest in three houses in Nicholas Street, and three in Castle Street.

The wording of the first two of these advertisements is of the sort used to announce a new business, a new department or a new product; it is not of the sort used to remind people of a long existing enterprise. It is therefore reasonable to believe that in 1782 Thomas was embarking on something new. He would have completed his apprenticeship quite some time before, possibly as early as 1779 or 1780. In the interval he may have worked in Waterford or in his father's business. The third notice tells us that he was associated with his father in the final collapse of the business in which his father had once prospered.

Finally, there are the letters written to Elizabeth Bennis, and originally published at Philadelphia in 1809 by her son Thomas under the title *Christian Correspondence*. Thomas did a certain amount of editing. For instance, at some points, presumably where the person mentioned was still alive, he substitutes an initial or initials for the name. Correspondents were sufficiently frank in dealing with the spiritual significance of Mrs Bennis's experiences for it to be likely that they were equally frank about their causes, but any reference to the causes of the collapse of the business have been removed. To a Methodist family, whose ethic laid such stress on earning one's living and paying one's way, the publication of commercial incompetence, over-ambitious speculation, or extravagant spending would have been acutely distressing. Patient endurance of the consequences, however, could have been seen as a Christian response to trouble. In the last analysis Thomas was anxious to present his mother's virtues, and not the weaknesses of other members of the family.

In November 1788 John Stretton wrote from Newfoundland to Elizabeth Bennis, partly to report on Methodist work there, but first of all to offer condolences in the losses the family had sustained. In the course of the letter he says:

> But, blessed be God, in the midst of affliction you abound in consolation also. O happy troubles, fortunate trials, blessed disappointments, that have turned all your family to seek the Lord: here is the answer of your many years' prayers, the fruit of your many supplications.

Setting aside the florid references to 'fortunate trials' and such, the twenty-first-century Methodist can still feel that the cloud was silver lined if adversity prompted others of the family to Christian commitment. A year later, in September 1790, John McGregor, the Methodist ex-soldier and Limerick tallow chandler, has this to say:

> You have had the comfort, the great comfort of seeing your

husband die in the Lord – that tender and affectionate partner of forty-three years; for whose eternal happiness you sent up many prayers. You have lived to see these prayers fully answered.

This is the evidence that, consenting as he was, however unenthusiastically, to his wife's Methodist work, it was only at the end of his life that Mitchell Bennis came to share her faith.

However, there is one enigmatic sentence earlier in the same letter from John McGregor:

David was scourged in his Absalom, Eli in his two sons, and my dear Sister Bennis in her E-----.

In the original letter the last name would have been written in full, but unquestionably it was edited out to avoid embarrassment. It would seem to hint at another son, whose name began with E, and whose behaviour brought disaster on the family. Careful search through the Limerick baptismal records, the ffolliot Index, the Hayes Index, and the Registry of Deeds has failed to reveal any such son. One of the more poignant features of Elizabeth's journal is the great thankfulness at becoming 'the living mother of a living child', and the subsequent record of the deaths of so many of them. This powerfully illustrates the dangers which women saw in childbirth, the high rate of infant mortality, and the way in which Elizabeth's faith supported her in successive bereavements.

From all of the written records it can be confidently maintained that only four of her children grew to adult life. McGregor's reference cannot be to either of her sons, Thomas and Henry, but both of her daughters had names beginning with E. The thought that one of them may have been the cause of grief to Elizabeth Bennis seems to be strengthened by a curious sentence in yet another letter, this one from Richard Condy, who had been the first master of the Free School for Boys, which the Dublin Methodists established in 1784 at Whitefriar Street. In the March of 1790 he wrote thus to Mrs Bennis:

The rains descended while you were yet in Limerick; when you were leaving it, the floods came; but now in Waterford the winds blow and beat against that house, and it falls not, for it is founded on a rock!

He is borrowing language from the parable of the houses built on rock and on sand, told in the seventh chapter of Matthew's gospel. It does, however, indicate that there was more than one tragedy in the years 1788 and 1789, but it tells us nothing of the nature of either.

Writing about William Curry, one of their more prominent leaders, the *Primitive Wesleyan Methodist Magazine,* on the occasion of his death, refers to his going at one time to Waterford, where he came under the influence of 'the godly Eleanor Bull'. That is not the sort of language that would have been used in the 1840s if in the 1780s Eleanor had brought disgrace on her family. So we are left with Elizabeth Finney. She had had the tragic experience of losing her husband within four and a half years of marriage. That was in 1785; what was she doing in 1789? How do we make sense of all of these hints and circumlocutions? It would seem reasonable to conclude that what happened to Mitchell Bennis was no different from what had happened to others before him, and would happen to others after. Having prospered with hard work, in his affluence he grew overconfident, and his business suffered accordingly. Given the Methodist insistence on industry and thrift, the bankruptcy would have distressed the family more than most, and could have precipitated his death. The death and the bankruptcy coming together, and indeed before the latter was finalised, would explain his widow's anxiety to leave Limerick.

The obvious refuge was Waterford, but there a further tragedy develops, the exact nature of which we as yet do not know. McGregor's language clearly suggests that whatever E---- did was a cause of shame, for only such would have justified the comparison with Absalom, Hophni and Phineas. It was certainly sufficient to persuade Elizabeth Bennis and her elder son to put the width of the Atlantic between them and their unpleasant memories.

According to her grandson George Geary Bennis, the date was 1789, but the American Henry gives 1792. Because the lists of immigrants were not then preserved in the American records, we have no means of verifying which, but the date of Condy's letter seems to support the latter. Their ultimate destination was

Philadelphia, where Thomas established a business at 166 Spruce Street. His son Henry's *Recollections*, from which we have quoted, tell us that it was a dry goods business. The registers of Union Methodist Church in Philadelphia indicate that he returned to New York in 1805, but Henry makes no mention of this and suggests that the family connection with Philadelphia was unbroken. In 1807 during Thomas Jefferson's presidency, an embargo was imposed on trade with Europe in an effort to persuade the English and French to respect the neutrality of American shipping. It was strongly enforced in 1808, and destroyed Thomas Bennis's business. For some time he kept a school.

The family joined St George's Methodist Church in Philadelphia, but when a division arose in that congregation, they transferred their allegiance to Union Methodist Church. This met in a part of the Academy, a building then owned by the University of Pennsylvania, but originally built in 1740 by George Whitefield for his work in the city. *A Brief History of "Union"*, published in 1914, is somewhat vague about the causes of the division, but quotes the Secretary of the Trustees in 1801, one Samuel Harvey, as writing, 'The difficulty originated in the Board about repairing the church building, and spread into the whole society.' More than fifty people, including four preachers, were involved in the secession.

The Methodists in the United States did not look very favourably on John Wesley, because he quite naturally took the British side in the American War of Independence, though not without some criticism of the folly of the British government. It may therefore be doubted if friendship with him would have done much to commend Elizabeth to the Philadelphians. Oddly, her name does not appear in the class lists of either St George's or Union. The names of her son Tom and his wife Ann do. They were probably married in New York where Elizabeth and Tom stayed for two or three years before moving to Philadelphia. Tom and Ann were never leaders in either place, but their son Mitchell was a class leader in Union for many years.

That Elizabeth did not make more of an impact on the church in Philadelphia was possibly due to her advancing years. At the time of her arrival there she was in her seventieth or seventy-first year; in eighteenth and nineteenth century terms she was an old woman. The United States was only twenty years old, and Philadelphia was still its capital city. It was a bustling, prosperous city giving consequence to the young and the active and the commercially successful.

Elizabeth died in the June of 1802 at the age of seventy-seven. She was in many ways a remarkable woman. In spite of a somewhat introspective and self-critical turn of mind, she could argue a case with sufficient conviction to persuade Wesley to change his plans. She had a considerable capacity for sympathy, from which the Limerick and Waterford Methodists greatly benefited. She seems to have had the rare ability to cope with both affluence and adversity, 'and treat those two impostors just the same'. Her contribution to the growth of Irish Methodism was invaluable.

'Let heart and pen flow together, to the glory of God:'

Faith, family and endeavour in the journal and correspondence of Elizabeth Bennis

On a spring morning in 1749 a young Limerick woman, Elizabeth Bennis, witnessed a disturbance in the street outside her house: at 'about ten o'clock' on the morning of 17 March, she remembered:

> I saw Mr Swindells ... pass by my door with a great mob after him. Upon my enquiring who he was, they told me he was one of the people called Swaddler ... the first time that any of those preachers had come here.[1]

This incident, minor enough in itself, was nonetheless significant as the earliest visit to the city by one of John Wesley's preachers. For Elizabeth, too, it was a momentous day. By nightfall she had embarked on a personal drama which would occupy the remainder of her life, which would transform her view of the world and of her place in it and which would give her a central part in the emergence and consolidation of Irish Methodism.

Initially, however, Elizabeth seems to have taken no more than a mild interest in the visitor or his teachings and, as the wife of a prominent local merchant, was certainly wary of association with the 'rabble' which followed Swindells.[2] But,

> Hearing a great account of the sermon, I resolved to go in the evening ... which I did, and was much affected ... and was determined I would not miss another sermon whilst he stayed in town, which was about three days ... In about a month after another preacher came to town, and finding many here willing to receive the word, they soon established a society, of which I was determined to be one ... I was one of the first that joined. Indeed, I did it in much fear and trembling, being perplexed by various reports ... concerning the wickedness and cunning of these men. But I had set a resolution that I would not believe any report, but would hear and

27

see for myself … I was as a sparrow upon the house top, not one of all my family or relations seeing the necessity of being born again, therefore was obliged to suffer much on this account.[3]

In the years ahead, this resolution and independence of mind, coupled with zeal and energy, enabled Elizabeth to overcome familial disapproval and a persistent sense of her own 'inabilities and unfitness'[4] to assume a central role within Irish Methodism. In doing so, she aligned herself with what was arguably the most dynamic movement within Protestantism since the Reformation. Initially envisaged as an evangelical force within the Church of England, the network of religious societies established by the Wesley brothers and their associates was already attracting both hostile and favourable attention. In England, where John Wesley had begun field preaching in 1739, Methodism was variously accused of 'enthusiasm' and of undermining the Established Church, of being a front for Catholicism and of Jacobite sympathies, of promoting democracy by organising its working-class followers and of preying on the gullibility of the ignorant and suggestible.[5] Wesley, convinced of an 'extraordinary call', countered such charges with the declaration that 'God commands me to do good work unto all men, to instruct the ignorant, reform the wicked, confirm the virtuous' and to do so, moreover, without reference to any of the conventional borders or boundaries. As he famously expressed it, 'I look upon the world as my parish',[6] and in a peripatetic ministry which lasted more than half a century he created a 'connexion' with its own organisational structures and regulations which spanned the British Isles and extended to North America and the West Indies.[7] By 1767, the first year for which a full set of membership statistics is available, Methodism could claim almost 26,000 members. At Wesley's death, in 1791, that number had grown to 72,468,[8] and his 'connexion' was well on the way to separation from the Established Church and to establishment as a denomination in its own right.[9]

In August 1747 John Wesley initiated Methodist missionary effort in Ireland when he made the first of twenty-one visits to the country. Although in his subsequent tours he travelled extensively throughout Ireland, on this occasion he confined himself mainly to Dublin, where he found an existing society of about 280 members and a population, as he considered, ripe for conversion, being 'in general ... of a more teachable spirit than in most parts of England'.[10] Wesley left Ireland on 23 August, but was succeeded a few weeks later by his brother, Charles, who shortly afterwards recorded the conversion of a widow, Mrs M-:

> A true mourner in Zion, till the Lord on Wednesday put the new song in her mouth. She set us all on fire with the warmth of her first love.[11]

As one of Methodism's first Irish converts, Mrs M- typified women's ardent response to the Wesleyan call to repentance, spiritual rebirth and evangelism. Methodism has been described as 'a woman's faith'.[12] It has been stated that women were in a majority, 'perhaps a substantial majority', in early Methodism, and this contention is supported by surviving membership figures for societies in both Britain and America, while in relation to the Irish movement, Crookshank's nineteenth-century *History* and his biographical studies of its 'memorable women', as well as more recent researches, have confirmed the vital part played by women during the first decades of its existence.[13]

Contemporaries themselves quickly became aware of the female response to Wesleyan revivalism, and reacted to it according to their own bias: while opponents accused itinerant preachers of taking advantage of the suggestibility of 'silly women',[14] sympathisers viewed it as a validation and matter for rejoicing. Thus, when Agnes Smyth, herself a recent convert to Methodism, reported in about 1776 on the progress of the movement in her own area of county Down, she specifically noted the welcome given to it by members of her own sex. 'I can give you but a small notion', she wrote,

> How the Word of the Lord runs and is glorified. All around, young and old, flock to the standard of Jesus, as the doves to their windows. I think the class in this town [Strangford] consists of thirty-six, almost all alive to God, and particularly some girls, who seem resolved to take the kingdom of heaven by violence.[15]

Elizabeth Bennis, then, was just one of a considerable body of women, convinced and galvanised by Wesleyan teaching, for whom conversion marked the opening of a new life chapter, and who saw it as their obligation and privilege to bring others to a knowledge of the truth of which they believed themselves to be in possession. What makes her exceptional is, firstly, the dynamism and effectiveness with which she promoted Methodism over an extended period and, secondly, the extensive evidence of her activism which has survived. This record consists, firstly, of her correspondence, edited by her son, Thomas, and published shortly after her death in Philadelphia in 1802.[16] Spanning the more than forty years from her conversion in 1749 to the eve of her departure from Ireland, as an elderly widow, in the early 1790s, these letters chronicle her own spiritual progress, the development and difficulties of the societies with which she was associated, and the condition of the Irish movement in general at this period, and have long been recognised as a valuable source of information on the early years of Irish Methodism. Elizabeth's best-known correspondent was John Wesley himself, but the collection also includes exchanges with some of his most notable – and colourful – lieutenants, among them the Irish-speaking preacher and Hebrew scholar, Thomas Walsh, Samuel Bradburn, known as 'the Demosthenes of Methodism' because of his oratory and wit, John Dillon, soldier turned itinerant preacher, and John Stretton – probably, like Walsh and Bennis herself, a native of Limerick – who emigrated from Waterford during the 1770s to set up as a merchant in Newfoundland, and went on to become one of the first Methodist missionaries in that remote and inhospitable region.

The second source on Elizabeth's life and activism is her journal. These volumes, which she took with her when she left Ireland for North America, passed from the hands of her descendants into the care of two separate repositories. The first set of journals, covering the years 1749 to 1764, was presented to Willamette University, Oregon in 1947 by a woman whose grandfather, a Methodist minister, had reportedly received it from Elizabeth's daughter.[17] The second, running from 1764 to 1779, was lodged in the archives of St George's United Methodist Church in Philadelphia, the oldest continuously-used

Methodist church in the United States and the congregation which Thomas and Ann Bennis, Elizabeth's son and daughter-in-law, joined when they arrived in Philadelphia in 1795.[18] These volumes, then, form a unique record, not least in their duration: spiritual diaries of this type, while not uncommon for this period, tend to cover a relatively short period of the writer's life. Elizabeth's journal, however, is an almost unbroken record of her existence from the moment of her conversion in 1749 through the thirty years to 1779.[19] It has exceptional value, moreover, in the wealth of information which it contains on the emergence of Irish Methodism, on the part played by Elizabeth – and, by extension, women generally – in that process, and on the day to day existence of a woman of the 'middle station' in mid-eighteenth-century provincial Ireland. Here we see Elizabeth Bennis not only as organiser and advocate of Methodism, but also as wife, mother, employer, household manager, business partner and friend. We witness her transformation from an un-sure young woman, isolated within her own family, to an as-sertive and matriarchal middle age. We share her trepidation at the prospect of giving birth, her hopes and fears for her children, her exasperated affection for her husband, and her sorrow at the loss of friends. We hear of domestic crises, of ill health and acci-dents, of servant problems and family feuds, of prosperity and retrenchment, of jaunts into the countryside and of journeys fur-ther afield, of social events and chance encounters, of books read and letters written and received, of fire, storm, epidemic and even earthquake. For Elizabeth herself, however, these were 'temporal' matters, and as such of infinitely less significance than the spiritual truths with which she was principally con-cerned. Despite their intrinsic interest and their value to the his-torical record, these details are incidental to the main business of the journal, which is essentially to record the progress of a soul – its growth in holiness, its developing relationship with God, and its journey, sometimes triumphant, more often hesitant, towards the ultimate ecstasy of salvation.

The keeping of a diary of conscience, or spiritual 'account book', was a puritan tradition, which was followed by Wesley himself and by many of his fellow evangelicals, among them some of Irish Methodism's most 'memorable women'.[20]

Elizabeth's journal is typical of this genre, in being intended not as a factual record of daily events but as a means of self-examination, as an aid to greater holiness and as an expression of the centrality of faith in the author's existence. Indeed, the first volume of the journal opens on the day, 23 June 1749, just a few weeks after she first heard Swindells preach, when she became convinced of her 'justification', or forgiveness of sins by faith through God's grace, thereby taking the essential first step, according to Wesleyan theology, towards 'sanctification' or 'perfect love' and, finally, salvation and everlasting life. As she described it, the discovery, though preceded by much prayer and heart-searching, was an instantaneous one:

> When conversing with Mr Haughton [the preacher] about the state of my soul, the light broke in upon me in a moment, and banished all the shades of darkness, all doubts were done away, and I could now believe in and lay hold of Christ as mine, and appropriate his mercy to my own soul ... My soul did cleave to him, and I was happy in his love, adoring and admiring this loving Redeemer. My soul in an holy ecstasy cried continually, 'My Lord and my God.'[21]

At the time of this conversion experience, Elizabeth was twenty-four years old, intelligent, active and devout, but troubled, as she had been since adolescence, by a sense of spiritual emptiness for which she had been unable to find relief in any of the 'visible congregations' to which she had access. This dissatisfaction may have originated in a childhood which she herself depicts as isolated, and which may also have lacked affection. Elizabeth never mentions her mother, and her father, Isaac Patten, merits just two appearances in the journal, neither of which suggests more than a correctly dutiful relationship.[22] Materially, the Pattens' circumstances seem to have been comfortable, and the household was evidently a literate and at least conventionally pious one. Certainly, Elizabeth must have received a decent education: she wrote an excellent hand, expressed herself fluently in writing,[23] and showed familiarity not only with the Bible and the hymns of Isaac Watts and John and Charles Wesley, but also with a range of devotional works, from Joseph Alleine's *An alarm to the unconverted*, which impressed her in adolescence, and the 'little Kempis' with which she solaced herself on a visit to the countryside, to the *Letters* of Mrs Lefevre, the posthumous memoir of yet another of Methodism's prominent women members.[24]

Isaac Patten died about 1743. Two years later Elizabeth married her cousin, Mitchell Bennis, and the couple set up home in Bow Lane, where Mitchell also carried on a saddlery and hardware business. A daughter, Eleanor, was born in 1748, two sons, Thomas and Henry, followed some years later, and a second daughter, also named Elizabeth, was born in 1765. In all, however, Elizabeth endured at least ten pregnancies, and suffered the loss of at least six of her children between 1750 and 1760, recording their deaths with pious resignation in her journal.[25]

Bow Lane, within sight and sound of Limerick's port and in the shadow of St Mary's Cathedral, was part of the medieval Englishtown, where most of the main administrative and public buildings and much of the city's trade were still concentrated. The spectacular development which characterised Limerick during the second half of the eighteenth century had not yet begun, and this was still a small and densely-populated city.[26] Mitchell's business activities would have made him a well-known figure in the area, and news of his wife's involvement in this novel and controversial movement seems to have given rise to gossip outside, and discord inside the family. In the months following her conversion, Elizabeth makes a number of references to 'trials', emanating 'from every quarter, from without and within, from friends and relatives, from strangers and acquaintances', and to being 'sneered and pointed at, and everywhere evil spoken of.'[27] What caused her most distress, both now and later, however, was the lack of support within her own family. Journal entries at this time record 'invectives against both preachers and doctrine' from 'a near relation' – probably her mother-in-law[28] – and her grief of spirit for her unconverted 'relations in the flesh', with particular mention of her sister and, most of all, her husband.[29] While the initial furore seems to have died down within a few months, the lack of a 'Christian friend' within her own household continued to be a grief to her. Two years later, she complained of

Not having any person in my family with whom I may converse, being looked upon by all as a poor, deluded creature, led away by the cunning craftiness of men, so that I have often experienced that truth, 'How can one be warm alone?'[30]

Despite these discouragements, however, and the onerous demands made by Methodism on its adherents, Elizabeth remained staunch in her pursuit of her spiritual goal. To be an 'altogether' rather than an 'almost' Christian, one must be unwaveringly vigilant, constantly on the alert, incessantly 'on the full stretch' after holiness – and even so, one might fall short of the goal, might even lose the 'blessings' already attained, as Elizabeth at one stage felt herself to have done. 'About the beginning of the year 1757', as she recalled, 'I was particularly stirred up to seek a total deliverance from all my inbred corruptions.' However, her zeal was disparaged by some 'friends in the society … till they had partly reasoned, and partly laughed me out of my earnestness.'

> Thus was the fervour of my desires abated, and some of my friends rejoiced at my deliverance … The Lord did often bear his testimony with my spirit that I was his child, but the reasonings of my enemy, the strength of my corruptions and the unbelief of my heart were ever questioning the work of God … till a kind of stupefaction had overspread my whole soul … The visits of his love grew shorter and seldomer, till at length I was left wholly destitute … Even then, the Lord did not suffer me to fall into outward sin or to quit the means of grace but, having lost the presence of God and being truly sensible of my loss, I became completely miserable.[31]

She was not to recover the certainty of her justification for a number of years, 'till the 22nd day of May 1763, being Whitsunday.'

> My heart had been much drawn out in earnest and sweet expectation for some days before that God would this day visit my soul … Under these expectations I attended the Lord's table and, being on my knees before I went to the Communion, I laid my case before the Lord, deploring my wretchedness by reason of the continual revoltings of my heart from him … when these words of our Lord were spoke to my heart: 'Believest thou that I am able to do this?' My

soul eagerly answered, 'Lord, I believe thou art able' … Thus I went to the table of the Lord … And in receiving the memorials my soul was enabled to lay hold on Christ for my complete salvation from all sin. But my busy enemy still pursued me and would fain have plucked it from me … Thus I continued grappling hard, sometimes up and sometimes down, till the 2nd day of June when, being at private prayer, I besought the Lord to deliver my soul from the power of my adversary … Whilst I thus prayed, the Lord did remove all my burden and enlarge my heart and admitted me to a closer communion with him than ever I had before …[32]

Although Elizabeth's 'grief of heart' and 'painful uncertainty' were not banished – and were, indeed, to trouble her throughout the period covered by the journal – this experience was a turning point, marking her unequivocal sense of God's pardon for past sin: as she recognised with hindsight, 'the witness of my justification was continually clear since the 22nd of May 1763, without one abiding doubt concerning it.'[33] However, it was not until two years later that she could finally believe herself to have received the gift of sanctification. It was, in fact, a friend's request for an account of her experience which prompted the breakthrough for which she had prayed for so long. The necessity of drawing up such a testimony, she wrote,

Made me cry the more earnestly to God for the witness of his spirit that I might see the more clearly the present state of my soul … till on the 30th day of September last 1765, as I was reading a letter which I had received from a Christian friend, the light again broke in upon my heart and I was enabled to believe. This was accompanied with much peace and comfort and joy, and afterward it was (at prayer) made indisputably clear to me that God had taken possession of my heart and that it was now wholly given up to him … Though Satan does endeavour to distress my mind by bringing in many doubts and questionings upon me … I trust my God will enable me to k[eep] my hold and to stand by faith till all doubt shall be done [away].[34]

Even sanctification, however, was not an end in itself, but a dynamic process: in Wesley's words, 'when we are born again, then our sanctification, our inward and outward holiness begins, and thenceforward we are gradually to "grow up in Him who is our Head".'[35] Hence the need for unremitting self-examination, the dispiriting emphasis on personal weakness, inadequacy and 'unfitness' and the, surely disproportionate, remorse for the most trivial of offences which characterise journals of this type, including, it must be admitted, that of Elizabeth herself. Thus, among innumerable examples, we find the following entry, in which she berates herself for impatience with one of her children:

O, what a wretch am I! I corrected my child in anger, thereby grieving the spirit of God ... The sense of his forbearing mercy is as a dagger to my heart, and with the weight of my sins sinks me almost below all hope, insomuch that this night I was afraid to eat lest God should cause the food to stop in my throat and send my soul quick into hell. I cast myself before the Lord, but could only sigh, but dare not pray.[36]

Or this, written many years later:

Yesterday parted with my dear friend, which affected me very much, even so as to affect my body ... My heart is foolishly tender in friendship but O, how hard and stubborn in the ways of God! During my illness yesterday I suffered much pain, but found my soul brought near to God in deep humiliation, sweet submission and thankful resignation. I admired the tenderness of the chastisement, and found the small visitation very precious ... Blessed forever be my God![37]

But the relentless self-denigration and the image of a jealous and vindictive deity were the shadow side of a faith which also evoked rhapsodic expressions of devotion to, and reliance on a boundlessly loving and generous God, as in the following passage:

My soul is happy, more than happy, in my God. The discoveries of his grace are sweet, and his love is better than life. I do find my heart, my whole heart, my every all, given up to him, and my whole soul rejoices in being his. O my Jesus, my Lord, my love, my delight, thou art my portion and my treasure, and in thee I have all, all that my heart can desire or my soul enjoy. I am satisfied, my desires are full, I ask no more. Thou art my God and O, how blessed, how extensive my inheritance, how transporting the view, to what delightful heights does it raise my enraptured soul, which turns to cast one look more on earth, and see if aught can there be found worth even one single desire! But O, how little, how insignificant does all appear! How poor, how trifling, how unworthy the toil, all the pomp and little pageantries of the wisest and grandest men that ever lived! How far inferior to my inheritance! My Jesus is my portion, my God is my all, and how little is Solomon in all his glory! O my God, I ask not wisdom or power or riches or honour or portion or inheritance here below ... My soul has tasted of thy love, and cannot relish, cannot be satisfied with anything below thyself. O my Jesus, my dear, dear, bleeding Lord, my desires are lost in thee. I only want to drink deeper into that ocean of love, to be still more closely united to thee, to be even lost to myself that I may be found in thee. This, thou knowest, is my one, my only wish, and thou has promised that the desire of their heart shall be given to those that fear thee. Amen, O my Lord, it is enough, for thou art a faithful God.[38]

Given the strength of Elizabeth's character and the intensity of her commitment to Methodism, it is not surprising that from an early stage she took a leading part in the organisation of the society in her native city. The first indication of this came in 1753, when her 'dear friend' and the leader of her band, Mrs Beauchamp, died, and Elizabeth, 'fearing the band ... might scatter' without direction, took the initiative of assuming the leadership. She did so initially as an interim measure, declaring her resolve 'to give it up when the preacher came to town'.[39] In the event, however, she retained the position, and by the beginning of the following year had become reconciled to her new role, while continuing to protest her inadequacy to the task. As she recorded following one meeting with her band:

Blessed be my God, it is not now a cross to me, but a blessed privilege, and I find my heart more closely knit to those who meet with me. Their trouble, I find, is my grief, and their joy my rejoicing, but O, the weight is heavy on me when I con-

sider my insufficiency! O my God, keep me humble, and
make me faithful, simple and obedient; instruct my ignorance, subdue my pride and strengthen my weakness, that I
may be able to give an account of this my stewardship with
joy.[40]

David Hempton, in noting the centrality of the class system to
Methodism, has suggested that 'for the ... faithful, especially
women, it was at the very centre of their allegiance'.[41] Certainly
Elizabeth's journal testifies repeatedly to the comfort and support she found in association with 'the people of God'. In the
only account which she gives of her life prior to her conversion,
she tells of her longing for

A Christian friend ... to whom I might declare all that passed
in my heart, and would have prized such a one as my greatest treasure below, but did not then ever expect to meet with
such.[42]

The band and class system within Methodism opened the door
to just such relationships, and for Elizabeth this was clearly an
enormously positive aspect of her new allegiance. As she noted,
recalling one particularly dark period, 'it is ... remarkable that I
seldom had either power or comfort in prayer during this state
of deadness, except in my band and class, and seldom without it
there',[43] and this claim is borne out by the frequency of entries
recording 'much comfort in my band' and 'blessed abundantly
in my band and class'. 'At such times', she wrote,

The Lord does enlighten my understanding ... and by the experience and understanding of others my judgement is informed, my questions answered, my difficulties solved and
my way made more clear, and in this exercise my soul is always happy.[44]

The intense fellowship forged in such gatherings inevitably extended beyond them, and intimate friendships were formed on
the basis of shared spiritual commitment. Elizabeth notes many
such instances, often briefly, with expressions of gratitude for
the blessings of 'Christian conversation' or 'Christian communion', but in a few cases in greater detail. Mrs Beauchamp was
one such friend. So, too, were Mrs Moore, 'a dear, a faithful, ten-

der, loving Christian friend and companion', Mrs Hosey, 'a dear, faithful, bosom friend, a sympathising companion', and Mrs Mason, 'a dear, faithful, praying, sympathising friend'.[45]

Rather more well-documented, because her exchanges with them were included in her published correspondence, are Elizabeth's long-term friendships with a number of the preachers. In such exchanges, as might be expected, Elizabeth frequently appears in the role of pupil to her correspondent's teacher, as when, writing to Thomas Walsh, she confessed that

> My heart is evil, very evil; my will perverse, my affection cold and dead, and my faith ... weak ... In this state may I expect or look for an entire, instantaneous change of heart? ... I shall anxiously expect your answer.[46]

Almost as often, however, it is she who takes the part of counsellor or confessor. Thus, responding to Samuel Bradburn's request for her opinion on a number of theological points, she protests her 'ignorance', but goes on to respond briskly to his queries and implicitly rebukes his over-scrupulousness and intolerance of others' views.[47] In a similar instance, recorded in the journal, she takes to task a preacher whom she accuses of having 'grieved the minds of many' by his denial of Wesley's doctrine of 'Christian perfection'.[48] However, as the journal – but not the edited correspondence – reveals, ardent and uninhibited friendships of this kind between men and women were liable to misinterpretation, and on at least one occasion Elizabeth found herself the subject of gossip and allegations of misconduct because of what does, indeed, appear to have been an exceptionally close relationship with one such 'Christian friend'.[49]

However, by far the best-documented friendship, the one which probably meant most to Elizabeth and which certainly ensured her place in the Methodist pantheon of 'memorable women', is that with the founder of Methodism himself. As an active and respected member of the Limerick society during the early 1750s, Elizabeth would certainly have had direct contact with John Wesley during his visits to the city at that time. The first mention of him in the journal is in 1752, when she records that 'my soul was comforted' at his arrival, and at 'the consideration of my not being amongst the number of those who have drawn back since he was last here.'[50] She certainly had an interview with him during his 1756 visit, since his own journal includes an account, received from 'one of our sisters', of Ann Beauchamp's death. The informant was undoubtedly Elizabeth, since the version quoted by Wesley is virtually identical to that included in her journal of three years previously,[51] and she herself evidently found this encounter and his preaching beneficial, noting during his stay that 'I find the coming of his messenger to this place has been a blessing to my soul.'[52] Wesley, for his part, was clearly impressed by Elizabeth's zeal and ability, and on his next visit to Limerick, in 1758, increased her responsibilities within the society by appointing her leader of a class. Elizabeth's first reaction was one of dismay:

> My mind much disturbed and weighed down with trouble on finding that Mr Wesley had appointed me leader over a class. My great inability and utter unfitness for this work makes it indeed a grievous burden ... I already find the charge of my band a heavy load on me, from which I would rejoice to be delivered, but the additional charge of a class makes my burden almost insupportable ... O Lord, have pity on me, and ... make me fit for it, I beseech thee ...[53]

Within a week, however, she had resigned herself to this new burden:

> My mind more calm and satisfied about the class, having determined that, as I have given up and made a solemn surrender of myself to God, so I will lay out all the feeble strength I have in his service and leave it to him to supply the rest ...[54]

Elizabeth certainly heard Wesley preach when he visited Limerick in 1762. This was a time of 'grievous and sore trials' for her: following on the death of a child in 1760 she gave up writing in her journal 'by reason of the deadness and distress of my soul'. Galvanized by Wesley's preaching, however, she recovered her 'power to wrestle and strive, till in a few weeks the Lord did heal my backsliding ... and filled my soul with abundance of peace and love', and gave her encouragement to 'seek the Lord, both for justification and sanctification'.[55] This episode seems to have been the impetus for the beginning of her correspondence with him: her first surviving letter to him, dated 2

August 1763, describes the 'dead formal state' into which she had fallen, the impact of his words on her and her recovery, so that now her heart 'was filled with love both to God and his people.' Nevertheless, she seeks Wesley's advice on her state, confessing to continued 'heaviness of soul' and 'deadness in prayer', and questioning whether she has, indeed, attained sanctification.

This letter, together with Wesley's almost immediate response, set the pattern for the first years of their correspondence: on Elizabeth's part, admission of her spiritual 'wanderings' and 'deficiencies'; on his, admonition and reassurance.[56] As her commitment to Methodism intensified, however, so did her militancy on its behalf: in her journal for 1769 she recorded her admiration for Richard Bourke, currently stationed preacher in Limerick, finding the 'opportunities ... of Christian conversation' with him 'exceedingly profitable and precious' and telling Wesley that his time with the society had 'proved a blessing to my soul, and to his also.' Bourke's one-year appointment was due to end in July 1769, but 'if you could spare him to us this year', she continued, 'I think it would be productive of good.'[57] Her successful request – the earliest example, according to Crookshank, 'of the voice of the people being heard in connection with a preaching appointment'[58] – marked the opening of the period of her greatest influence within Irish Methodism. While she continued to seek, and Wesley to offer spiritual guidance, their correspondence was increasingly concerned with organisational and disciplinary matters. So, in 1770, Wesley solicited her views on the condition of the society in Limerick:

> How does the work of God go on at Limerick? Does the select society meet constantly, and do you speak freely to each other? What preachers are with you now? Do you converse frankly and openly with them, without any shyness or reserve?[59]

In return, Elizabeth supplied Wesley with accounts of the progress of Methodism in the locality: numbers, she told him, were increasing, and the members 'meet openly and freely, but mostly in a complaining state'.[60] Some of these complaints may have related to finance: in the following year she reported that

> We are rather cast down by having another married preacher, with a young family, sent to us, before we could recruit our finances; we now owe a heavy debt, and the weekly collections are not equal to the weekly expenses. The bulk of the society are poor, so that the weight lies on a few.

This was not a new problem. The wife of another preacher, she noted,

> Finding the affairs of the society much embarrassed, refused the usual subsistence, and supported herself and children by working at her trade while here, though she had a young child at the breast.

And she suggested, as a possible solution to this difficulty, 'could we not have a single preacher at least every other year, till we are out of debt?'[61]

Whether or not this advice was adopted, Wesley's letters certainly reveal a growing reliance on Elizabeth – a reliance which took little account of conventional assumptions about the role of women within institutional religion. The weak organisational structures of early Methodism, together with the exigencies of a missionary movement, allowed female members to assume a more active and interventionist role than would have been possible for them in any of the mainstream Christian denominations, and Wesley himself was quick to acknowledge the valuable part which women could play in dispersing the Word.[62] So, as he had sanctioned the activities of female preachers such as Alice Cambridge by urging that conscience 'will not permit you to be silent when God commands you to speak',[63] so he now overruled Elizabeth's plea of inadequacy by insisting that she use her talents on behalf of Methodism: as he urged early in their correspondence,

> If God has given you this light, he did not intend that you should hide it under a bushel ... It is good to tell the loving kindness of the Lord.[64]

In response, Elizabeth redoubled her exertions for the movement, nurturing and encouraging members, making contact with potential recruits, and urging on the preachers. Many years later, one of them, John McGregor, recalled her inspirational role at this time:

> Whose parlour can I now turn into a study? What woman
> will throw away her work, to meditate and converse with me
> on the things of God, and consult together to make our call-
> ing and election sure? Who will now counsel, instruct, or ad-
> monish me; and spur me on, to run steadily my course to the
> end? Who will thrust me into the jail, among the malefactors;
> to the barracks, amongst the soldiers; to sick beds, and dis-
> tressed souls? This have you often done, when I was able, but
> not always willing. Have I not rightly styled you my golden
> spur, that often brought (as it were) blood, but never left a
> festered wound behind?[65]

At least partly because of such zealous supervision, Methodism
established a firm foothold in Limerick over the following years,
and in 1772 Elizabeth was able to report that

> The select band in particular, and the society in general, are
> much stirred up ... the class-meetings are lively; the prayer
> meetings through the city are revived; the public congreg-
> ation is in general much larger, and a deeper seriousness and
> spirit of enquiry observable.[66]

Elizabeth's growing assurance in exerting her authority and the
status which she enjoyed as Wesley's agent and confidante are
evident in the part which she played in the settlement of a dispute which threatened the unity of the Limerick society. In May
1772 she expressed concern about 'a particular affair'[67] and in a
letter to Wesley written at this time she reported animosity between the appointed preachers and a former stationed preacher,
James Deaves, who was evidently stirring up controversy within
the membership. As she explained, following a visit from the
preachers,

> Both Mr Goodwin and Mr Hudson were grievously dis-
> tressed after they came here, and seem determined to go
> home rather than continue in connection with him. As they
> opened their minds only to me, I advised them to write to
> you and to give you an exact account of the matter. Indeed, if
> Mr Hudson had not done so, I must have taken upon me to
> do it, for their trials affected me very much.[68]

As Elizabeth had feared, Deaves's stay left the Limerick society 'in a decline and in confusion'.[69] Significantly, it was to her rather than to one of his preachers that Wesley turned in this crisis, commissioning her to re-establish discipline by inviting Captain Webb, a noted preacher, to the city. He also urged her to exert her own influence among the membership: 'Speak a little to as many as you can. Go among them, to their houses. Speak in love and discord will vanish.'[70] A month later, Elizabeth was able to report that the society was

> ... once more re-adjusted. We all seem to be in love and in earnest. Captain Webb's visit has proved a blessing: our house was not large enough for the congregations ... If we could now have a succession of strange preachers from the neighbouring circuits, perhaps poor Limerick might once more raise its head.[71]

This suggestion was approved by Wesley as 'preferable to any which I have heard proposed',[72] and the strategy was apparently successful. In August 1773 Elizabeth reported that numbers were once more on the increase and that unity had been restored:

> Some are added, some converted, and are renewed in love. The young men are again stirred up and I hope more in earnest than they have been for many months. The select band meet well and our meetings are comfortable because preacher and people are all of one mind, and whilst this is the case the band will thrive.[73]

By this time Elizabeth had expanded her sphere of activity beyond Limerick. In 1768 her daughter, Eleanor, married and moved to Waterford, and in late 1769 Elizabeth visited her there for the first time. On the evening of her arrival, following a 'very fatiguing' journey of three days, she attended a meeting of the local society and made contact with the current preacher, Hugh Saunderson, with whom she established an immediate rapport.[74] During her two-month stay in Waterford, she immersed herself in the life of the congregation there: on 5 December, for instance, she 'had a comfortable hour of conversation and prayer with two women of the society', and in the evening 'put myself in the way to speak to a person who I feared had substituted his opinions in the room of Christ'.[75] A week later she spoke with 'a Christian woman' who, in the course of conversation, recovered 'the witness of her sanctification'[76] and a few days later spent the evening 'with a lady who ... had sent to request my company on Mr Wesley's character of me'.[77]

Having acquainted herself with the society in Waterford, Elizabeth kept Wesley informed of its progress. Six months after this first visit, she noted that 'the people here go on at a poor rate', and passed on their request for a stationed preacher.[78] In response to Wesley's irritation at the confused accounts which he had received,[79] she explained the situation in more detail:

> The people are poor, and think the expense of a preacher's horse and family more than they can well bear; but if it were possible to let them have a single preacher resident in the city, or even to exchange monthly with the circuit preacher ... I think it might answer a good end ... I feel much for the city society – a handful of poor simple souls, that need every support and encouragement.[80]

Evidently feeling that she might have taken too much upon herself, she ended with an apology and an excuse: 'Dear Sir, I hope you will not think me too presumptuous in dictating, but I find my soul knit to these poor sheep.'

In fact, Wesley approved her intervention on this as on other occasions.[81] 'Be not idle,' he told her, 'neither give way to voluntary humility. You were not sent to Waterford for nothing, but to "strengthen the things that remain".'[82] On her frequent visits to the city over the next few years, Elizabeth devoted much of her time to Methodist business,[83] and by August 1772 was able to report that

> This society is increased in number and grace since I was last here; I do meet a band and a class; we all speak with freedom. I love the people, and I believe they love me. There are three preachers on the circuit, and all have work enough.[84]

Although Limerick and Waterford were Elizabeth's primary fields of activity,[85] she also played a part, through her twenty-year correspondence with John Stretton, in the Methodist mission to North America. Stretton, who left Ireland in 1770 to set up as a merchant in Newfoundland, found on his arrival that the movement there consisted of no more than 'a few professors scattered through the different bays',[86] and went on to make a major contribution to establishing Methodism on a firm foundation in the region. In 1776-77 he travelled on foot to introduce Methodism to the Trinity Bay area, in 1778 he journeyed to Conception Bay and St John's, and in 1788 he built the first Methodist chapel at Harbour Grace.[87] According to Crookshank, Elizabeth had been instrumental in Stretton's conversion.[88] She may have been in Waterford to bid him farewell when he sailed for Newfoundland, and his first letter to her, dated October 1770, assumes some knowledge of the state of Methodism there, and reveals a dependence on her interest, judgement and support which intensified in the course of their long correspondence.[89] In annual letters, he confided news of his personal affairs and details of his difficulties in business, admitted to his sense of isolation in the harsh and often hostile environment in which he found himself, and kept her informed of the progress of Methodism in the region.[90] In 1776, confessing that 'there has not one soul been awakened by my speaking that I know of, now near a year', he requested her 'to consult Mr Wesley about my doubts of being called to speak in public, and let me have his opinion through you.'[91] A decade later, he asked her to support his appeal to Wesley to send a preacher to 'this benighted corner', adding, 'I know by experience that sweet persuasion dwells upon your tongue.'[92] In the only two of her letters to Stretton to have survived, Elizabeth set aside her own diffidence – 'I forget that I am writing to a *preacher* from whom I should *receive* instruction' – to steel him against depression and disappointment, and to encourage him to persevere in his task of evangelisation:

> What hinders your deliverance? The Lord has given you to feel your need, to feel the bitterness of sin, and has also discovered to you the remedy; then what hinders? Will you plead your poverty? Why, this is the very thing which should drive you forward; the good physician came not to heal the whole, but to cure the sick of every malady.[93]

And in her next letter she offered some advice based on her own experience – and in the process encapsulated the purpose and content of her own journal, as an aid to meditation and self-examination, as a record of a spiritual journey and as a forum for prayer and praise:

> I wish you to pursue the diary that I formerly recommended;
> you will find it a great help. I have often experienced much
> comfort in reading over past experience, and have often felt
> happiness and support in comparing past with present ...
> Only do not write much at a time, that it be not burthensome,
> except when your heart is particularly enlarged; then it may
> not be well to cramp yourself, but let your heart and pen flow
> together, to the glory of God.[94]

Yet, while Elizabeth's surviving correspondence, as well as her
journals, are primarily concerned with the state of her conscience, her relations with God and her efforts on behalf of
Methodism, it should be remembered that she was also immersed throughout this period in the more mundane 'hurries
and bustles of life',[95] which included the care of her family and
household and involvement in the family business. While
Elizabeth lamented these duties as a distraction from the pursuit
of holiness[96] and fretted that her husband and children were
'idols', usurping the love which should have been God's alone,
family relationships inevitably remained an enormously important element in her life.[97] Indeed, the story of the Bennis marriage as it emerges over this extended period forms one of the
most intriguing subplots within the journal. While the union of
Elizabeth with her cousin Mitchell may have had its prudential
aspects, this was clearly much more than a marriage of convenience. 'My husband's affections are very dear to me – nothing on
this earth so dear', Elizabeth wrote in the immediate aftermath
of her conversion.[98] After twenty-five years of marriage she
recorded 'the tenderest affection for my husband, and have no
doubt of his love for me',[99] and her account of reconciliation following a quarrel conveys an impression of conjugal intimacy
and mutual attachment:

> When I did speak, I found my heart filled with the tenderest
> affection towards him, so that I could use no other language
> than the language of love, and found by this means the Lord
> had wrought also on his, so that peace was made in both
> breasts, and our hearts more closely united together.[100]

However, this is far from being the only marital dispute recorded, and the relationship was evidently a stormy as well as a loving one. While the journal is tantalisingly discreet on domestic and business affairs, and the numerous 'trials' of which Elizabeth complains are rarely specified in any detail, it is clear that she and Mitchell were frequently in disagreement. The first, and on-going, cause of conflict was Mitchell's rejection of Methodism. Throughout the period covered by the journal he seems to have veered from tolerance of his wife's all-consuming involvement to an understandable irritation at being the object of a sustained campaign of prayer, from mockery of religion to outbursts of hostility and short-lived attempts to assert his authority. Certainly, in the months following her conversion, Elizabeth had to contend with opposition from various quarters, and her journey to the country shortly afterwards, at her husband's re-quest, may have been an attempt to dissuade her from this new involvement.[101] An already difficult situation was exacerbated by the interference of her mother-in-law, who reportedly sought 'to sow discord' between Mitchell and herself.[102] In the short term these efforts were evidently successful: nothing else but love of God, Elizabeth lamented, 'could enable me to bear the in-difference of a husband so dear to me', and shortly afterwards she recorded that 'the loss of my husband's affections weighs me down to the dust'.[103] The estrangement proved temporary, however, and the affection and sympathy between them sur-vived this, as it was to survive other difficulties. In the coming years Elizabeth was, for the most part, able to practice her faith without restriction,[104] while Mitchell, notwithstanding her con-stant prayers on his behalf, remained resolutely secular in his views and behaviour. On just one occasion during the course of thirty years did Elizabeth have cause to believe – very briefly – that her most fervent wish had been realised:

> My heart was much drawn out in prayer and hope and desire for my dear husband on seeing him come to the preaching, so contrary to my expectation … But alas, how disappointed, how cast down when I found he had sat under a sermon that would if possible have waked the dead without being the least moved![105]

Even misfortune, it seemed, could not turn Mitchell to religion:

thus, as Elizabeth recorded with some irritation after he had been injured in falling from his horse:

> The Lord is graciously restoring my husband to health, for which I feel my heart thankful, but cannot help being distressed at seeing that this visitation has brought forth no fruit to his soul's advantage ... Lord, it is thou alone that canst break the rocky heart and manifest thyself to the stubborn soul ...[106]

The second principal cause of friction between Elizabeth and her husband related to his behaviour as it impacted on the family finances, and on his management of the Bennis business enterprises. A series of infuriatingly cryptic entries describes one particularly protracted crisis, in which, it would seem, Mitchell's conduct, and perhaps involvement in undesirable company, threatened disaster. The first inkling of a problem surfaces in autumn 1751, with Elizabeth recording 'outward trials ... and grief for my husband's soul and body', going on, mysteriously, to imply that she was in some way 'the cause of his extravagancy and so of his ruin, both spiritual and temporal.'[107] A succession of entries over the next few months suggest concern for her husband and discord between them, together with continuing 'worldly trouble'.[108] Matters apparently worsened in the early weeks of 1752, and in March Elizabeth confided:

> My heart ... sorely grieved and heavily burdened for my husband, now visibly in a decay. I spoke to him in much love, beseeching him to alter his manner of living, even for his body's sake, but my tenderness was only returned with all the harshness and unkindness he was capable of.[109]

A few days later she described herself as

> ... grievously afflicted for my husband. I see both his body and soul going to destruction, but dare not reprove him ... If I do, with even tears of love, his blasphemies frighten my very soul, and condemn me for speaking.[110]

Two months later, Elizabeth, already worried about the 'bad success' of what was apparently an ongoing lawsuit, hinted at some wrongdoing on Mitchell's part, confessing to

> ... trouble of mind concerning my husband. I find not anger against him for bringing trouble on his family, but am griev-

ed for his soul.[111]

Over the following weeks, 'trials' and 'troubles' intensified, and Elizabeth expressed 'fears for the time to come, and doubts how my present worldly trouble should end, from the bad prospect that appears at present to human eyes'.[112] Her apprehensions, however, were clearly not realised on this occasion: the summary of her affairs which opens the 1753 journal included a rather cautious estimate of her temporal affairs, as 'better than intended by my enemies, and at present, though wearing a dull aspect, yet I can trust my God with them.'[113]

However, this was far from being the end of the family's financial difficulties, references to which punctuate Elizabeth's record. In 1756 Mitchell was actually confined to his own house for a month on account of a debt of £600 – described by Elizabeth as 'unjust' but which in any case he was compelled to pay – and the journal lists numerous fluctuations in his business and some considerable losses, which Elizabeth clearly felt were at least partly due to his own 'extravagance and bad management'.[114] 'His manner of conducting his affairs is a continual cause of distress to me,' she wrote in exasperation during another crisis, and she worried that his 'indolence and obstinacy' might endanger the welfare of their children and 'be the ruin of him and his family'.[115] So, as she confided to her journal,

> I ... am often constrained to act a part which does not belong to me, and which is indeed very grievous to me ... I desire to be as helpful to my family as I can, both from inclination and duty, and if I would be so I must come out of my place, and take many things upon me which otherwise would be neglected.[116]

On this occasion, indeed, Elizabeth did manage to dissuade her husband from a course of action 'which I see will be the ruin of him and his family',[117] and was sufficiently informed about and involved in the running of the Bennis enterprises – which included dealings in property as well as a saddlery and hardware business – to deputise for Mitchell when he travelled to Dublin on business. 'Being obliged to act for my husband in his absence', as she noted on one such occasion,

> I found my spirit a little hurried in being surrounded with

clamorous and unreasonable men but, blessed be my God, he did preserve me from anger, and gave me a watchful spirit.[118]

If Elizabeth was able to assist and exert a certain influence in business affairs, at home she enjoyed a much more untrammelled authority. Elizabeth was a loving, if sometimes irritable and over-anxious mother, concerned about her children's happiness and material prospects as well as their prospects of salvation. This was, however, undoubtedly her primary consideration, which she professed even in the most difficult circumstances as, for instance, that described in the following extract:

My child very ill, and have found this day many distressing fears and much anguish of spirit even so as to affect my body very much. This ... put me on searching my heart, and on the strictest scrutiny do not find one desire contrary to the will of my God. Indeed, I find the most tender and distressing feelings of nature such as cannot be described, yet cannot ask the child's life ... Nor do I desire to receive my child back into life on any other condition than that the Lord would make him his own child, that he might live to his glory ...[119]

Resignation on this heroic scale may, however, have been more easily attainable in theory than in practice: in November 1756 Elizabeth, following the death of one of their children, recorded the impact of the tragedy on both herself and her husband:

I went with a heavy heart to the table of the Lord, seeking a blessing, but I fear I did not seek it aright, for I came away heavy and dead ... The loss of my child is ever before me, and the grief of my husband strikes to my very soul, whose heart was pent up in this child, being his first, and only son.[120]

Nevertheless, when Mitchell insisted on the inoculation of one of the children a few years later, Elizabeth confessed to

... many conflicts and much uneasiness of mind ... My mind is not clear concerning it, whilst out of obedience to my husband I submit to it. But it is not my act. O my God, take the disposal of me and mine ... as seemeth good in thy sight.[121]

Elizabeth's 'uneasiness' may have been prompted by a fear that medical intervention of this kind would be a flouting of God's will, but she may also have been alarmed by the dangers involved. Certainly, while one of the children recovered, another was dead 'with the same disorder' within a few weeks.[122] Although Elizabeth 'found power to thank my God for the life of my one child and for the death of the other', subsequent entries make clear her wretchedness as she struggled to reconcile herself to the loss and to recover her trust in her God.[123] Such was her unhappiness, indeed, that it seems to have precipitated some sort of collapse and an inability or unwillingness to record her feelings: in June 1760, just two months after her child's death, the journal fell silent and, except for a single entry in 1762, was not resumed until May 1763.[124]

While Mitchell, on the evidence available, was far from being a distant or unloving parent, it does appear to have been Elizabeth who took the initiative in matters relating to the future of their children. In September 1768, for instance, she confided to her journal her concern about 'a particular temporal affair' which, as ever, she went on to lay before the Lord, 'desiring to be directed by him, and beseeching his gracious interposition either to forward or frustrate it as he shall see best.'[125] This was evidently the proposed marriage of her elder daughter, Eleanor, to Jonas Bull of Waterford, which, judging by Elizabeth's reference to 'fears, distress, anxious cares' and 'paternal conflicts' was a cause for some concern and perhaps controversy within the family.[126] The point, however, is that it appears to have been Elizabeth rather than her husband who favoured and forwarded the marriage, which took place on 3 November 1768. A few weeks later, Elizabeth returned to the subject:

> I know it was lawful for me to marry my daughter, and was enabled through the whole of this affair to submit it entirely to the Lord, beseeching him if it was not agreeable to his will that he would frustrate it, and in all my transactions about it have endeavoured to act agreeable to my profession and with an eye to the will and glory of God, yet could not help a constant agitation of mind ... so that I found need continually to cry to the Lord for help and succour.[127]

In fact, the hint of foreboding in this entry was well-founded: some years later Bull was revealed to be 'an unkind husband', and the discovery of her daughter's 'sufferings' caused Elizabeth great distress.[128] Nevertheless, the affair does reveal her as having at least an equal voice on an issue of considerable importance within the family. It was she, too, who on one of her visits to Waterford made arrangements to have Thomas apprenticed there, once more deriving her authority from her assurance of divine approval:

> I have for some time past been asking of the Lord to direct me in the choice of a business and place for my eldest son and requesting that he would point out my way in this matter and, from every circumstance which has attended it, I think the Lord has interposed and directed me. A place offered here: I brought him with me, and have put him to business here.[129]

Elizabeth was also able to make her feelings known when she and her husband clashed over the education of their second son, Henry, Mitchell wishing to have him 'bred a scholar', Elizabeth opposing this,

> … as I have an entire dislike to the law from the dishonesty of its professors, and would not have him thrust into the church except he was called of God to it.[130]

Ultimately, in what was probably a compromise with his wife's strong views in the matter, Mitchell proposed sending Henry to Kingswood, the Methodist boarding school near Bristol, and Elizabeth concurred, 'much depressed' by the separation from her son, but convinced that 'the thing is of God'.[131] Nevertheless, when Henry unexpectedly arrived home, 'a poor, starved, dejected figure', having run away from school 'on account of the ill-treatment he received' there, Elizabeth set aside her 'disappointment' and her customary devotion to all things Wesleyan to engage in a vigorous correspondence with 'the masters' at Kingswood in Henry's defence.[132]

As her children grew to adulthood, Elizabeth maintained her involvement in their lives. When Eleanor married and left Limerick, she missed her sorely, corresponded with her regularly, and looked forward to her periodic visits to her in Waterford.[133] Having established her elder son, Thomas, in an apprenticeship, she anxiously followed his progress and fretted about his health and conduct. Some years later, when Thomas returned to Limerick to set up in trade on his own account, she found herself 'busily employed day and night, assisting my son in his business', thanking God 'for having it to do, and for a measure of health to enable me to do it.'[134]

However, her children's resistance to her evangelising efforts continued to be a cause of sadness. Thus, when Eleanor was reported seriously ill in 1776, she 'found it hard to give her up, and harder still to resign her in an unconverted state', going on to lament 'the unchanged state of my husband and children'.[135] Ironically, perhaps, the only one of her children to give her momentary cause for hope during this period was Henry, whose 'deeply serious' demeanour following his precipitate departure from Kingswood,

> ... made me willing to forget all the trouble and sorrow I have had ... and gives me hopes that the Lord will visit the souls of my other children also.[136]

Henry's conversion, however, was not lasting: within a few months, Elizabeth was saddened to observe him 'growing slack in the service of God' and to discover some weeks later that he 'had quit the society'.[137]

Although Elizabeth could not know it at this time, ultimately all of her children were to find and follow their own routes to holiness: Eleanor as 'the godly' Mrs Bull of Primitive Wesleyan record, Thomas as a member of St George's Methodist Church in Philadelphia and as the editor of his mother's correspondence with John Wesley, Henry as a member of the Society of Friends.[138] Of the four surviving children, the one who has left least trace is the youngest, Elizabeth. As the only one of the siblings living at home for much of the 1770s, she was clearly the focus of her mother's anxious care and attention, as well as of her occasional irritation and impatience. We know that she married young.[139] We know, too, that she was widowed five years later at the age of twenty, but nothing of her life after that time.[140] However, John Stretton, writing in 1790, specifically congratulated Elizabeth on seeing 'all your children with their faces Zion-ward',[141] suggesting that her younger daughter, too, had come to share some measure of her mother's faith.[142] Even Mitchell, it seems, succumbed at last to his wife's zeal on his behalf. After so many years of intransigence, he did, reportedly, at last, 'die in the Lord', leaving Elizabeth, at what must have been a time of great sorrow, with the realisation of the 'strong and confident hopes' of his conversion which she had nursed for so long.[143]

However, Mitchell's death in 1788 seems also to have precipitated a collapse of the Bennis family fortunes. At least until 1779, the year in which Elizabeth's surviving journal ends, these appear to have been prosperous enough to weather the periodic crises which beset them. In 1773 Elizabeth rejoiced that 'the Lord has blessed my husband's industry, far above our expectation'.[144] Five years later she thanked God for supplying her with 'food to eat, and raiment to put on, a comfortable habitation, fire and warm' and 'servants to attend', and in the same year she and Mitchell helped Thomas set up shop in Limerick.[145] The journal, however, does also record a number of losses as well as some misgiving on Elizabeth's part about the conduct of business, and John Stretton, writing to Elizabeth in the year of Mitchell's death, referred to 'troubles', 'trials' and 'disappointments'.[146] By 1790 Elizabeth had left Limerick to live in Waterford[147] and, although no longer the power which she had once been within Irish Methodism, was still in contact with a number of preachers and with the local society.[148] However, her temporal difficulties, whatever they were, had clearly not abated, since one of her correspondents, writing to her in that year, made reference to the 'furnace of affliction' in which she was still suffering.[149] It was presumably these unspecified troubles which decided Elizabeth, then nearing seventy, to leave Ireland. Sometime after 1791 she and Thomas emigrated, settling eventually in Philadelphia, where she died in June 1802.[150]

Elizabeth's conversion, described by Crookshank as one of the 'blessed triumphs of redeeming grace' which marked Irish Methodism's advance,[151] gave her a forum in which she could employ her considerable talents to their fullest extent, and the record shows her to have been among the movement's most active and effective agents during these years of missionary endeavour. In the forty years between her first encounter with 'one of Mr Wesley's preachers' and her apparent retirement in about 1790, she recruited new members, rallied doubters and rebuked backsliders, fostered and encouraged young and struggling societies, acted as confidante and advisor to the preachers, as a

conduit for contacts between John Wesley and his Irish followers and as Stretton's mentor and mainstay in his mission to
Newfoundland. In the short term, Methodism made demands of
its female members and permitted a degree of autonomy, or
'boldness' as Elizabeth termed it,[152] which transgressed conventional assumptions about women's role in religion and society.[153] Indeed, in her activism and assumption of moral authority,
as well as in her own evangelising efforts and the support which
she gave to missionary projects overseas, Elizabeth anticipates
the evangelical women of the following century, whose efforts
on behalf of religion and morality had profound implications for
the female role in wider society.[154]

Yet, while the journal supplements the record of Elizabeth's
activism, its greatest value lies in the insight which it provides
into the private individual and the window which it opens onto
the day-to-day existence and inner consciousness of an 'ordinary' eighteenth-century Irishwoman. Here Elizabeth Bennis is
revealed in her weaknesses, her vulnerabilities and her strengths,
her internal conflicts, her agonies of soul and victories over the
self. This is a personality which is not always easy, likeable or
even explicable in today's terms, but is nonetheless admirable in
its rectitude, in its unswerving sense of purpose and in its un-
flinching honesty. Above all, however, this is the narrative of a
spiritual journey, and an exploration and celebration of a personal faith. If at times the creed which Elizabeth espoused appears narrow, harsh and prescriptive, it was also one which
challenged assumptions, authorised action, and offered guidance in prosperity and consolation in adversity. Most crucially,
this was a dynamic faith, a never-ending struggle against temptation and human weakness, a hazardous progress towards the
pilgrim's ultimate, joyous goal of salvation and eternal life. So
the journey which Elizabeth describes is one of change and of
discovery, from the exultation of the journal's opening entry[155]
to an awareness of the costs involved in conversion,[156] from self-
condemnation for 'a slothful, careless spirit'[157] to gratitude for
the blessings which 'crowd so thick upon my mind',[158] from the
weariness and discouragement of the final entry[159] to the serenity
and confidence of what were to be her last recorded words, written more than a decade after the journal's end, on the eve of her

departure from Ireland and at a time of evident difficulty and unhappiness.[160] With this declaration of a system of belief informed by a lifetime's experience and tested both by time and misfortune, Elizabeth disappears from the historical record, leaving untold the story of those eventful final years, with their challenges of emigration, resettlement and old age in an alien environment. What remains is the profession of a faith which, in its optimism, its goodwill towards 'all mankind' and its sure trust in a loving God, was surely capable of sustaining her through the time which remained, as it had done since that day so long ago, 'when the Lord sent his messenger into the streets and lanes of this city and inclined my heart to receive his truths.'[161] 'My faith', she wrote,

> Is not founded on St Peter, or St Paul; on Pope or Bishop of any sect; but on the Lord Jesus Christ alone, who died for my sins, and rose again for my justification, and now intercedes for me at the right hand of God … I came to him by faith, under a deep sense of my necessities, and he does not send me empty away; but enables me to rejoice humbly before him. My heart is open in prayer to him for all mankind. I believe through his merit and death, all might be saved … I would not dare to confine the mercy of God to any particular body of people; nor would I strain any text in the book of God to exclude any from his mercy. I believe the whole Christian church of every denomination is the visible church of Christ; but that those only who worship him in spirit and in truth, who love him and keep his commandments, are members of his invisible church, and are accepted of him. This is, and has been for many years, my faith; in which I find myself happy in life, and willing to die; and by the grace of my God resolve not to change.
>
> Wishing you all happiness in time and eternity, I am, dear Sir, your friend and humble servant,
> Eliza Bennis.[162]

The Journal
1749-79

I wish you to pursue the diary that I formerly recommended; you will find it a great help. I have often experienced much comfort in reading over past experience, and have often felt happiness and support in comparing past with present ... Only do not write much at a time, that it be not burthensome, except when your heart is particularly enlarged; then it may not be well to cramp yourself, but let your heart and pen flow together, to the glory of God.

Elizabeth Bennis to John Stretton, 24 July 1777,
XCVII, Christian correspondence

The reading over your papers ... makes me love you abundantly better than I did before: I have now a more intimate knowledge of you; I enter more into your spirit, your tempers, and hopes, and fears, and desires; all which tend to endear you to me.

John Wesley to Elizabeth Bennis, 24 July 1769,
XII, Christian correspondence

1749

23 June

The Lord spoke peace to my soul in this manner: I had been deeply convinced of sin and unbelief and earnestly groaning for redemption for about three months before[1] ... I saw that by my original stain I had forfeited the divine favour, that my nature was corrupt throughout ... and could produce only corrupt fruit ... I saw that he that believeth not must be damned, and he that believeth only could be saved, and that I was a condemned unbeliever. In this manner, I was bearing my burden and groaning for redemption till the 21st of June, whilst John Haughton[2] preached, and offered Christ freely to all, I found my burden in a moment taken off and felt my soul at liberty, but was still afraid to lay hold of Christ as mine ... In this manner I was till the 23rd when, conversing with Mr Haughton about the state of my soul, the light broke in upon me in a moment and banished all the shades of darkness, all doubts were done away and I could now believe in and lay hold of Christ as mine, and appropriate his mercy to my own soul. The spirit of God bore witness with my spirit that I was his child and I could say, 'He hath loved me and given himself for me'[3] ... O, thou who hast been the Alpha, be thou the Omega, and carry on thy work in my soul till thou shalt finish it to thy glory. Uphold with thy right hand the feeblest soul that looks to thee, and suffer not my enemy to take advantage of my weakness or ignorance, but lead and instruct thy helpless child till thou hast fully perfected thy good work in my soul ...

30 June

My spirit is grieved for my relations according to the flesh ... O, that thou wouldst now open their eyes and snatch them from the brink of the precipice! O, that thou wouldst even give me my husband and sister,[4] how happy should I be! ...

5 July

Received an invitation to the country, and my husband will have me go. But alas, what shall I do there, where I shall hear the truths of God every day evil spoken of, and be myself separate from the Gospel and from my dear, dear brethren in Christ? …

9 July
Parted my spiritual friends after we had sung and prayed together. My dear father in Christ[5] prayed earnestly for me that the Lord would keep me steadfast and immovable …

10 July
The Lord has brought me here safe, glory be to his name. I first retired to give … thanks for his gracious protection and care over me, and to beseech him for the family of this house and for myself and for my dear absent brethren, and the Lord gave me sweet comfort …

13 July
Wrote to my brother and father in Christ,[6] and found much comfort in opening the state of my soul to him and requesting his prayers for me. There is nothing wanting here to make life agreeable but the preaching of the word and the conversation of my dear Christian friends. Everything around me bears the image of their great creator: the green fields and bleating flocks, the trees in full blossom, with the spacious firmament and all its shining host fill my soul with an holy awe and reverence to the great Contriver, and there is something so solemn in the silence of this place and such matter for contemplation in the works of creation all around as sometimes carries me beyond myself.

19 July
Gave way to light and trifling conversation,[7] which brought condemnation on my conscience …

26 July
It has been my usual custom since I came here to retire at preaching hours when the children of God are met together to seek his face, and I find it is a time when the Lord delights to bless me …

30 July
Received some letters from my dear friends in Limerick … O,

may we have cause continually to rejoice over each other, and may none of us ever draw back to perdition!

3 August

Glory be to my God, who has again brought me home in safety to my own house and to the house and people of God. I find my enemy has been at work in my absence and has stirred up even them of my own household against me ... When I came to town I was sent for by a near relation whom I had left burdened with sin, but found her now perfectly at ease in a carnal security and breathing out invectives against both preachers and doctrine, and (fearing lest I should be carried away with their delusions) took much pains to persuade and caution me of their deceit, as she called it. But in all this, I found my soul sweetly stayed upon God ... making no other answer than this, that when I found all she said to be truth I would immediately quit all communion with them, but till then was fully determined to take nothing on hearsay, but to hear for myself, and by this answer was delivered for that time from any further importunity ... I have counted the cost and ... think I am willing to give up all, even the friendship of my nearest and dearest relatives ...[8]

13 August

I find myself now touched in the most sensible part. The enemy is endeavouring to sow discord between my husband and me, and has employed his mother in this work ... My husband's affections are very dear to me – nothing on this earth so dear – which makes my trial grievous to be borne, but through the strength of my God I can and will bear it ...

17 August

Still more trials ... from without and within, from friends and relatives, from strangers and acquaintances ...

20 August

... I am again to go to the country. O Lord, do thou sustain me and keep me still unspotted from the world ...

1 September
Received some letters from my dear friends in Limerick ...
Blessed be God for the success of the gospel everywhere, and for
the prospect of deliverance to our brethren in Cork![9]

25 September
Blessed be my God who has brought me in safety to my own
house again ...

30 September
... My heart rejoiced in coming again under the word ... but I
find I am come home to suffer much. I find the fire was only
spreading still further, though unperceived by me, and now I
find this trial begin to lie heavy on me. To be thus wounded in
the house of my friend, I find is grievous to be borne, but the
Lord ... will sustain me ...

10 October
I do find my trials bear hard upon me ... If an enemy had done
this it would not grieve me, but a friend whose natural affection
should have prevented this, and one who has so often proved
my kindness – the consideration of this, joined to her present
success, make these things often very grievous to me ...

18 October
O, what it is to have Jesus in a time of trial! ... Nothing else but
this could enable me to bear the indifference of a husband so
dear to me ... Indeed, Satan could not have touched me in a
more tender part, but in the Lord have I put my trust ...

3 November
I find my enemy is determined to leave me nothing of all that
was precious to me: my character was to me, as the wise man
says, as precious ointment[10] but I see I must ... give it up,
though, indeed, I find a grief at my heart to be sneered and
pointed at, and everywhere evil spoken of ...

10 November
... The loss of my husband's affections weighs me down to the

dust, and if I would dare to choose I would say, let me lose all this world can give, but leave me happy in this. But … O Lord, let me lay my hand on my mouth and say, thy will be done.

20 November
… The evils I suffer come constantly to my mind, and I find my heart ready to start against her who is the cause. O Lord, set my mind at rest, and pardon her …

1750

8 February

… I foolishly thought I should have nothing to do after I had believed but to bask continually in the sunbeams of God's love … I little thought of the mystery of iniquity that has since been revealed to me, which lay unseen in my heart …

23 February

Being in great heaviness and under many doubts concerning my state, I went to bed … and dreamed … I was surrounded with a glorious light, which darted its rays to every corner of the room, and with this my soul was filled with comfort and joy … The ecstasy of my spirit awoke me, but the comfort and joy of my soul remained …

20 April

The mercies of my God are new to me every moment. He has … made me a witness of his power to save by making me the living mother of a living child[1] … In my pain I found my soul trusting in the Lord, and after my delivery … my soul drawn out to God in love and gratitude. During my confinement had many comfortable visits from my God but, being left but seldom alone, my comforts were often interrupted. Was often weighed down with grief for the trouble of our brethren in Cork, and when the assizes came suffered much in my mind.[2] Being in much trouble one day on this account, and Satan suggesting many things to my mind, a friend came into my room (who also laboured under many fears of the same kind, as the preachers had that day left Limerick to stand their trial in Cork) and desired I would open the Bible in their behalf and see if God would give us any comfort … It opened on the 41st of Isaiah, beginning at the tenth verse. This revived my hopes and O, how has the Lord accomplished it, doing even according to his promise in that very text! …[3]

23 June

My heart has this day been much drawn out in thankfulness and gratitude to God … I look upon it as the birthday of my soul[4] and O, what hast thou done for me! …

2 July
Rose to the morning preaching[5] and met my band in the evening and my class at night[6] ... This has been a comfortable day indeed to my soul ...

26 July
Went to visit an aged sister whom the Lord has lately brought into his family. She has been long seeking, but has at length found him ... My soul was much comforted with her and humbled to the dust under a sense of my own vileness, yet filled with joy and thankfulness to God on her behalf ...

18 October
... Had much comfort at the morning preaching ... The Lord has blessed me this day with his presence amongst his people, and has made it a Sabbath indeed to my soul ...[7]

6 November
Met my band, and had many evil surmisings concerning a person in the band, which I freely and in love told her of, and she satisfied me in, which eased my mind and cured all my suspicions ...[8]

30 November
Was much revived at the morning preaching from a sense of Christ's love to his church ... But alas, this vanished like the morning dew, and I grew cold and lifeless again, till the bands met in the evening, when a general blessing revived the whole ...

20 December
Cold and comfortless all day, till somewhat refreshed by the evening preaching. But alas, this was but a glance, vanishing as soon as it appeared ...

1751

10 January

My soul dead and clouded – a few days ago happy in the love of God ... but alas, where am I now? Grovelling here below, shorn of my strength, wretched and miserable ...

3 February

Went to the sacrament weary of myself and heavy-laden with my own corruptions ... but blessed be my Rock who, after a dark and cloudy night, brings a bright and joyous morning ...

22 February

Much backwardness in duties and deadness of soul till evening when, reading Young's *Night Thoughts*, my soul soared aloft with his, beyond all created beings[1] ... O Lord, as the hart panteth after the water brooks, so does my soul after thee[2] ...

6 March

A blessed evening in meditating and hearing the word. The Lord gave utterance to his messengers, and comforted my soul in his own house ... O my Lord, how sweet are these thy words to poor, unworthy dust and ashes:

> What mighty wonders love performs
> To put a comeliness on worms.[3]

14 March

My soul has been cold and dead all this day, the just reward of my neglect for suffering worldly business to take place of my morning devotion ...

1 April

... My heart was much drawn out in prayer and hope and desire for my dear husband on seeing him come to the preaching so contrary to my expectation ... but alas, how disappointed, how cast down when I found he had sat under a sermon that would if possible have waked the dead without being the least moved! ... O, hear my prayers for him who prays not for himself, and let the same free grace that found out me reach him also ...

8 May

Went to see a sick friend and found him just launching into eternity, with his soul stayed upon God and longing to be dissolved and to be with Christ. O Lord Jesus, leave him not in this his last struggle, but finish thy great work in him ... ...

9 May

... Glory be to thee, O God, who hath fought the battle and got the victory for this our brother ... He cried with a holy rapture, 'Come, Lord Jesus, come quickly and take me home', and so took his flight to the realms of bliss. Thus, O my Jesus, thus may I end my tedious pilgrimage and share in the glorious conquest ...

12 May

Alas, how dry and barren have I been under all the means of grace[4] this day. My mind has been fixed upon things below, and not on things above ...

23 May

The Lord sweetly refreshed my soul in prayer this day. Was particularly drawn out in behalf of my husband, and had strong assurances that the Lord would have mercy on him ... O Lord my God, hear my weak petitions on his behalf, and let there be joy in heaven at the conversion of this sinner. Unbelief would lay many bars in the way, but ... the same almighty power that caused water to flow out of the rock in the wilderness can bring tears of repentance from this rocky heart also ...

29 May

Heard a comfortable sermon ... but was overcome with sickness, drowsiness and heaviness of soul ... Whilst everyone around me received comfort, I alone remained comfortless, though the Lord's ambassador declared the whole counsel of God, both in the sermon and at the meeting of the bands ...

30 May

No life all day till I met with the society[5] at night, when the Lord softened my heart ...

3 June

Was so busied preparing for a ride that I am to take with some others tomorrow that I neglected prayer this morning without even thinking of it ... Met my band in the evening, but had no comfort ... Met with some harshness from my mother-in-law (who continues to persecute) which had like to disturb me, but when I found my danger I retired to prayer ...

4 June

... Having a fear upon me lest I should offend, I requested earnestly of my God that he would bless me this day ... and keep me from joining in sinful or unprofitable discourse, and my God heard my prayer and kept my mind stayed upon him. And at our coming home, my horse and the horse of another in company tired, which occasioned us to join and wait for each other and, falling into conversation about the things of God, my soul was so rapt up that I scarce knew where I was. ... Everything around me – fields, flocks and herds, the running brooks and blossomed trees, the clear, serene sky with its various figured clouds – all heightened the devout rapture of my soul and spoke their great Creator's praise.

5 June

Weak and weary, both in body and mind ... Was even tired of the sermon and the exhortation to the bands ...

6 June

Cold and dead indeed, even so as to fall asleep at prayer ... Found anger rise in my breast, which increased my guilt. The most terrible thunder at night that I ever heard, every clap of which revives a sense of my guilt ...[6]

11 June

... Heard a comfortable sermon on these words, 'How shall we escape if we neglect so great salvation?' and, whilst the man of God preached, the spirit of God applied the word to my heart ...[7]

12 June

Had many temptations concerning the person who preached

this evening which robbed me of my comfort, but my soul was sweetly watered afterwards in the bands under the exhortation of another ... The Lord restored me my husband safe out of danger, and found my heart full of thankfulness to my God. O Lord, have pity on his soul and deliver that also, for ... it is in imminent danger and he sees it not ...

13 June
Heard a good sermon from the Reverend Mr Whitefield[8] ...

14 June
... I have found comfort in everything this day: at morning preaching, at prayer and in writing to a Christian friend ... Heard Mr Whitefield preach in the evening ... My soul was exalted even to heaven and so overcome with the glorious prospect which was then presented to my view that ... for a moment I knew not whether I was in the body or not, so far was I drawn above all earthly things. O, this was the happiest moment of my life! ...

15 June
Heard Mr Whitefield preach in the morning ... and, though all around me seemed refreshed by his discourse, yet my heart remained hard and unaffected ... But the Lord was pleased to refresh me again in the evening whilst he preached from these words, 'Behold the Lamb of God'[9] ...

16 June
... Heard Mr Whitefield preach ... My heart echoed back the same words and had a sweet, calm peace in my soul ... Heard him preach again in the evening ... but had no comfort, so unstable is my soul ...

23 June
Met my band. Satan had been hard at work to make breaches between some of us, but the Lord ... would not suffer him to hurt us and gave us a blessing before we parted ... This was also the happy day when my Jesus first made up the breach between my heavenly Father and me[10] ... O, how many mercies might I re-

count, spiritual and temporal! How have I and my family been kept safe and unhurt in the midst of deaths and dangers and, when I imagined my worldly affairs to be in a tottering way, how did my God graciously interpose! ... And when ... he was pleased to chastise my husband by sickness ... even then did he step in to my relief and restore back my husband from the jaws of death. O Lord, bring back his soul also from the jaws of hell, and let him not remain an insensible sharer in all these blessings! ...

28 June
Had much comfort in my soul this morning in talking with a person about the things of God. The Lord did put words in my mouth to plead his cause ... But woe is me, that am constrained to dwell amongst, and converse with those continually that are strangers to my God, and speak evil of his ways and watch over me for evil and not for good ...

20 July
Was much refreshed under a comfortable sermon from Mr Larwood[11] ... O Lord, ... make him an instrument in thy hands of much good to the souls of all thy people here!

23 July
Mr Larwood met and examined the class to which I belong, and it proved a blessing to my soul. He preached in the evening from these words: 'What shall it profit a man to gain the whole world and lose his own soul?'[12] ...

28 July
Spent some time in company with Mr Larwood, and found his conversation sweet and reviving to my soul ... Found some risings of pride whilst Mr Larwood reproved the society for some things which I had already laid aside ...

30 July
Was hindered from going to the preaching by company coming in to me, in whose trifling conversation I joined, without having

courage to speak to the glory of God, for which I was condemned afterward. O Lord, give me courage and zeal for thy glory, that my discourse may be seasoned with salt![13]

13 August
Found anger rise in my breast on correcting my child – or rather, I did it more from an angry spirit than a point of duty, for which I found condemnation and trouble ...

15 August
No comfort in praying, reading or hearing, nor scarcely power to send a thought to God all day. Was overcome with drowsiness at the society and at the last prayer fell asleep ...

28 August
Found anger rise in my breast at my servant ... Alas, how does the anger of a worm rise whilst the wrath of God sleeps! ...

31 August
Went into the country and returned September 6th, during which time I laboured under much deadness and barrenness of soul and many scoffs from the thoughtless and profane, and had no friend near to help my weakness up. O, the blessings of Christian communion! ... It is easier for a camel to go through the eye of a needle than for a rich man to enter into the kingdom of heaven[14] ... I saw the truth of our Lord's words, and could not but thank him for withholding from me these things which my corrupt heart still hankered after ...

12 September
... I find now no comfort in anything. I attend the ordinances but alas, they are dry and barren to me. Others come away refreshed by the word of the Lord, rejoicing in their privileges, whilst I alone am found, like Gideon's fleece, dry under the gracious dew of heaven[15] ...

17 September
Was much offended with a brother for attempting to preach, and on examination found much of it owing to the pride of my

heart that would reject such a person as a teacher. O Lord, sub-due this in me, and send by whom thou wilt send! ...

22 September
Was so indisposed that I could not go abroad. I purposed much satisfaction to myself in private, but was disappointed in this by acquaintances coming in continually to enquire about my health, but none enquired about my health of soul ... O, how much more welcome and comfortable would the company of one Christian friend be, who would search my heart to the bot-tom, and to whom I might disclose all my griefs! ... I could nei-ther find comfort in reading or prayer, but the short time I had to spend in private was only spent in fruitless struggles with my-self.

25 September
How do the mercies of God every day abound toward me! I see on every side the hand of the Lord stretched out, and numbers bewailing their dead. Many have the desire of their eyes taken off at a stroke, and yet me and mine remain unhurt[16] ... O, what am I that thou shouldst be thus mindful of me? ...

27 September
... This was kept as a watch night but, on account of my want of health, could not stay longer than ten o'clock[17] ... My heart ached to leave the people and service of God ...

28 September
Found my child sick this morning. Went to prayer and resigned her to the will of my heavenly father ...

29 September
Could not go to public worship this day on account of my child's illness, till evening went to the preaching and stayed to the love feast, which proved a feast of love indeed to my soul.[18] O my God, what great things art thou doing in the earth! Thou choos-est one here and another there out of every sect and party, and all join hands, not to contend for useless opinions or ceremonies, but earnestly to contend for the faith of the gospel, provoking

each other to love and good works. O Lord, increase their number and their faith …

30 September
Was hindered of going either to preaching or prayer this day by the illness of my child. I find my spirit weighed down by the fatigue of my body …

3 October
… Part of my kitchen chimney fell in this evening, and none hurt, though we were all present and in danger. Here is a remarkable instance of the goodness of God …

5 October
… I find outward trials beset me sorely, and grief for my husband's soul and body weighs down my spirit, and Satan cries, 'This you have got by serving God', and would fain condemn me as the cause of his extravagancy and so of his ruin, both spiritual and temporal[19] … O Lord, take this matter into thy hands …

7 October
Found my mind something eased by laying open my heart in my band, but when I came home the same cause of grief presented itself …

13 October
Having so many watching over me for evil, and endeavouring to sow the seeds of discord between my husband and me, I see I have need to watch, and the fear of laying a stumbling block in his way, who is already too embittered, has hindered me of going to the monthly sacrament … But Lord, I commit this and all my care to thee … After I came from public worship I retired to prayer at the time that the people of God were receiving the sacrament in the great church,[20] and found much comfort.

14 October
The mercies of my God are new to me every moment. My child well recovered from the smallpox, whilst numbers, young and old, have been taken away by the same disorder …

20 October
An uncomfortable day. Found myself much beset by the world and troubled for some disappointments which till then I was ignorant of …

30 October
Found many struggles concerning one of my children whose illness appears to be the smallpox … O, make me resigned to thy will! …

31 October
Found much thankfulness at the prospect of my child's life … Only my earnest prayer is, whom thou shalt see fit to spare to me, O, let it be for a blessing and make them children of thine! And, I beseech thee, rather leave me childless than suffer me to have any that may be rebels against my God.

13 November
Met my band and afterward the preaching and public bands[21] in much deadness of soul …

20 November
I find worldly trouble bear hard upon me …

21 November
My soul much weighed down on account of my husband. His manner of life is every moment as a dagger to my heart. I am burdened on account of his soul and body … Alas, what shall I do?

24 November
The Lord … gave me comfort under the word and in private, and by a comfortable letter from a dear friend …

25 November
Met my band … The Lord gave me a blessing … but find my trials grievous …

2 December
… Was much tempted not to meet my band this day, Satan urging many inconveniencies – the weakness of my body, the distance of the place, the coldness and wetness of the day, and the deadness of my own soul, so unfit to receive a blessing in this duty, but … I broke through and went, and found it a great blessing to my soul …

5 December
Have been detained from the preaching by bodily weakness …

11 December
Went to the preaching and love feast. Rejoiced to find myself again amongst the people of God …

12 December
Scarce a thought of God all day … Martha-like, careful and troubled about many things, but neglecting the one thing needful.[22]
…

17 December
After a heavy, cloudy day, the Lord did visit my soul in private, gave me a glimpse of his love and a steadfast assurance of being accepted through Christ …

29 December
Heard a good sermon this morning from these words, 'Remember the Sabbath day, to keep it holy,'[23] most of which condemned me for neglects and shortcomings in this duty … Deadness of soul, backwardness in holy duties, wandering and worldly thoughts still beset me, and draw off my mind from God. Neither in my conversation do I keep this day holy, not having any person in my family with whom I may converse, being looked upon by all as a poor, deluded creature, led away by the cunning craftiness of men … But I will trust in my God for this also … I will not hold my peace. I will importune thee for the soul of my husband; I will not cease asking till thou hast granted this my request …

1752

1 January

My soul thankful and rejoicing on hearing that the Lord had given a clear manifestation of his love and an appearance of pardon through Christ to one who … now rejoices in the Lord … triumphing in the weakness of her body from the prospect it gives her of being forever with him …

14 January

Have been confined from the preaching by the weakness of my body …

17 January

Finding my extremity drawing near, I retired to give myself up into the hands of my gracious God … O Lord … be present with me in my extremity, and suffer not the fierceness of my pain to draw my heart from thee, but make me patient and submissive under thy hand …

1 February

Blessed be my God who has answered all my requests and has made me a living mother of a living child! … O, may this life which thou hast spared be ever devoted to thy service! In the time of my extremity, found power to lift my heart to God, and patience under my trial. During my confinement, found my heart much affected with the goodness of God to me, and a deep sense of my unworthiness, and often drawn out in prayer and praise. The Lord did thus sweeten my confinement, and in some measure make me amends for the want of Christian conversation and other helps.

9 February

Went again amongst the people of God to hear his word with a thankful heart, and … was refreshed in all the means of grace …

10 February

Met my band. The Lord gave us to see each other's faces with joy, and comforted us together.

16 February
Was much comforted on being sent for by a young relation at the point of death, whose insensible state had often grieved me, yet dare not mention it to her ... But soon the Lord relieved her and gave her perfect peace ...

19 February
Stayed with this young saint, till I saw her breath her last ... She prayed that God might ease her pain that she might die in peace, yet in this also submitted, saying 'Thy will be done.' Her fear of offending God was so great that she would not put herself in an easy posture to die till she first asked her minister if he thought it would offend God. Her words and thoughts and desires were all in heaven, and thither she followed, sweetly resigning her soul into the hands of her faithful creator and blessed Redeemer ...

21 February
Found my faith much strengthened in reading a chapter in Arndt's *True Christianity*[1] ...

6 March
Well may the Christian's life be called a warfare, for every moment brings its own work – at least, I find it so ... But my God has his way in the whirlwind, and when he has tried me, I shall come forth as pure gold, fit for my Master's use.

12 March
In reading a chapter in *True Christianity* this morning, my soul was much refreshed ...

19 March
Being amongst fashionable folk this day, and finding no place for the things of God, I remained altogether silent. I received some witty reprimands for it but ... I had comfort in my own soul, rejoicing to be counted a fool for Christ's sake.

24 March
My heart much lifted up at the preaching ... but I found after-

ward that God was strengthening me for the trial I was to meet with, my heart being sorely grieved and heavily burdened for my husband, now visibly in a decay. I spoke to him in much love, beseeching him to alter his manner of living, even for his body's sake, but my tenderness was only returned with all the harshness and unkindness he was capable of … My enemy … did not fail to aggravate every unkind expression, still laying before me the excess of my love and the ill return I receive for it, and placing before me every former trial of the same kind, till my soul was even overwhelmed with grief …

27 March
My soul under much heaviness, and grievously afflicted for my husband. I see both his body and soul going to destruction, but dare not reprove him. I am condemned for not speaking, but if at any time I do, with even tears of love, his blasphemies frighten my very soul and condemn me for speaking … O Lord, I give up all to thee!

29 March
… My thoughts stayed upon God and taken up with the solemnity of the day, and a thankfulness in my heart for having my part in this glorious resurrection[2] …

4 April
… Whilst the preacher spoke from these words, 'Let the inhabitants of the rock sing', my soul was even transported with a sense of God's love to me[3] … I was got beyond myself, and wished earnestly to be dissolved, that I might be with Christ, never more to part …

10 April
… Went to see a sick person who was a gainsayer of the truth, but now convinced by the spirit of God and groaning earnestly for redemption …

13 April
Went to meet my band, but we concluded to defer it and go to see the sick person before mentioned, who declared to us how

the Lord had visited his soul ... He often praised God for his sickness, which had confined him to his bed and brought his spiritual friends to seek, and save, his soul. Our souls felt the flame that glowed in his, and we had a little Bethel[4] in the place.

20 April

My soul was much rejoiced at hearing of the happy end of my friend, who died rejoicing and triumphing over death. My heart rejoiced at finding him safe landed ... and almost envied his state ...

21 April

... From the fall of Thomas Williams,[5] many sophistical reasonings did Satan bring into my mind ... but God did deliver my soul out of the snare. In talking to a person who I thought tinctured with predestination, whilst I endeavoured to reason them out of this opinion, I found I had insensibly almost reasoned myself into it, but out of this also my God did deliver me ...[6]

2 May

My young child brought home to me in a dying way. This I found bore very heavy on me, but I flew to the strong for strength ... and now I think I can resign my child to him, trusting in him for patience against the trying hour.

10 May

Was detained at home till evening with my sick child, but ... could neither pray nor read nor meditate, nor lift my heart to God in any wise. Went to the preaching in the evening, but had no comfort there ...

14 May

This morning the Lord called home my child and gave me such a sense of his love and such resignation to his will as I have never before experienced, insomuch that I had power not to shed one tear. Blessed be God, who gives suffering grace for suffering times ...

20 May

Had many temptations to stay from meeting my band, Satan urging the length of the way, the wetness of the day, and the danger of cold, but I broke through and went and God was surely in the midst …

21 May

… No comfort under the word, but rather a prejudice to the preacher[7] … I have besought the Lord in prayer to take it away …

23 May

My prejudice in part removed, but yet there is something in me concerning him which I would not desire to entertain. I can receive him as a brother in Christ, but cannot honour him as a teacher in the church … O my God … give us teachers after thine own heart, that may lead us into all truth, men fearing God, and hating covetousness.

25 May

Met my band, where I opened my heart concerning the preacher and found every person there labouring under the same temptation concerning him. This was some comfort to me …

26 May

Was much comforted under Mr Wild's preaching. My heart rejoiced at seeing him, who was but a few months ago an unconverted soldier in this place, now a preacher of the gospel …[8]

28 May

Was much comforted in conversing with Mr Larwood, finding that these things which cause me to go on heavily in the ways of God are his burden also …

31 May

Had an account from Dublin of the bad success of my affairs now in law, which to all human appearance will … bring my circumstances very low but, blessed be God, I found … an entire resignation to his will … knowing that not a hair of my head can fall to the ground without his permission …

4 June

Trouble of mind concerning my husband. I find not anger against him for bringing trouble on his family, but am grieved for his soul. O my God, take this matter into thy hands and disappoint his and my enemy!

6 June

Found great stirrings of anger at some abuse I received, and said some angry words, which as soon as said were as a dagger to my heart ...

8 June

Much comforted at my band and class, and by a letter from a dear friend in Dublin. His account of the sufferings of the children of God there, and their wonderful deliverance (God raising up friends for them even amongst those that knew him not) filled my soul with thankfulness and love to God ...[9]

11 June

... One affliction comes on the back of another ...

16 June

Still I find my worldly trouble bear very hard upon me, and the grief for my husband's soul weighs me down. These things distress my mind so that I cannot stay my thoughts one moment upon God, nor find comfort for my own soul ...

19 June

The Lord has restored my husband, and preserved him safe from the power and stratagems of his enemies ... Gracious God ... order all my temporal so as may best advance my spiritual concerns, that all I have and all I am may be thine ...

7 July

Found my mind much disquieted on hearing some evil things that had been said of me ... and the injury appeared before me in the most heinous light, being done by one whom I had many times obliged and who had always pretended the most sincere friendship for me, and who himself was conscious of the falsehood of his assertions. These, together with my husband's taking part against me, weighed me down and the absence of God from my soul completed my distress, insomuch that I wept bitterly for a long time ... But ... I see that I should have calmly committed my cause to God ... seeing that in this I suffer for righteousness' sake ... for could I be prevailed upon to quit the service of God, I might live in quiet as I did before, but O, what are all earthly things when put in the scale with the favour of God? ...

22 July
I often find the care of the world break in upon me, and fears for the time to come and doubts how my present worldly trouble should end from the bad prospect that appears at present to human eyes, but one look to Jesus calms all my fears ...

25 July
I have been much busied about temporal things, but ... I often find, whilst my hands are employed below, my heart and affections are set on things above, and my God gives me strength for my day as he sees I have need and, having less time for retirement, the Lord does abundantly make up the want to me by pouring his love into my heart whilst employed in my business, and makes the few opportunities of private prayer which I am now obliged to snatch precious to me, and I find my soul strengthened and refreshed by them as a parched ground after a gentle shower ...

1 August
... O, when shall the time come that every thought shall be brought under the dominion of grace, when shall I love my God with all my heart, and serve him with every thought and desire? ... I have ever found thee a gracious God, and my soul desires to be given up to thee. And now I do here in thy presence most solemnly renew my former engagement, and bind myself to thee forever. I accept of thee upon thine own terms, and do now declare that I would not, if I might, be saved any other way than the way laid down in thy gospel. I accept of thee in all thy offices: as my prophet to teach me, ... as my priest, to atone for me, ... as my king, to rule over me, freely and willingly submitting

myself to thy government, desiring no longer to yield obedience to the god of this world, but do here give myself up to be ruled, governed and directed by thee … All this I promise and purpose with a dependence on divine grace and the daily and hourly intercession of my bleeding advocate, humbly beseeching that … thou will grant me thy aid and support, and that unallowed miscarriages contrary to the settled bent and resolution of my heart shall not make void this covenant. Thus do I now solemnly and deliberately, in the presence of all the heavenly host, renew my former engagements and give myself up to be the Lord's, and let surrounding angels witness to the solemn transaction to which I now subscribe. [signed] Elizabeth Bennis[10]

13 August
Received a great deal of ill usage without being moved to anger, and found power to pray for the person who had used me so. My soul was comforted at the arrival of Mr Wesley, and the consideration of my not being amongst the number of those who have drawn back since he was last here …[11]

15 August
Found much trouble for the present state of the church of Christ here … O Lord, let Zion prosper, and teach me to trust in thee!

19 August
Mr Wesley met the classes, and my soul was sweetly refreshed in meeting. My heart was filled with peace and love, and much drawn out in prayer for him… Give him many children of faith that may be as so many stars in his crown, make him a living witness of the great truths thou hast raised him up to declare … O Lord, spare him yet many years for the good of thy church, till thou has fully ripened him for thy glory …

20 August
Mr Wesley met the bands and the Lord poured out a large blessing upon us …[12]

24 August
Had much comfort in meeting my band … but much grieved for

Mr Edwards.[13] My soul was even weighed down with grief for him ... O, may I never prove unfaithful, or sell my heavenly inheritance for a poor morsel of pottage! ...

25 August
Found stirrings of anger in my breast at hearing the people of God evil spoken of, and found I was offended at the person or persons whose evil conduct had brought this reproach upon us ...

26 August
Received much abuse from one in my own family, which God enabled me to bear with meekness and without answering again, neither did I find anger in my heart toward her, but when she would not be pacified, I retired to pray for her, and had much comfort ...

2 September
Found much trouble of mind this day on being represented as a hypocrite and receiving much abuse from a bitter tongue. Having received much evil treatment from the same person, I began to fear lest there might be any, even the least act of injustice in my dealing with her ... I laid the case before the preacher, simply and faithfully, and received his approbation, yet ... being in great heaviness of soul, I besought the Lord to speak to me by his word ... and, taking the Bible, it opened on the 12th chapter of Daniel and the 10th verse: 'Many shall be purified and made white, and tried, but the wicked shall do wickedly, and none of the wicked shall understand, but the wise shall understand.' This was some comfort to me, knowing that the way to the crown is by the way of the cross.

[14 September]
Yesterday the 2nd, and this the 14th – here the style alters.[14] My soul in much heaviness this day, and full of doubts and fears ... The fear of my acting wrong in this affair perplexes my mind, though on the strictest search I cannot see any injustice in my part. In this state I begged of God to give me a text to bear me up ... and after prayer I opened the Bible on the first epistle to the

Corinthians, and the 10th chapter and 11th-13th verses. This comforted my soul and I took it as an answer from the Lord ...[15]

23 September
Was much grieved and weighed down on occasion of some disturbance between some in my band and a teacher in the church, in which art and hypocrisy had got the upper hand (because lodging in a preacher), when truth, a tender conscience, zeal for God's glory and the good of the church, and grief for a fallen brother, were all represented as prejudice, evil speaking, backbiting and the like.[16] In this, I often besought the Lord to direct me and my friends, and to show me if, in taking this thing in hand in so sanguine a manner, we were right or not. After much prayer, I opened the Bible on these words, 'It is good to be zealously affected in a good cause.'[17] This strengthened me much, being sure of the goodness of my, and my friends' cause, and I strengthened my brethren as the Lord enabled me, and God gave them strength and courage and cleared their innocency in the presence of their adversary. And in all this affair, I can see the hand of God guiding and directing it and ... have a conscience clear and void of offence, being able to appeal to my God that my whole design was ... that sin might not be countenanced in any, and to hinder hurtful and dangerous opinions from spreading in the church of Christ ...

25 September
Met my band, and the Lord poured out a great blessing on us, and removed prejudice from some. We prayed earnestly for those who had injured us, and ... the Lord did abundantly water our own souls. The Lord gave me a great blessing in my class also ...

3 October
Suffered much this day from an evil tongue without making one word of answer ... But, notwithstanding this, I found it indeed hard to bear insults, abuses and bitter curses from a person who I had never injured, nor even answered a word to all her evil treatment of me ... O Lord, give me patience and heavenly meekness, that in this, and all things, I may approve myself in thy sight!

11 October
... I poured out my soul in prayer before my God ... and was again much refreshed at the public bands ...[18]

23 October
Breakfasted with some Christian friends, and my soul was much refreshed in talking and hearing of the things of God ... Met my band in the evening, and the Lord poured out a great blessing upon us, and at the preaching my heart was so filled with joy and comfort that I only wanted death to complete my happiness. O, what a blessed day has this been! ...

11 November
I spoke in much love to a sister concerning some things which I thought wrong in her ... I prayed for her, and the Lord removed the evil, and I received her thanks for dealing plainly with her ... O, blessed be God for Christian freedom and openness of heart! ...

15 November
I have resolved ... to set apart some time every day, besides morning and evening, as an hour of intercession, to offer up petitions for my friends and enemies, for those of my own household and for the church of Christ, for the messengers of Christ, for the ungodly world, and to ask counsel of God in doubtful matters ... This day I began to put it in practice, and the Lord made it a blessing to my soul ...

20 November
Having been long in trouble about a person who, from many circumstances, I have reason to believe lives in sin, and yet shelters himself in the society, and finding it impracticable, or at least dangerous to speak to himself, I laid the case before the Lord ... I then discovered the whole to the preacher, and gave the matter up to God ...

23 November
Had an accusing message sent to me from one who I believe is a Christian ... desiring I would clear myself of what was laid to my charge. I answered ... that it was a small thing to me to be

judged of man's judgement, and almost equal whether I be looked upon as a Christian or a hypocrite so long as I keep a conscience void of offence, that I freely forgave my enemies, and did, and would continue to pray for them, but to clear myself of their assertions I would not, except to those who came to me for information about the matter ... that if there was a scandal brought upon the church of Christ, it was not through my misconduct ... I then retired to examine myself, and found no ill will to this person for taking part with my enemies, nor any trouble at what the world might think of me ...

24 November
My enemies have stirred up themselves again to distress me, and have given out most shocking things of me ...

5 December
A fire broke out in the house of one of our brethren, which was likely to consume all his substance. When I heard it, my heart failed me and I was ready to cry out, 'What profit is there in serving the Lord?' but ... went to prayer, and had a steadfast assurance that the Lord would quench the violence of the flames, and not suffer him to be entirely destroyed. And so it proved: the Lord quenched the fire, and gave his servant a wonderful deliverance.

15 December
Being alone with a person in a natural state, I took occasion to speak to her of the things of God. Had much comfort in my own soul, and found her much affected ...

22 December
I found the thoughts of death comfortable to me this day ... O Lord, prepare me for that great change that I be not then found without oil in my vessel![20]

25 December
Rose this morning about three o'clock to join in celebrating the nativity of our Lord. My heart was melted down into thanksgiving and love for the abundant grace of God ...

27 December

Being all day confined to the company and conversation of worldly people, my spirit was quite wearied and my soul burdened. O Lord, one day spent in thy courts is better than a thousand spent in vanity!

1753

1 January
Blessed be the God of my salvation, who hath brought me in safety to the beginning of another year, upholding me in the midst of many dangers and preserving me alive amidst a thousand slain! How many have been afflicted by losses, crosses and disappointments; how many summoned away by death, their day of grace at an end! ... Yet ... I am ... preserved from sickness, death, the world, the flesh and the devil ... my temporal affairs better than intended by my enemies and at present, though wearing a dull aspect, yet I can trust my God with them, being assured that all things shall work together for my good ...

13 January
My soul is grieved and my spirit pressed down on account of the sinking state of the church of Christ[1] ...

15 January
Had much comfort in my band and class but O, my soul thirsts for the prosperity of Zion! O my God, remove the cause of this deadness, and revive thy work again in this place.

20 January
I find many anxious thoughts about the event of my temporal affairs ... I do commit them all to the Lord, with a steadfast assurance of his care over me and mine, but Satan raises many storms within ...

10 February
Blessed be God, he has taken my temporal affairs into his hands, and has delivered me out of my trouble ... But ... I find a hardness of heart, a deadness and slothfulness of spirit, which I endeavour in vain to shake off ...

23 February
My soul thirsts after God, desires, longs and sighs for his appearance:

> With longing eyes and lifted hands,
> For thee I long, to thee I look,
> As travellers in thirsty lands
> Pant for the cooling water brook.[2]

15 March

Finding my thoughts much taken up with a prospect of worldly good ... I was grieved to find my heart thus departing from God, and retired to prayer, earnestly beseeching the Lord ... to frustrate all my hopes, if it was not to his glory and my soul's good ...

17 March

Found my heart more thankful and more power to meditate this day. Looking back on what the Lord has done in this city and in my own soul since this day four years (when I first heard the gospel) has been a blessing to me ...[3]

26 March

Had my thoughts much taken up with temporal things this day ... Whilst, like Martha, I am carefully employed, I am apt to neglect the one thing needful ...

12 April

I find my thoughts often carried away with a prospect of worldly good ... but God shows me the danger of it ... and gives me a will resigned to his ...

14 April

One of my children being taken ill, I found my mind much disturbed, and not that entire resignation that I would desire ...

20 April

I find nature shrinks at the thought of parting with my child, yet can truly say, if a wish would restore her, I would not bestow it on her contrary to the will of my heavenly Father, but am often afraid lest, in the grief that nature feels, there should be sin. O my God ... uphold me now in the time of my need.

23 April

This morning my child died. The Lord gave and the Lord hath taken away ... In this trial, nature could not refrain, but found my soul patiently submitted to the will of God.

27 April

My husband being taken ill, I find it bear very hard upon me, and many anxious fears of things to come break in upon me ...

1 May

Met with a great disappointment in my worldly affairs which at first troubled me but ... do believe that this also shall work together for my good.

5 May

... My days are consumed in vanity, and my years in the bitterness of my soul. In vain do I daily attend thy word – all is dry and sapless, for I cannot find my God. O Lord, what shall I do? ... I cast me at thy feet and here will I lie, and if I perish, I will perish here.

11 May

My other child being taken ill, I find my mind much burdened lest the Lord should lay more on me than I should be able to bear. But why should I not trust God? ...

13 May

I find my present affliction bear very hard upon me: the death of my child, the illness of my other child, the illness of my husband, and my own approaching time of trial, but above all, the absence of my God – all these together burden me sore, and press me down to the dust ... It is my desire that the Lord should deal with me according to his own good pleasure, yet find I have not strength to bear the worst. It is my desire that the Lord should now take this child also, rather than that she should not live to his glory, choosing to be childless rather than rear a child for hell, yet ... find nature shrink at the thought of losing my only child. Indeed, I find a continual struggle between nature and grace ... O, who can explain this struggle for life, this travail and pain, this trembling and strife? ... Lord, I ask not the life of my child, nor the prolonging my own life ... I only ask grace to bear thankfully the sufferings thou shalt see fit for me, that in all things I may say, with humble resignation, thy will be done.

15 May
My child appearing to be better, I find a measure of thankfulness and gratitude of heart to my God, who had pity on my distress.

30 May
Weak in body and mind ...

2 July
Blessed be my God, who does magnify his grace toward me! The Lord did visit my soul, and made me the living mother of a living child. O, may my reprieved life be spent in the service of my God! In my trial, I found the Lord present with me. During the time of my confinement I often found a hardness of heart and deadness of affection, notwithstanding the goodness of God to me ... O my God, pardon, and apply thy blood for my daily trespasses and shortcomings.

13 July
Both my children being taken ill, I found myself more than ordinary troubled, and my will not wholly resigned to the will of God, but I besought the Lord in prayer, and found my spirit more calmed.

15 July
Blessed be God, I find an entire resignation to his will concerning my children ... Having received much ill usage from one in my family, I find it bear heavy on me, and my spirit grieved thereby.

20 July
Blessed be my God, he hath restored to me again both my children. But O, how hard and unthankful is my heart after all the blessings conferred upon me! ...

26 July
Was violently attacked by an abusive tongue, and falsely accused. I found grief and anger war in my breast, but durst not suffer it to break out, lest I should sin against God …

27 July
My yesterday's trial bears hard upon me … If an enemy had done this, I could bear it. Satan lays it before me, with all its aggravations, and brings former injuries to my mind which I would desire to forget forever, so that my mind is much disturbed and I find a shyness to the person, which I pray against …

6 August
Satan has this day thrust sore at me concerning my husband's illness, bringing in desponding thoughts and fears of things to come upon me, but my God does … enable me to resist and to trust in him …

8 August
Being in great heaviness of soul by reason of inbred sin, I took the *Homilies of Macarius* to read, and in reading found my soul much refreshed …[4]

12 August
The leader of my band (to whom I find my spirit close united) being sick, I went to see her, and found it a great blessing to my soul. The Lord refreshed us both whilst we spoke together of the things of God.[5]

17 August
My dear friend, the leader of my band, being to all human appearance near her end … I find a secret reserve in my breast, an earnest desire that she might live, but in this I can trust in the Lord for strength in the time of need …

18 August
Went again to visit my dear, dying friend … The Lord blessed us abundantly together, and gave us the immediate answer of our prayers. Sister Beauchamp had been before her illness in much

heaviness and deadness of soul for some days. I asked her now concerning the state of her soul. She answered, 'I am quite happy ... I have now a steadfast assurance of the pardon of my sins, and I find my heart comforted with the presence of God ... It would go hard with me to live now. But pray now that the Lord would perfect the work of sanctification in my soul before I depart.'[6] On being asked if she could freely part with all her friends, she answered, 'Yes, and as for my children, I have cast them upon the Lord, and I know that he will take care of them ...' She then prayed for all her friends and acquaintance, and for ... her band in general, and then for each person in it in particular ... She prayed earnestly for Mr Wesley, desiring to be found at his feet in the day of judgement ... She then prayed over her mother and kissed her, taking her leave of her, and called for her sister, whom she exhorted in like manner, then prayed for her and took her leave of her, kissing her. She thus took her leave of all around her, one by one, exhorting them, praying for them, and kissing them, then, calling for her servants, took her leave of them also in like manner, speaking to them as their several states and tempers required, and praying for them. Then, seeing one of her neighbours in the room she called her, saying, 'O Mary, it is time for you to repent. You are old in years, and old in sin. The Lord has borne long with you, and you don't know now the day or the hour. You see I am young, and the Lord is now calling me away, and what should I do now without an interest in Christ? ... And this you also may attain if you seek for it, for none ever sought the Lord in vain. Up, then, and be doing, repent before it be too late ...' Here her strength failing, she cried, 'I am almost spent, but had I strength I could exhort you all till morning.' Then, recovering herself, immediately she turned to another, and said, 'O Mrs Moore, I love you dearly, and I am sorry for you. You are careful for the things of this life ... This one thing you have neglected, and what should it profit you to gain the whole world and lose your own soul? ... Your glass is almost run, and what will all your toil and care profit you when you come to be as I am? O, it is a dreadful thing to delay repentance to a deathbed! ... My neighbours used to wonder how I could find time, and thought me very foolish for spending it after that manner, but now I know ... I shall, by and by, receive an exceeding great reward ... I exhort every one of you to seek the Lord ... I am now a-dying, and if you repent not, these my dying words shall rise up in judgement against you.' Then, calling her mother-in-law, she said, 'Mother, I forgive you all that you have ever done against me, and I have prayed the Lord to forgive you, but O, your soul has often been a great trouble to me. You are old, and a great sinner, and what will become of you if you die in that state? ... You have had many calls, but you have neglected them. Don't think the Lord will work a miracle upon you when you come to a deathbed, as he did on your husband. The Lord was gracious, very gracious to him, indeed, and wrought a great work in him in three weeks' time, but are you sure that he will do so by you? ... But if you now return, he will receive you, and freely pardon all your sins ... ' Then, calling for her husband, she said, 'My dear, the Lord has borne long with you and has given you many calls, even by dreams, but you have been disobedient and trifled away your good desires, and it is often the Lord's method, when we will not hear his call, to make us feel his rod, perhaps by removing our darling in this world from us. And so it is now: I was your darling and ... he is now about to take me from you, if by any means he may bring you to himself. O, then take care and let not this also be in vain.' She then prayed over, and took her leave of him. She then desired to be left alone with me. ... I then went to prayer with her, and when we had continued in prayer for some time she found the answer of our joint petitions in her heart ... This was, indeed, a comfortable day to my soul. I was abundantly blessed in the conversation of my dear friend, and my faith much strengthened, but O, I find not power to give her up ... O Lord, assist me in the trying hour ...

19 August
Visited my dear, dying friend again, and found her raving a little now and then, but whilst we spoke to her of the things of God, she never wavered ... On seeing me, she said, 'Sister Bennis, now this is your time. Lift up your heart in my behalf.' ... The leader of her class coming in, she said, 'Brother Burriss, I am now so spent that I can say but little to you ... but ... the Lord brought you and all my dear friends to my remembrance ... I shall soon be with him, but you must come ... and when you see

me near my end, go all to prayer, and continue so till I am quite gone, and let there be no crying or bawling over me, but all of you sing praises and rejoice over me.' ... She never complained of her pain, or discovered any peevishness under it, but bore her sickness with that patience, resignation, Christian meekness and love to all around her, that could only be found in a soul who knew herself just entering into her Lord's rest ...

20 August

This morning my dear, dear, happy friend took her last farewell ... I stayed with her all night, and strove with God for a resigned will, and about an hour before she died, I obtained my request: the Lord gave me freely to resign her without any reserve, and at present I find my will so wholly given up to the will of God with respect to her, that if one wish could bring her back, I would not bestow it on her ... O my Lord, keep me ever low at thy feet ... till at last I shall, with this my dear friend, and with all these who have washed their robes and made them white in the blood of the Lamb, rejoice before thy throne for evermore.

21 August

This day we committed the remains of our dear friend to the grave, at which solemnity my soul was much refreshed. We sang and praised God together, and talked of the goodness of God to each other, and instead of grief we had much comfort, and joy in the Holy Ghost.

22 August

Met my band. We missed our leader from amongst us, but the Lord strengthened our weakness, and we ... had much comfort together.

27 August

Fearing the band to which I belong might scatter, I again met it as leader. I found Satan ... would fain raise pride in me. This I laid before the Lord, and besought him to subdue, and declared to the band my resolution to give it up when the preacher came to town, and this, by the grace of God, I am resolved to do ...

3 September
Met my band again … I knew not what to say or how to pray, nor could I look straight at anyone in the band, and upon examination found this proceeded from pride …

10 September
Was constrained by business to neglect meeting my band this day. I … was troubled at the disappointment, but yet found a secret satisfaction for missing meeting it, hoping that we should have a preacher before the next time that I might give it up …

17 September
Met the band as leader again in much shame and confusion of face, and found neither words nor power in prayer with them, and came away quite confounded … I applied to the preacher to provide another leader, which he refused to do.[7] This distressed me much …

20 September
Still the leadership of the band distresses me. It is before me continually, and my mind fearful and a dread upon me concerning it. I laid open my mind to a spiritual friend, and found his words strengthening to my soul …

24 September
Met my band again, but before I went I laid my case before the Lord … My soul was much refreshed, and my God kept every hindrance from me.

26 September
My soul much comforted these two days … but this evening resentment rising in my breast (though it did not break out) yet robbed me of all my comfort, as water spilt on fire, and left nothing behind but darkness and confusion.

30 September
My soul was much blessed in reading Arndt's *True Christianity*. It solved many difficulties, and strengthened my confidence in the Redeemer …

8 October
Met my band, with a single eye and a simple heart, and the Lord, according to his promise, was in the midst and comforted all our hearts ...

9 October
The Lord does comfort and refresh my soul ... but find some fears at times lest this should be a preparation for some heavy trial. O Lord, thy will be done! ...

11 October
My eldest child ... taken very ill ... But, blessed be my God, ... I find an entire resignation and submission to his will.

13 October
... My child appears to be dangerously ill and, though I find this indeed trying to flesh and blood, yet find my soul quite submissive and resigned to the will of my God ... My child growing worse, I retired to prayer, and whilst I prayed (not for her life, but for a will wholly resigned and for strength in the trying hour) I found it ... spoken into my heart, clear and beyond all doubt, that the child's sickness is not to death, and I found at the same time a strong assurance of this ...

27 October
... Blessed be God for my child's recovery. O Lord, give me a grateful heart!

12 November
I find the unholy walking of some proves a temptation to me, and often robs me of comfort, but this does drive me closer to Christ in prayer, lest I also should become a stumbling block in the way of any.

26 November
Had much comfort in my band this day, though Satan strove hard to keep me from it ... I am often ready to give it up, and am only restrained by the fear of offending God ... I think I was only nominated for this by man, who has not penetration to see my

heart and my great unfitness for this office, therefore often think it is not the will of God that I should hold it. Could I see it was his will I should rejoice to do it, however grievous to flesh and blood. O my God ... direct me, I beseech thee!

29 November
Was much comforted and my soul refreshed this evening in Christian conversation. Blessed be God for this sweet communion of saints. These are the happiest hours of my life ...

9 December
My heart ... alive and earnest after God this day, but the news of Mr John Wesley's being at the point of death was like a dagger to my heart.[8] ... I was for some time overwhelmed with grief at the great loss that the church of Christ should sustain by the removal of so great, so shining a light, so wise a pastor, so zealous an apostle and father of the church, and fearing lest his death might give our enemies an opportunity of triumphing over us. But ... the God whom we serve is able to deliver us, and able also to raise up another in his place and endow him with gifts and grace suitable to the great work. O Lord, thy ways are in the deep. Do as seemeth best in thy sight, only keep thy little flock, for whom thou hast reserved the kingdom.

13 December
Perplexed with many fears of what may come upon the church if the Lord should remove Mr Wesley, but ... am enabled in this to trust in the Lord ...

14 December
Was much comforted this day with the good news that Mr Wesley was recovering ...[9]

16 December
... My next door neighbour has his only child dead this morning, whilst the calamity has missed my door, and me and my family dwell in safety. O my God, let not these thy mercies pass unheeded by me! ...

25 December

I found not my thoughts exercised on the solemnity of this day. Endeavoured to meditate, but could not keep my thoughts stayed one moment ... O, thou who wast veiled in flesh for me, give me power to overcome the flesh, that my heart may continually aspire after thee.

28 December

I have been much taken up with the things of this life, and find this hurry about temporal things leaves my soul less fit for God ...

1754

14 January
Was much refreshed in my band, but O, how unfit am I for this
office! The deadness and barrenness of my own soul and the littleness of my grace almost stop my mouth from speaking to
these, or make me often speak an unfelt truth. But yet I find the
gracious Lord … sends down his blessings amongst us …

22 January
One of my children being taken ill and some disappointments as
to worldly affairs weighed me down very much …

24 January
My child's removal, to all human appearance, drawing nigh, my
spirit has been grievously pressed down … but the Lord gave
me power to wrestle in prayer with him till I received an entire
resignation to his will …

29 January
The Lord has … restored me my child from the jaws of death. O
my God, let the life thou hast spared be dedicated to thee …

6 February
I find reading the scripture a great strengthening to my soul …
Therefore am determined, by the grace of God, to read a portion
of it every day …[1]

11 February
The Lord did refresh my soul this day in meeting my band.
Blessed be my God, it is not now a cross to me, but a blessed
privilege, and I find my heart more closely knit to those who
meet with me … O my God, keep me humble, and make me
faithful, simple and obedient. Instruct my ignorance, subdue my
pride and strengthen my weakness, that I may be able to give an
account of this my stewardship with joy.

12 February
Being in a large company this day, I found it hard to stay my thoughts upon God, but was often carried off with their trifling discourse. O Lord, pardon, and give me to see the world in a true light, and to esteem all things in it only as dross and dung …

25 February
So busied about temporal things that I could not go to meet my band, and found it hard to keep my mind patient under the disappointment.

1 March
I found many things rising in my heart this day, particularly desires after the world, which grieved my soul …

> Lord, arm me with thy spirit's might,
> Since I am called in thy great name.
> In thee my wandering thoughts unite,
> Of all my works be thou the aim.
> Thy love attend me all my days,
> And my sole business be thy praise.[2]

22 March
I find that much care for the things of this life often takes off my thoughts from God … and robs me of spiritual comforts. O Lord … give me power to cast all my care upon thee, and to die to the world that I may live wholly to thee!

12 April
This day being the anniversary of our Lord's crucifixion, I besought the Lord to make it a blessing to my soul[3] … The solemn transactions of this day were deeply impressed on my mind and, as the hours passed, the sufferings of our Lord each hour, and the benefits accruing to me therefrom, were clear to my mind and deeply impressed on my heart …

14 April
Blessed be my God, he hath made this day a day of blessings to my soul, a Sabbath indeed. I could see by faith my blessed Lord

rising, ascending and interceding for me, laden with blessings for my sinful soul ... But O, what shall I render to thee, my God, for all thy bounty? ...

21 April
Still I find the world beset me, even in my best duties, and my thoughts often carried off from God in contriving how to lay up treasure upon earth ...

4 May
Being about to settle some affairs of consequence this day, I found my thoughts too much taken up with them and my mind too anxious lest they should not be settled as I would have them. The Lord ... gave me power to look to him for a resigned will and ... he heard and delivered me, giving me power to resign all to him, and ... gave me success, and ordered it as I would have it ...

15 May
I found pride rise in my heart this day greatly on my husband's requiring my making a submission where I was conscious I had done nothing wrong. Yet, in obedience to him, I did, but not in lowliness of mind or humility of heart, for my heart was so swelled with pride that I could have cried tears for being obliged to do it. My conscience condemned me for this ...

31 May
A cloud hangs over my soul, and I am, as it were, veiled in darkness, groping my way forward, feeble and helpless. I strive to pray, but cannot. I drag my body before the Lord, but cannot give him my heart, and when I would lay all my complaint before him, my enemy comes in as a flood upon me, and easily leads my thoughts astray ... O Lord, in this distress to thee I flee! ...

24 June
Much comfort in my band this day ... yet weighed down and distressed because of my own unprofitableness. Alas, alas, what have I been doing these five years? How ought I now to be as a

lamp held out to enlighten others, as an example to those under my care, but O, how short, how far short do I come of this and how near the condemnation of the slothful servant, who buried his talent in the earth![4] ...

5 July

My soul was much comforted in conversing with a Christian friend and, though we differed in opinions, yet we ... found in our hearts that love of Jesus that unites his people ...

7 July

... Being in company with a person whose words and behaviour I thought not answerable to his profession, I spoke plainly and in love to him ...

10 July

The sermon this morning probed my heart to the bottom and tore away almost all my hopes, and made it appear to me very doubtful whether I be in the faith or not, Mr Bastable's description of living faith and the marks attending it being far above what I ever have experienced.[5] This has filled my soul with the deepest distress ...

11 July

Grieved, troubled and distressed about the state of my soul, yet ... provoked to anger by a mere trifle ... My grief and distress of soul was heightened this day by my husband's debarring me of the morning preaching ...

12 July

... This being appointed a day of public intercession[6], I was filled with expectations of a great blessing with the congregation but, missing the hour, I met them coming out, at which my soul was filled with grief and distress ...

13 July

I was this evening obliged against my will to go on a tour of pleasure with a few worldlings ... I retired before I went to pray that the Lord would keep my mind stayed upon him but, no sooner had I come from prayer into my family, than anger got again the better of me. It raged in my heart like a fire, and broke out in expressions which, though not unreasonable on the occasion, yet were sinful as proceeding from an evil heart ... I stood confounded and condemned before the Lord ...

22 July
... Some doubts again arising in my mind concerning a person in my band, I besought the Lord earnestly to direct me ... I cannot speak in the band for prudential reasons, and am afraid to speak at all lest I should grieve a child of God's ... whom I believe innocent of every aspersion ... This matter being long a burden to my mind, I some days ago laid it before the Lord, beseeching him ... if it was his will that I should open my mind to her on this matter that he would put her on speaking to me first about it ... Being to meet with her in band this day, I prayed the more earnestly about it, and after our meeting was over she told me she wanted an opportunity of speaking privately to me. We set a time, and are to meet ...

25 July
This day being the time appointed between my friend and me for an interview, she came, and my fears returned. But casting myself before the Lord, I besought him earnestly to direct me ... I then opened to her all my heart, all I heard, all I feared, all I thought and what others thought concerning her, with my reasons for speaking now and my reasons for not speaking before ... I found power to speak in love, and had a solemn sense of the presence of God with me all the time ... Whether I have acted right or wrong, I have done it with a single eye to his glory, and according to the best of my knowledge. O Lord, forgive, if ignorantly I have acted wrong.

31 July
Finding that, notwithstanding my acting with so much caution with the person in my band before mentioned, yet I had only laid myself open to the censure of others and what I intended for good cast back on myself in bitterness – this, I say, troubled me, and for some time grieved my spirit lest I should have done

wrong, but on searching into my heart, can say truly in the presence of God that I did intend it for the better, that I did not act hastily, but earnestly sought counsel of God in prayer and, if I have acted wrong, it proceeded from my ignorance and here, indeed, I may soon be led into error, having but little wisdom to guide me, but find my conscience clear and my God reconciled …

2 August
My soul has been much grieved for a person in my band, who in the above affair has acted a bad part, but I trust the Lord will enable me to deal faithfully with her also …

5 August
Had much comfort in meeting my band, and spoke freely and plainly to a person in it, who I think has not acted a Christian part by another who was not there, but found my heart much drawn out in prayer for her. My soul was much blessed in this meeting and in talking to some sick persons of the things of God, though all strangers to me …

15 August
Had much comfort in talking with two sick persons this day, whose necessities had brought me to visit them …

18 August
Was detained from the preaching by a shower of company coming in upon me. I found it hard to resign myself to this disappointment, but prayed earnestly to the Lord to keep my heart with him … But O, my heart mourned over the ignorance of those who are even counted religious! I could not but admire at that mercy and free grace that plucked me, unworthy me, out of that number, and I rejoiced in being accounted a fool for Christ's sake … Had much comfort in visiting one of my sick folk this day. My soul was even rejoiced to find that the Lord had manifested himself to her, so that she now desired to die that she might be with Christ, as indeed she did soon after. Blessed be the Lord for this! But, on the other hand, my spirit was grieved with another of them, who I found had armed himself against

my words, though always accounted by all his acquaintance as an extraordinary Christian (and I believe very justly). What a pity that such should refuse the blessings and comforts that God is willing to give his children! ...

19 August
Was much comforted in meeting my band, and particularly at seeing one there who I feared was offended with me for speaking plainly to her. I found my heart thankful for her, and earnest in prayer for her ... This evening there was great thunder and lightening, at which I found great terror ...[8]

21 August
Rode a few miles off to dine, and found my heart often wandering from God, and taking more pleasure in the beauties of nature than in the author of them ...

25 August
The Lord has made this a blessed Sabbath to my soul ... Yet one thing troubles me – that I cannot receive Angel Mounsel as a preacher.[9] I know not the cause ... I told this to a Christian friend this day, who answered that he believed the fault to be in me ... O my God, if thou hast sent him, give me grace and power to receive him as thy messenger!

9 September
Had much comfort in my band this day, and had great power and freedom to speak to them. Found my heart closely linked to my dear Sister Parry, and thankful for her. I now see how Satan has been at work in my band, by stirring up another person against her, and Satan has now drawn the other quite away. This brought grief on my mind from two quarters: first, for the soul of her who is turned aside, and next for the distress of mind brought on her who is sincere of heart. O my God, forgive, if in my dealing plainly I have in any wise offended or grieved this thy child ...[10]

10 September
I walked out to the country this day to dine. I had a dread on me

lest I should by lightness or forgetfulness offend my God and lose my comfort, but I besought the Lord for help and, leaving my company for a while, I took my little Kempis[11] and sat down under a haystack, where for about an hour I had sweet communion with my God, even as a man with his friend ...

2 October
... I am easily taken in the snare of my enemy, who this day again provoked me to anger ... Such is the cursed pride of my heart, that cannot bear to be ill-used without falling into sin, so that the very thing that would tend to my spiritual advancement and growth in grace, if borne with patience and resignation, now through my own stubbornness, impatience and unwatchfulness hinders me in my spiritual journey, and causes me continual grief and sorrow of heart ...

14 October
Had much comfort in my band, but very little anywhere else ...

20 October
A dull Sabbath. Much, very much disordered in body, and weighed down in spirit, and but little comfort in any duty ...

21 October
So ill in body that I only kept out of bed to meet my band, and the Lord made it a blessing to my soul. I find the disordered body does press down the spirit ... and my enemy, taking advantage of my weakness, buffets me sorely. O Lord, have pity on me! ...

4 December[12]
Blessed and forever praised be my God, the God of my salvation, whose mercy I have always experienced, and whose loving kindness has followed me all my life long, and has now added another instance of his loving kindness and tender mercy to the thousands that are gone before! ... When all human help failed and my mourning friends stood weeping round, then did my God graciously interpose and, as in the days of his flesh, rebuked the fever and bid me live. O, how great that mercy that

spared me, seeing my unfitness to die! O my God, may this life which thou hast spared be dedicated and wholly given up to thee, may my added days be spent in thy service and to thy glory! During the time of my illness, the Lord kept my senses entire, but found my heart cold and dead, nor could I at all lift it to God as I would desire ... Some short visits the Lord graciously afforded me, but was for the most part in distress for God, and found this far more grievous than the fever on my body. But ... he knows what I have need of, and orders all things ... One remarkable instance of the goodness of God in this his visitation to me was this: a beam in the floor over the room where I lay sick took fire but, my sickness keeping me awake, I discovered the fire, which would otherwise in all probability have consumed the house before it could be overcome. Thus, the Lord brought good out of this evil, and showed me to be still the care of his watchful providence.

22 December
Went abroad this day for the first time since my illness, and found ... my soul filled with love and gratitude at the consideration of the goodness of God ...

23 December
The Lord ... brought a Christian friend to see me, and blessed our conversation to both our souls ... I found great trouble and sorrow of heart afterward in speaking to a very dear friend, whom Satan and the world have kept back for a time. My heart was enlarged, and I found power to speak in much love, yet plain and home ... O Lord, deliver him, and keep me that I fall not!

24 December
My thoughts have been this day much employed on the solemnity of the season. God manifested in the flesh – O, how solemn the thought, how deep, how mysterious! The mighty becomes base, the infinite becomes finite, the immortal becomes mortal, the rich becomes poor, he who bestows every blessing is ministered to by his creatures, the strength of Israel is supported by a feeble woman, and all this for man ... O, the wonderful condescension and mercy of our God! ...

28 December

I find I have lost by being much in company these two days. My heart is corrupt, light and trifling, and is soon carried away to like, and join in foolish and unprofitable conversation, and hereby I suffer loss …

1755

1 January

O, how innumerable the mercies I have received the past year …
and yet how few returns of gratitude from me! … And now, O
Lord my God, I beseech thee, continue to me thy wonted goodness and, as thou hast graciously brought me to the beginning of
another year, O, may I now begin to live to thy glory! Subdue
my corruptions and renew my heart, dig about and dung this
barren tree, that it may henceforth bring fruit to thy glory.

15 January

Glory be to my God, whose signal mercies are ever engaged on
my behalf, and keeps me still amidst ten thousand snares: one
whom I thought stronger in grace than I, and whose standing in
the church has been as long as mine, has now drawn back and
given way to sin, and yet I am upheld …

27 January

My band not meeting, I was grieved lest the cause should be in
me, knowing my unfitness for so great a work. This put me
upon examination and prayer … and had much comfort with
my God.

1 February

Spoke plain and home to a person fallen from grace, and found
that the Lord blessed my words, both to him and me, and was
condemned for not following after him before …

3 February

My soul was much comforted in conversing with a Christian
friend about Christian diligence. It stirred me up to search my
heart, and found the exercise a blessing to my soul …[1]

7 February

This day found anger work in my breast whilst I corrected my
child, for which I was immediately condemned, and cast myself
before the Lord in prayer …

10 February
Was reproved publicly in my class for what I did not intend ill,
yet found my heart so knit to the person who gave the reproof
that I could grasp her to my bosom for dealing so plainly with
me …

11 February
Had a remarkable dream this morning, which I would desire
ever to remember … I dreamed that, being in a large company
where my father was at the head, they wanted me to drink of
their liquor, which I refused, but to induce me to drink my father
gave 'Mr Wesley' as a toast … At this … I drank, giving glory to
God, then retired to entertain a few female friends … Whilst I sat
with them, my husband came in, and was surprised to see his
countenance entirely altered, and methought I saw nothing but
perfect wickedness in his looks. This grieved my spirit, but
made me the more obliging in my behaviour toward him, but he
seemed bent on evil and aggravated at me … I shed showers of
tears, and used much entreaties with him to remember his eternal state and repent before it was too late, but his answers cut
me to the heart, and increased my grief for him, he telling me he
would never repent, that he would be damned, and that he
chose to go to hell, where he would have much company, and
many such answers as these … But in my dream I thought he
lived thus and died thus, and then indeed was my grief increased for the loss of a beloved husband, but much for the loss
of his soul. I shed abundance of tears, insomuch that my pillow
was wet, and my heart even broke. Thus, filled with grief and
distress, I went to the corpse and lay down on it to indulge my
grief, but had not been there long when I felt the corpse move. I
arose, and saw that life was again coming into him, but whilst I
looked, I had an inward, confident persuasion that this was an
evil spirit that had animated the corpse of my husband, and that
his business was to tempt me and try if, either by subtlety or
force, he might prevail. The confidence I had of this made me
deaf to all the congratulations of my friends, who assisted at his
recovery and wondered to see no abatement of my grief and
could not receive my opinion of this matter. I sat looking and
waiting the event, till he at length arose (but his person and vis-

age quite altered into the likeness of another man) and ran up and down like a madman, but this did not fright or move me, my heart being filled with the love of God, and so confident in his care and protection that I thought I could encounter all the infernal host. In this confidence I looked round and asked, 'Is there never a child of God's here who will come with me, that I may speak to this fiend, and know what is his business with me?' Then, seeing Sister Parry near me, I took her with me, and going in search of him, we after a little time found him in another room. As we approached him, I said, 'I charge you in the name of the Lord Jesus that you do me no hurt ... I know you are a messenger of Satan's, sent to tempt me, but you shall never be able to prevail, for the Lord is my strength and my defence.' ... 'Why so confident?' said he, 'What is it you think I cannot do?' 'I think', said I, 'you have not power so much as to lay your hand upon me'. 'Have I not?' said he, smartly striking his hand on my shoulder. 'What do you think now?' This action of his made me start, being so confident before. But, recovering myself, I said, 'Indeed, I ... am still confident that you cannot hurt me.' By this time I found myself placed at a large table whereon was laid a white basin with blood in it and a white saucer in the blood with which I continually kept the blood stirring, covering the inside of the basin with the blood so that no spot might appear where the blood was not ... I observed whilst I was at this exercise that when I stopped my faith grew weak, but when I again stirred the blood ... my faith again strengthened. My adversary had also a mug with some liquor in it, of which he often pressed me to drink, but I obstinately refused, still telling him it was blood and not liquor, and that I would not touch it. I did believe that this my adversary had a limited time allowed him to remain in this body, at the end of which the evil spirit should be obliged to depart and leave the body inanimate again ... In this agony of soul I clasped my hands and cried to God for help, and so awoke, my body weak and my animal spirits sunk through the agony of spirit I suffered in the above dream, but ... with my soul happy in God ... but what I may infer from it I know not ...

17 February
Met my band in much grief and distress of soul because of my

great unfitness, but ... the Lord ... did bless us indeed, and made our meeting comfortable to us all ... Was also much blessed in meeting my class, particularly in speaking plain and home to a person in it who I thought too careless ...

19 February
Was troubled on hearing that the person who I spoke to in the class was offended, yet am not sorry that I delivered my own soul ... ...

27 February
Both my children being taken very ill caused me some exercise of mind. I found it hard to give up all, yet it is my earnest desire that the Lord would work his mind in me ... I desire that his will may be done, however grievous to nature, and that he would take from me every earthly comfort that would draw off my love from him ...

29 February
I find it hard indeed to possess Martha's hands and Mary's heart. In a hurry of temporal things I find it hard to fix my thoughts upon things eternal. These two days my mind has been much taken off from God, forgetful and wandering ...

1 March
Having received some harsh, angry language, I also found anger rise and returned two or three answers which, though right in themselves, yet were spoke with an angry spirit, which brought trouble and heaviness on my soul ...

3 March
... One of my children the Lord has graciously restored ... The other is under his afflicting hand, perhaps an innocent sufferer for my sins and O, that my will may be wholly given up to his! ...

9 March
In praying for my husband, the Lord gave me a strong and comfortable assurance that one time or other the Lord would restore him ... O my God, I ask in thy name the soul of my husband! ... I

ask with all the power and faith I have … Let thy blood plead for him and thy mercy pursue him, till thou hast forced his stubbornness to yield, that he may be saved by grace …

11 March

… The Lord has graciously restored my other child. O, may I be thankful! …

12 March

One of my children being scalded, and might have been worse had not the Lord wonderfully preserved him. Instead of considering the mercy and being thankful, found anger rise against the person who was the means of it, and spoke angry and cross to her. Not considering the goodness of God in the present mercy or in the late restoration of both my children from sickness but yielding to my own evil, wicked nature, I brought condemnation on my own soul, and after this my other child fell in the fire and was not hurt. This discovered still more of the wonderful goodness of God, and could not but admire at his preserving care over my family whilst I myself was sinning against him, and would have thought it just had the Lord suffered the fire to kindle upon her as a punishment on me …

2 April

One of my children being taken suddenly ill, my mind was burdened with many uneasy thoughts but, looking to the Lord, I found my soul comforted …

3 April

The Lord has again restored my child …

17 April

I find it hard to keep off the world. It often comes in as a flood upon me, and I find my heart desiring it and ready to wander after it. O Lord, what shall I do? …

24 April

I received great abuse this day from an unruly tongue, but my God enabled me to answer in meekness …

27 April

The sermon this morning from the 2nd chapter of the Revelations and the 5th verse cut me to the heart, and gave me to see the necessity of repenting and ... of coming to God as at the beginning, with a broken and contrite heart ...[2]

5 May

Met my band in great distress and, being before intended to give up my band because of my great unfitness at present for so great a charge, I now laid my intent before them but, all speaking against it, I was obliged to be silent ...

7 May

This day laid before the preacher, Mr Bastable, my intent to give up the band, with my reasons for it, but was by him dissuaded from it. O Lord, if thou wilt employ me, give me grace suitable to the work! ...

1 June

In my present state I find a difficulty in almost everything – a slothfulness in spirituals and a peevishness in temporals, so that every thing is a cross to me ...

12 June

... This day, being in the country minding my business there, and having no place within for prayer, I retired to a private corner of the garden, and there the Lord did visit my soul and gave me a comfortable sense of his love.

21 June

... I corrected my child in anger, thereby grieving the spirit of God ... The sense of his forbearing mercy is as a dagger to my heart, and with the weight of my sins sinks me almost below all hope, insomuch that this night I was afraid to eat lest God should cause the food to stop in my throat and send my soul quick into hell ...

27 June

Being this day about my affairs in the country, and retiring into a private corner in the garden to prayer, the Lord graciously visited my soul with his presence and sweetly comforted my heart with his love ...

4 July

My mind has been busied about temporal things and forgetful of God. It is, according to the alteration of the style, six years this day since the Lord first spoke peace to my soul[3] ... and O, what need have I to be ashamed and confounded before him, seeing how little glory I have brought to his name and how small the advances I have made in his ways! ...

18 August

I met my band, and opened my whole heart before them, begging their prayers, and laid before them my resolution of giving up the band, as I cannot see how I can be of any use as a leader, seeing my ignorance is very great and my grace exceeding small, and am often afraid that I hinder a blessing amongst them ... I fear God has not called me to this, else he would give me gifts and grace suitable to the work ...

19 August

Laid my resolution before the preacher, Mr Walsh, with my reasons for it, opening to him the whole state of my soul, but he would not take the band from me, only exhorted me to patience, prayer and watchfulness ...[4]

24 August

There being a love feast this night for the band only, I attended there. The sight of it filled my heart with thankfulness and my eyes with tears, and during the whole time I had such a brokenness of heart and such a deep sense of my own baseness, and my heart so filled with love to God, that I could be content to suffer anything for him, and found my spirit so united to all his people there present that I could put them all into my bosom ...

26 August

Went into the country this day, and retired to my usual corner in the garden to prayer, and there the Lord did condescend to visit my soul and comforted me with his presence, so that for a time I was truly happy in the love of God. But alas, the comfort soon vanished, and I remained dead as before.

20 September
Last night a fire broke out in the Abbey, which consumed a great part of it and was in danger of spreading into the town, which would, in all likelihood, have consumed the whole town had not God in much mercy restrained it.[5] During this time I found my heart drawn out in thankfulness to God that it was not in my house, or near my house, that it broke out … How does his goodness preserve every moment from every evil me and my family! How many poor creatures has the last night's fire drove to want and beggary! Yet the good Lord gives me to lie down in peace and rise in safety, and suffers no evil to come near my dwelling …

5 October
Was sorely troubled for making a bargain this day, being the Sabbath[6] …

13 October
One of my children being taken ill of the measles to all appearance, I found many uneasy thoughts passing through my mind …

28 October
The Lord has graciously restored me my child, all glory be to him! My time of trial being near at hand, I have been examining myself concerning my state and … think I see cause for rejoicing and much thankfulness. I know that my Redeemer liveth, I know that in him, and for his sake alone, I am forgiven …that, if he shall make this my entrance into an eternal state … he will also finish his work in my soul before he calls me hence, and … whether life or death, do find myself wholly resigned to his divine disposal …

6 November
On hearing this day of the earthquake which happened in Cork

on the first of this month, I found my heart much affected – grieved for the ungodly and unthinking, and filled with gratitude and thankfulness to my good God ... for all his goodness and mercy to me and mine ...[7]

7 November

This day ... set apart as a day of public fasting and prayer throughout all the societies in England and Ireland on account of the late dreadful and alarming earthquake, to beseech the Lord in behalf of these kingdoms that he would keep us from the hands of our enemies and give repentance to these nations and turn away his threatening judgements from us, and that he would uphold his own gospel and cause it to prevail in the earth ...

22 November

... On the morning of the 9th day of this month the Lord showed his mercy to me, and made me the living mother of a living child. In the time of my extremity I found power to call upon the Lord in faith and received a gracious answer ... O my gracious God, let this life which thou hast spared be dedicated to thee and spent in thy service and to thy glory! ...

4 December

This day we received an account of the great city of Lisbon being wholly destroyed by an earthquake at the same time that the shock was felt in Cork, and here my soul stands amazed at the goodness and mercy of God to these kingdoms, who gave us only to feel his threatenings whilst he poured out his judgements on other places ...[8]

6 December

This being my first time of going abroad, I found my heart in some measure thankful ... But was condemned in the evening for joining in trifling conversation ...

14 December

Yesterday being the Sabbath, and I, by reason of the illness of one of my children, being confined at home, yet resolved to spend the day well, but ... spent it thoughtlessly and unprofitably, for which my soul was much weighed down. This day found my mind in some measure stayed upon God and comforted by a letter from my dear brother Walsh, but all these cannot suffice or satisfy, so long as my heart remains unchanged.[9]

22 December

Had an opportunity of the preacher this morning and told him as well as I could the present state of my mind, and was in some measure comforted, but ... this was followed with such an hardness of heart ... as cannot be expressed ... Went heavy-laden to the preaching after much struggling all the day, but there was so overcome with drowsiness that the most part of the sermon passed unheard by me. Thus, in much heaviness, went to meet my class, and there the Lord was pleased to remove my burden and comfort my soul, and afterward the Lord blessed me much in private prayer ...

1756

4 January

… This day my heart is hard as the nether millstone – dead and unable to move towards God …[1]

17 January

… Last night, being very ill in body and grievously distressed in mind, I cast myself before the Lord, unable to pray. I groaned out my requests, beseeching the Lord to have pity on my state, and not to call me hence till he would perfect his work in my soul, and that he would now show me a token for good, in releasing both my body and mind from the present indisposition of both. With this request I laid me down to rest, and the Lord heard my request, gave me comfortable rest and raised me up this morning in perfect health of body and strength of soul, and comforted me this day with his gracious presence …

26 January

Had a comfortable meeting with only one of my band. Blessed be our God, the fewness of our number did not hinder his blessing upon us … The preacher this evening enlarging on that text, 'The Lord shall pour out his fury on the nations that know him not, and on the families that call not on his name'[2] … I was filled with distress, and cried in my heart, 'Lord, what shall my family do, seeing they know thee not?' … Immediately these words came to my mind … 'What is that to thee? Follow thou me' … and I was filled with peace and joy …

8 February

Being confined from the public worship this day, some friends came to sit with me, but was much condemned for joining with them in speaking my own words and thinking my own thoughts on the Lord's day … My disorder being a sore breast (which above all things I have much dreaded), I find the pain of my mind little inferior to the pain of my body, but this brings distress on my soul as it argues a will not resigned to the will of my God …

16 February
The Lord gave me power these two days to praise his name, though under great pain … I have been much drawn out in thankfulness to God under the consideration of others' afflictions, where pain and poverty often comes together …

18 February
My infant[3] being taken ill … I cannot keep nature quiet from unprofitable fears and forebodings about her. I strive and pray against it, yet still it remains. My breast having broke, I found much power to lift my heart to God in thankfulness and gratitude.

22 February
My child being better, I found my heart in some measure thankful …

13 March
I met with a sore trial in my family this day, and found anger ready to rise against the person, but the Lord restrained it …

15 March
Had a happy meeting in my band and class this day, though somewhat ruffled in the morning by my mother-in-law. O Lord, convert her soul, and give me grace to stand in the time of trial!

21 March
… In the morning I found anger at one of my children … but my Lord … graciously forgave my sin, and sweetly refreshed and comforted my soul …

22 March
Was much comforted in the happy death of a dear, Christian friend and one of my own band … my dear Sister Bethel.[4] … The day before she died, looking at her hands which were swelled, she cried out with joy, 'O, blessed be God for this first sign of my departure!' Thus she continued rejoicing in spirit, though in great pain of body, till this morning, when she sweetly fell asleep in the arms of her beloved Lord …

9 April

My eldest child being taken ill, I find my mind much disturbed about her ...

12 April

... Last night a woman who was walking about in tolerable health dropped dead suddenly, and why was it not I ... nor any of my family? The Lord has kept the destroying angel from my door, and only gave me to see the evil afar off ...

23 April

My child being better, I find in a measure my heart thankful to God ... But alas, I find pride and self in everything I do ...

27 April

Another of my children being taken ill, I find my mind much disturbed and my soul distressed because I find not power to give her up ...

1 May

My mind and heart much drawn out in thankfulness and gratitude to God for all his common blessings and for his distinguishing mercies, and the sight of some criminals going to be hanged heightened my gratitude, so that, whilst my eyes were filled with tears and my heart drawn out in prayer for them, my whole soul was filled with thankfulness and praise under a sense of the abundant goodness of God to me.

8 May

Blessed be God, my child is better, and likely to do well ...

8 June

My soul was much comforted this day, and I found a thankfulness of heart and a flow of love and gratitude to God at seeing that dear man of God, John Wesley.[5] It drew my heart out in earnest prayer in behalf of myself and of the church in this city ...

17 June

... I was in heaviness, filled with doubts, fears and perplexities, but my God has again caused the light of his countenance to shine on my soul with cheering and comforting rays, dispelling the clouds of darkness and unbelief, and causing me to rejoice in God my Saviour …

23 June
My soul happy in the Lord, but much grieved at parting with that dear man of God, Mr John Wesley.[6] O gracious Lord, prosper his way before his face, and let thy blessing attend him. Make him everywhere a messenger of glad tidings to thy people, and a son of thunder to the careless ones … Comfort his soul in every trial and give him strength of body and soul for the great work thou hast given him to do. And … give us grace, that we despise not the weakest but still open our hearts to receive thy word with thankfulness from whom thou wilt, simply looking to thee for a blessing … and … stir us up to greater diligence, that we may redeem the time and take up our cross henceforth and follow thee.

This should be a day much to be remembered by me, a day of praise and thanksgiving to my God, the day of my espousals with my Lord, when he looked upon mé in mercy, and bid me live[7] …

26 June
… I know not whether it be the forebodings of my own timorous heart or not, but methinks there is some trial near. If so, O my God, proportion my strength to my need, that I faint not, and then thy will be done.

27 June
… This was in some measure a comfortable Sabbath to my soul, but one of my children being taken ill, I find it bear upon my mind more than I would have it …

29 June
… My child to all human appearance sick unto death, and my husband taken and confined in his house for an unjust debt, and unable suddenly to pay it – these things I find bear hard upon me, so as even to affect my body.[8] Yet I find my soul stayed

upon God, and a comfortable calm within, and for this my heart is thankful …

30 June
I find not my heart so fully resigned as to my child as I would desire, but I am resolved to pray till I can give her up. O Lord, assist me … As to my other trouble, I find power to give myself and all my affairs up into the hands of my God[9] … Indeed, the Lord has already interfered in my behalf, in raising up friends for me where I least expected it, so that he has not been sent to gaol, but only confined to his own house. This I acknowledge as a particular instance of the goodness of God to me and my family …

5 July
Having received a great deal of wicked, ill-natured language from my mother-in-law this day, I found it affected me very much, being conscious that I never injured her, even so far as a disobedient expression. I found her behaviour a grievous trial to me, and found stirrings of anger within, which broke out into expressions not sinful in themselves, but as they proceeded from an angry spirit must certainly be so. In this Satan was not wanting to aggravate, bringing to my remembrance all her former behaviour, part of which I was wicked enough to repeat, which has brought my soul into much heaviness. And still Satan returns, crying, if any other person had done this it might be borne, or if even she had done it at any other time, but thus to behave in the height of my troubles! – these suggestions still keep my soul pressed down, and even my body is affected with the weight of inward and outward trouble together …

10 July
I found some stirrings of anger in my breast at meeting with some ingratitude and inconsideration where I had a right to expect better. This brought trouble and condemnation again upon my soul …

13 July
Was again brought under condemnation by finding anger work within, till my gracious Lord showed me still his readiness to

forgive … My child being better and likely to do well, I find my heart in a measure thankful, but grieved that it is not more so …

20 July
The Lord … enabled me to meet my band with a thoughtful heart … and gave me there a particular blessing. I find that my mother-in-law has been saying many evil things concerning me to many of the people of God, as well as others. This troubled me much, yet … upon close examination I find no ill will to her for this …

31 July
I have this day been in much trouble and distress. I have found man changeable, and earthly friends but as a broken reed, and all their professions of friendship but as a blast that passeth away, and fear lest I have trusted too much in them, therefore has God wisely disappointed me … My husband being this day enlarged, I found my heart thankful, and no fretfulness at his being obliged to pay so large a sum – £600 – in his wrong, but rather thankful at the Lord's enabling him to do it. Satan did, indeed, thrust sore at me to make me curse my enemies … yet my God knoweth I do not wish them evil …

25 August
Had much comfort in my band … and was this night particularly drawn out in earnest prayer for my husband, and found power to believe that God will at last save his soul. Yet I often think it will be so as by fire. O my God … do thou rescue him as a brand out of the burning.[10]

30 August
… The Lord made it a Sabbath indeed to my soul, and blessed me abundantly in private prayer, and in speaking to a papist whom God has convinced … of the errors of the Church of Rome, and in some measure of the method of salvation laid down in the gospel.[11] … O Lord, lay hold on her, and rescue her soul from the power of crafty and designing men … This morning I dreamed that I went to the Abbey to the morning preaching, and as I went I saw men on the top of the abbey church who

were mending and pointing the house. I went in and sat with the rest of the congregation a considerable time, waiting for a preacher, but in some time two of the workmen who I had seen on the roof came in with such a striking solemnity in their countenance and behaviour as filled my soul with awe and comfort. They both went into the pulpit and prayed and gave out a hymn, then, desiring the attention of the congregation, one of them spoke as follows. 'We', said he, 'were at our work yesterday on the top of this house, and we looked and saw the heavens opened, and God the Father seated on his throne with the Son seated at his right hand, and there was brought before God an accusation concerning this church, and there were called two angels, and commission given them to come down and search into the state of the church and try if the accusation was true … And we … saw the two angels descend, and they came into this house … and they examined into the state of the church and found adultery in the church, and we beheld them ascend again, and the heavens opened and the angels brought their report and laid it before God … And behold, the church was called to appear before God, that she might hear her accusation and receive her punishment, … and the angels were called and gave in their accusation against her, and the Lord's anger waxed hot against her and we saw him lift his hand to strike … but God the Son laid hold on his Father's hand and stayed it … and, standing up between them, he screened her from his father's wrath whilst he himself pleaded for her.' Here he ended, giving a short exhortation and prayer, and so dismissed the congregation. In my dream my soul was much comforted, and woke with my heart filled with love and joy.[12]

26 September
… How easy is it for a person to sin, even whilst in their duty! In telling a person whom I love my objections to and thoughts of him, I at last found a hastiness of temper for which I was condemned …

4 October
Had much comfort this morning in conversing with the preacher, but observed some stirrings of pride within, which grieved my

spirit ... Soon after Satan brought me low in the dust by provoking me to anger ... O Lord, have pity on me, and bruise the serpent's head.[13]

9 October

The Lord kept me these five days from any risings of anger ... but alas ... this evening, being off my watch, I corrected my child in great wrath, and immediately I had a hell in my breast. Not for correcting my child am I condemned, but for the passion that raged in my breast ... Even my body bears a part, and is weighed down with the guilt that presses my soul ...

17 October

A comfortable Sabbath ... The Lord kept my mind stayed upon him. In the evening my mind was much disturbed: my maidservant, who is to me even as my right hand, honest, faithful, useful and affectionate, was taken very ill, and by every symptom it appears to be a fever. This brought fears and forebodings into my mind, but I cast myself before the Lord and ... besought him to consider my present distress and (if he saw fit) not to take from me at present so useful a person, and whilst I prayed I had a steadfast assurance that God would not either remove her, or afflict her in suffering this sickness to continue. This comforted my soul ...

18 October

Blessed be my God ... my servant is better, to the astonishment of many ...

24 October

I found this day that I could not bear with the mockers of Christ's gospel as I ought. O Lord, give me meekness and patience, and pity for the enemies of thy cross, and give me a holy boldness in thy cause, that I may never be ashamed of thy cross but may thereby be crucified to the world, and the world crucified to me.

29 October

... This day one of my children has been taken ill ...

31 October

My child's disorder appears to be the smallpox, and this day another of my children took ill. At first I was something alarmed but, casting myself before the Lord, I received strength and power and comfort from him, and was enabled to give up my two children to him without any reserve. My soul was filled with comfort, so that I could not help praising God for my afflictions, neither could I pray for the life of my children, my will being wholly resigned and given up to the will of my God ...

3 November

My children appear to be in danger, and I find not myself as wholly resigned as I should be. Yet I dare not ask their lives of the Lord lest I should offend ...

6 November

Yesterday my child was better, and I had strong hopes that the Lord would spare him, but it pleased him at night to frustrate all my hopes, and this morning the Lord took him to himself.[14] I found it, indeed, a heavy trial, the most severe I ever felt – it was taking away the desire of my eyes at a stroke ... In my distress I cast myself before the Lord often, and at last received power to resign him up to the Lord, though my soul is clouded and grievously distressed, but it is my Father's will ... O my God, I thank thee for all thy gracious dealings with me. O, let thy will be done, though it be grievous to flesh and blood, and give me power to thank thee with all my heart, from a grateful, feeling sense of all thy mercies.

7 November

I went with a heavy heart to the table of the Lord, seeking a blessing, but I fear I did not seek it aright, for I came away heavy and dead ... and was all the day barren and dry and unable to lift my heart to God. The loss of my child is ever before me, and the grief of my husband strikes to my very soul, whose heart was pent up in this child, being his first, and only son. I can truly say if one wish would bring him back, I would not bestow it on him contrary to the will of my heavenly Father, yet I find something in my heart with which I am not satisfied.

9 November
My other child seems to be near her end, and I find this double stroke coming very heavy on me. My mind is much disturbed, and do not find my heart so wholly given up to God as I would have it. My body and soul are both weighed down, so that I have not strength of either even to pray ... Upon the closest examination I can truly say I am resigned to the will of my God ... but I am grieved that I do not feel my heart thankful and acknowledging, under all the mercies I have and do daily receive ...

12 November
The Lord has now taken away my other child also – two out of three in one week.[15] Yet I know it is for good, and would not have his will reversed. He has graciously left me one child still, and many other comforts in life. O, that I could be thankful for this and all his gracious dealings with me! O my God, I beseech thee, sanctify this my affliction to my soul, and ... remove this deadness of soul, that I may have power to serve thee aright in loving obedience to thy will ...

17 November
Distressed and perplexed on every side. My mind is, indeed, like a troubled sea, full of doubts and fears and forebodings of more ill to come, and dreams disturb my rest, so that day and night is alike to me ... O Lord my God ... why dost thou hide thy face, and hearken not to the voice of my groaning? O Lord, help. O Lord, visit. O Lord, deliver my soul, lest my enemy be too strong for me.

23 November
Met my band in much trouble of soul, but dare not pray with them as usual. My husband being taken ill, my trouble and distress is much increased ... O Lord, if I must still suffer, give me more strength ...

25 November
Blessed be God, my husband is better ...

3 December

I know not how to describe the state of my soul, only by saying I am unhappy and miserable without God. My soul is dead and dark, and in this state I find a peevishness of spirit beset me, which continually renews my guilt and increases my trouble.

18 December

... There is a void in my soul which nothing but God can fill ... I am prone to evil continually, my proud, evil heart is every moment ready to go astray, and my grand enemy never leaves tempting ... Yet through the strength of my Redeemer I am hitherto conquerer, though I think I sometimes escape with the skin of my teeth, and sometimes with less ... O Lord, how long, how long shall I labour in the dark and cloudy day? When wilt thou chase away these mists and speak uninterrupted light into my soul? I am weary of my groaning, weary of sinning ... O, raise up upon me the light of thy countenance, and cause me to see my way and see my guide, and go on rejoicing, giving thee the glory.

21 December

Much backwardness in prayer, but had much comfort in my band. Though I cannot rejoice for myself, yet my soul rejoices for others, and much for the prosperity of the church in general. Blessed be thy name, O Lord, that thou art again reviving thy work in the midst of us[16] ...

25 December

I met this morning at four o'clock with the people of God to praise the Lord for his love to man. But alas ... I was as Gideon's fleece, unwatered and dry in the midst of a plenteous, gracious shower! ... I endeavoured to lift my heart and keep it stayed upon God ... but all in vain. I cannot, cannot pray ... O Lord, what shall I do? ...

1757

1 January
... O, how innumerable the blessings I have received this last year, and how astonishing my ingratitude! ... But, as thou hast graciously brought me to the beginning of another year, so, Lord, keep and protect me still from sin ... that, if thou shalt graciously prolong my life till the close of this year, there may be still greater things opened to my view ...

3 January
My mind ... drawn out much these few days on the perfection of the saints.[1] My soul earnestly desires it ... I spoke to a Christian friend who is also seeking after it, requesting her prayers for my information ...

5 January
... Being to dine abroad in worldly company, I feared greatly lest I should give way to lightness or trifling and thereby contract guilt, but I sought help of my God by prayer, and found power ... to watch and often to lift my heart to God whilst in company, and in the evening, when they all went to see a play, I solaced myself in the enjoyment of my God, and my whole heart was drawn out after him in gratitude and thankfulness for delivering me from these abominations and snares of the devil ...[2]

8 January
... Yesterday my soul was much enlivened by conversing with an experienced Christian, but this day I found much disturbance ... on hearing of many base, unkind things which my mother-in-law has said of me. O Lord, reward her not according to her dealings with me, but change her heart and have mercy on her, and ... enable me to bear all injuries with patience and an entire resignation to thy will ...

21 January
Much disturbed on hearing of many evil and wicked things which my mother-in-law had said of me, and on seeing other evils in her. But, on looking up to the Lord, I found his presence

with me, and something reminding me that my time of trial[3] should not be long, and my soul rejoiced in the thoughts of approaching death, but in this was condemned ...

22 January

... Going into company in the evening, I found I suffered loss ... but when I came home the Lord sweetly refreshed my soul, and my heart was drawn out in thankfulness and gratitude to my good God for not placing me in a high rank in this life, where much company would be likely to rob me of much communion with my God ...

25 January

... I had much life and comfort in meeting my band. I could not help speaking much to them concerning perfect holiness ... notwithstanding my great ignorance and, whilst I spoke to them about it, the promise (which before seemed to be at a distance) now seemed to draw night to my soul ... and all this day I am ready to lay hold upon it ...

2 February

Under the sermon this morning ... my soul was unspeakably happy, my hunger and thirst after holiness of heart was insatiable, my whole soul was upon the full stretch after it, and it was brought near, even within my reach. The glorious prospect filled my heart with joy and delight, and my soul sprang forward to grasp the prize and for a moment thought myself in the possession of it, not knowing whether I was in the body or not ... But at night, entering into a conversation about this great work of God on the soul with the preacher, and his opinion concerning the manner of it not agreeing with mine, I found my hopes and earnest expectations in a moment damped as water cast on fire ... I ... looked upon this to be an instantaneous work, that would immediately deliver me from this hell of inbred sin, but Mr Olivers thinks it first gradual. Sin dies by degrees, and at last expires. This, I say, damped my hopes ... O Lord, help me ...[4]

11 February
This being kept a public national fast, the Lord enabled me to join in keeping it ...[5]

17 February
My thoughts much taken up in the world, and absent from God. O my Lord, shall I ever live at this poor, dying rate? ...

29 March
I found it a great cross to meet my band this day, and would gladly have missed it because of the deadness of my soul ... but the Lord did there comfort me.

9 April
My mind often disturbed this day by the risings of pride and stirrings of anger occasioned by a little dispute between my husband and me ...

30 April
Distressed with many anxious fears concerning my approaching trial ...

14 May
Much heaviness of soul, and many fears concerning the trial which is before me and now apprehend to be very near ...[6]

24 May
Blessed forever be the God of my salvation ... The Lord my God ... delivered me in the time of my distress and made me the living mother of a living child ... I have had many of the fiery darts of Satan shot at me, but my God has stood by me, and ... blessed me this day in conversing with a Christian friend ...

5 June
Sabbath day. My heart much affected this morning under a thankful sense of the goodness of God to me in bringing me again in health and safety to the public worship, but afterwards ... was twice or thrice condemned for speaking of worldly things ...

12 June

Was obliged to dine in the country with my husband, which hindered me of the preaching in the evening. This disappointment raised peevishness and fretfulness in me when I should rather have exercised patience.

24 June

Have been busied about temporals these three days, and my thoughts absent from God. This day my soul was much refreshed and drawn out in thankfulness for past mercies. There being a sight (desirable to the eye) to pass under my window, I found a desire to see it, but thought it would be more pleasing to God to sacrifice this desire to him, and accordingly when all flocked to the window I retired to prayer, and had sweet access to my God and communion with him …

3 July

A dull and cloudy morning, but … in the evening the bright sun of righteousness arose on my soul … At the love feast my soul was much blessed …O my Lord, I give myself up wholly to thee – spirit, soul and body, all I have and all I am – and now make a solemn surrender of all I have, am and enjoy to thee without reserve, desiring to be wholly thine, to be ruled, governed, guided and directed by thee alone, and do take thee only as my portion and my inheritance, my lot in the land of the living and choice to all eternity, my friend, my helper, my teacher and my guide, my sure and only Saviour and Redeemer. Disclaiming all things else, I betake me to thy blood and righteousness for pardon, peace and safety. Abhoring my own filthy rags, I cast my soul upon the multitude of thy mercies, desiring to have or enjoy no blessing, either spiritual or temporal, but what flows through thy wounds and blood. I take thee, my Jesus, for my husband and head, and do accept of thee in all thy offices as my prophet, priest and king, humbly desiring to renew my former engagements and covenants with thee, begging pardon and forgiveness through Christ my Redeemer for my many and numberless miscarriages, and begging thy grace for the future, without which I can do nothing, and in an humble dependence on which, for the performance of this covenant, I subscribe myself to be the Lord's. [signed] Eliza Bennis[7]

4 July
This being the day according to the present style[8] in the which the Lord first spoke peace and pardon to my soul, I found my heart much drawn out in thankfulness and gratitude to my gracious God for his goodness to my worthless soul …

5 July
My soul much blessed under the word and in meeting my band, but found anger rise in my breast in speaking for God – a bad spirit in a good cause …

8 July
My soul much strengthened in hearing that dear man of God, Mr Whitefield, preach on Christ the sure foundation …[9]

31 July
My soul was happy in God this day whilst I heard his truths spoken against. Glory be to thee, O Lord, that hast revealed these things to babes, which lie hid from the wise and prudent! …

4 August
… My young child being taken ill, I have found it often bear heavy on me, and undutiful thoughts coming in upon me concerning my disappointments in all my children, but I find when I do look to Jesus he comes in with help …

13 August
Being much in worldly company, my thoughts and desires also have been much there, and consequently my soul much clouded. O, that I could live in the world as thought I were not of it! …

25 August
My mind much distressed with temporal cares and disappointments, which haunt me in every duty …

17 September

… Much hurried about temporal things. O Lord … sanctify every disappointment in temporals to the rooting and establishing my soul deeper and firmer on thee …

25 September
Sabbath day. Much blessed under the word but, being obliged to dine abroad in worldly company, I found it hard to keep my thoughts stayed upon God. A cursed desire to please often draws me into sin …

28 September
My child still continuing ill, I find my mind much disturbed, and not yet power to give him up. O my Lord, proportion my strength to my day …

4 October
On being told much of my mother-in-law's ill will to me and her endeavours to lessen and expose me, I found much trouble of mind and many heart-risings against her, and the remembrance of former injuries stirred up in my mind. But, by going to God with my distress, I found … power to pray for her and forgive her …

4 November
A sleepiness of soul is come upon me. I feel my deadness, yet cannot arise … O my God, raise me up again, awake me though it be with thunder, lest I sink down with the ungodly.

27 November
… Being informed that many of my fellow travellers to Zion had set apart every Sabbath night between the hours of eight and nine as an hour of intercession for our fleets and armies in particular, for these kingdoms in general, for the church and cause of God, and for his majesty the King of Prussia and the protestant religion,[10] I determined also to meet my friends at that hour at the throne of grace, and was somewhat straitened to get it accomplished, but by the help of my God I broke through and retired and, though absent in body, yet found myself present in spirit with the many individuals who at that hour had also se-

questered themselves from the world to humble ourselves before the Lord and to send up our joint petitions … in behalf of ourselves and our guilty lands …

14 December
Much coldness, deadness and unbelief …

26 December
My mind troubled about a temporal affair which has proved a disappointment to me, and justly so, because the lawfulness of it was not entirely clear to me when I took it in hand. O Lord, give me grace to make a right use of it …

29 December
I dined in a large company of worldly people, where not one word of God was to be heard except in an oath. I called upon God before I went and, blessed be God, I was not led away by their carnal mirth and found no relish for their enjoyment. I was amongst them as a fish upon dry land, labouring to keep my thoughts stayed upon God …

1758

1 January

Blessed be God for the beginning of another day, of another week, of another year ... O Lord, still let thy good spirit strive with me till thou shalt cause me to bring forth fruit to thy glory. O, quicken my pace, increase my faith and enable me now to begin again, that in thy strength I may go on, and in thy might may overcome, and at last obtain the victory through thy merit and death ... I found this night some risings of anger within, whilst my spirit was grieved at my husband's railing at and abusing the truths and people of God. O my gracious Lord, forgive him for he knows not what he does ...

14 January

I have only been adding sin to sin these four days, indulging a dissatisfied spirit and keeping resentment to my husband because of his extravagance and bad management, when it rather became me to look to Christ and exercise patience ...

11 February

... So depraved is my mind that I am often amused with the world, with company, with trifles, but O, there is ... a wound which nothing earthly can cure, and many fears of falling yet lower ...

3 April

On seeing some of the foolish vanities of the world, my heart was particularly drawn out in gratitude and thankfulness to God for delivering me from it, and for not giving me a higher station in this world than what I possess ...

14 May

Sabbath day. My soul refreshed under the morning preaching, but was hindered from the evening service by the illness of one of my children, and found but little comfort at home.

26 May
Alarms all around, sickness and death knocking at almost every door. Yet O, how stupid and insensible is my heart in the midst of all! ...

1 June
Weighed down with weakness, both body and soul, equally unfit for spirituals or temporals. O Lord, do as thou wilt with the body, but ... quicken my soul, I beseech thee ...

11 June
Sabbath day. Stupid and dead under a searching sermon from Mr Walsh[1] ...

16 June
My heart much rejoiced at seeing that dear man of God, Mr John Wesley, yet still cold and dead under his word.[2]

23 June
... I expected that when Mr Wesley was come, then surely my soul should be quickened, but justly has God left me worse than before as looking for any blessing from man.

28 June
My mind much disturbed and weighed down with trouble on finding that Mr Wesley had appointed me leader over a class. My great inability and utter unfitness for this work makes it indeed a grievous burden ... I already find the charge of my band a heavy load on me, from which I would rejoice to be delivered, but the additional charge of a class makes my burden almost insupportable[3] ... O Lord, have pity on me, and if thou hast appointed me for this, O, make me fit for it, I beseech thee ...

30 June
This day being set apart by us as a day of solemn fasting and humiliation preparatory to a solemn covenanting with God, I found my heart in some measure given up to God, but O, not in any wise as I would have it, and the thought of this class is, indeed, a grievous burden upon me.

2 July

My mind more calm and satisfied about the class, having determined that, as I have given up and made a solemn surrender of myself to God, so I will lay out all the feeble strength I have in his service ...

3 July

Met my class for the first time under a deep sense of my weakness and inability ... In the evening met with the society and joined with them solemn covenanting with God, and received the sacrament from Mr Wesley, during which solemn transaction I think my heart was sincere with God. Thus have I publicly renewed the solemn contract which I have aforetime privately and heartily subscribed my hand to, and do now openly avow ...[4]

7 July

Much grieved at the departure of that dear servant of God, Mr Wesley[5] ...

9 July

Sabbath day. My husband being taken ill, my mind has been much distressed and weighed down ...

12 July

My heart thankful for the recovery of my husband ...

30 July

Cold and dead as to my own state, but rejoiced in spirit and thankful to God on account of a deserter condemned to die tomorrow, and for whom the Lord hath done great things, and made him a blessed witness of his pardoning mercy ...[6]

1 August

My soul thankful and comforted for the happy end of the above person, but cold and comfortless as to my own state ...

9 August

My mind much disturbed on my husband's being taken ill ...

12 August
Yesterday and this day my husband appearing to be in great danger, I found then indeed that I had need of more grace, not being able to support under my great distress ... But this evening the Lord has given me a better prospect ... Pardon, O my God, pardon my undutiful grief ... and if thou wilt strike, O Lord, make me able to bear it, that I sin not.

13 August
... My heart much drawn out in thankfulness to God for a prospect of my husband's recovery ...

30 August
My time of trial being near at hand, my fears are many and my mind much perplexed, but more for the state of my soul than that of the body ...

4 September
O, how do the mercies of God surround me continually! The Lord has graciously turned the evil from my door, has ... restored my husband from the jaws of death, and has called away my next-door neighbour ...

9 September
Met my class in much deadness of soul, and was constrained to press others forward to that diligence which I do not find in my own spirit. O Lord ... how shall I bear the weight of this class?

1 October
... On the 19th of last month the Lord looked graciously on me and helped me in my distress, and made me the living mother of a living child. I have since found my heart much drawn out in thankfulness and gratitude to God for all his mercies, but often wandering away from him, full of worldly cares and fears ...

7 October
This morning my young child died, and I think in this I found a resigned will and a thankful heart for so tender a chastisement ...

10 October
Met my band in much deadness of soul and pain of body …

1 November
During the above space[7] the Lord has been pleased in much mercy to afflict my body but O, how tender, how loving are his chastisements! … I found during my illness many impatient thoughts and desires and much deadness of affection, worldly-mindedness and coldness and stupidity and a hardness of heart which I can only feel, but not express. O Lord, have pity …

18 November
Much beset with an angry spirit, and had much ado, even by prayer, to keep it down. I found it a heavy cross to meet my class this night …

9 December
I found it a grievous cross to meet my class this night. O my God … I am not fit for thy work …

25 December
A blessed, joyful day to every happy soul. Mine alone remains like Gideon's fleece, unwatered in the midst of falling showers …

1759

1 January
… These many years have I been a barren tree in my Lord's vineyard … O Lord … cause that this year I may bear fruit to thy glory, for the merit and sake of Jesus Christ, my saviour and intercessor.

2 February
… One of my children being taken ill, my mind was much distressed, but by prayer was relieved …

6 February
My soul comforted in meeting my band, and as to my child, I think I do not desire to dictate to God …

16 February
This being kept as a public national fast[1], I endeavoured to stay my mind upon God, but my heart was hard as a rock. The Lord has restored me my child, but again laid his afflicting hand upon my husband, and find this a grievous trial …

25 February
… Blessed be the Lord my God for all his mercies! A prospect of my husband's recovery has raised my dropping spirits, and put a song of praise and thanksgiving in my mouth. O, that the restoration of his soul might be the next happy theme! …

17 March
In obedience to my husband, I went contrary to my conscience into sinful, carnal company. The Lord gave me power to pray beforehand and in some measure to watch whilst among them, yet in some things I was condemned …

1 April
Heard Mr Trembath[2] preach, and was in some measure emboldened to plead with God … but alas, I came still empty away.

9 May

Went this day to see a poor sick woman, the richest soul I ever saw. A Lazarus indeed[3] – miserable to behold, yet rich in possession ... having nothing and yet possessing all things, destitute of the common necessaries of life, her highest cordial being a little sour milk, yet praising God, and crying out in raptures, 'I want nothing. I have as much of this world as I desire. I have Christ, and in him I possess all things.' Her body so spent as to be past all hopes of living longer than a very few days, which adds to her comfort, she praising God that she is past all hopes of recovery ... exhorting all around her and preaching Christ to all who come to see her. My heart was broken at the sight and filled with grief and trouble of soul because of my own distance from God, but filled with thankfulness to God for her ...

1 June

My thoughts and hands these few days busily employed in temporal things, settling and contriving my earthly habitation.[4] But alas, on how sandy a foundation are such buildings reared! ...

6 June

Still darkly feeling after God ... In this state I find my class a grievous burden to me. I have made many applications to get rid of it, but in vain, and am afraid to give it up positively lest I should offend my God ... but ... I have neither grace nor abilities. O Lord, pity my state.

12 July

The Lord this day broke in upon my soul whilst at prayer with light and power, so that my soul was humbled to the dust before him. My heart was broken, yet filled with love and gratitude, and my hopes sweetly revived. I cannot describe the comforts of this short space ...

16 August

Went sometimes to visit a person troubled in mind. I was, as it were, pushed to pray with her, and was kept back for some time from a sense of my own unworthiness, but at length I broke through, and the Lord gave me power in prayer and blessed me in my own soul.

20 August
Went to see a sick person, and found power to speak a little of
God to him, but after I came away was condemned for saying so
little.

24 August
My thoughts and time taken up in helping one in distress …

25 September
The only description I can give of my state is that I have no joy,
no peace, no life, no power and often no desires. I am sensible of
my misery, but as utterly unable to shake myself out of it as to
create a new world. O, thou who alone art able to create my
heart anew, look in mercy upon me, and deliver me out of this
my misery! …

27 October
My soul is indeed in great distress because of my vileness, besides a time of trial being near at hand …

19 November
… The 4th of this month the Lord was pleased to look in mercy
on my distress, and made me the living mother of a living child.
Blessed forever be his name! A sense of this, together with former mercies, humbled me low before the Lord …

29 November
Went abroad for the first time and, this being a day appointed by
authority as a day of general thanksgiving for the success of his
Majesty's arms,[5] I endeavoured to fix on my mind a thankful remembrance of the particular blessings vouchsafed to me …

28 December
Sore distressed for want of God, and grievously burdened by
the charge of a class. It is a heavy, weighty cross, which I will not
be allowed to lay down, and am not able to carry. O Lord …
thou knowest I am not fit to lead thy people, that I have neither
power nor ability, neither light nor life nor grace nor strength …
O, grant me the cheering light of thy countenance, and I ask no

more than all my strength and talents shall be employed for thee, nor shall ever complain of the hardness of the task assigned me.

1760

1 January

Great and wonderful, indeed, are the mercies of God to me! His long-suffering and forbearance how great, that has still spared a sinful wretch, a cumberground indeed, and has brought me in safety to the beginning of another year! The passing bell this day declared a tree cut down ... This soul perhaps brought forth fruit and is cut down, and I, a dead stock, remain a monument of his sparing mercy ...

24 January

... O dear Redeemer, deliver me from this cursed Laodicean state,[1] rouse my sleepy soul from her lethargy, and let me hear thy voice that I may live.

8 March

... My heart is hard as the adamantine rock, and my whole soul estranged from God ... I am, indeed, looked upon by the world as a good Christian, and the thought of this is often as a dagger to my heart ... O Lord ... graciously receive me into thy favour after all that I have done ...

8 April

Many conflicts and much uneasiness of mind concerning the innoculating one of my children. My mind is not clear concerning it, whilst out of obedience to my husband I submit to it. But it is not my act. O my God, take the disposal of me and mine ... as seemeth good in thy sight ...[2]

30 April

This space[3] has been spent in tending my child, whom the Lord has been graciously pleased to restore to me, and has taken another from me with the same disorder ... During my confinement with my child, I suffered much anxiety of mind concerning him, but had my heart more than usual stayed upon God, and sweet comfort in private prayer ...And, blessed be my God, I found him a present help in the time of my trouble. I found power to thank my God for the life of one child and for the death of the other …

12 May
My heart still cold and dead to God. How then can I do his will? In everything I fall short, and am condemned …

1 June
I see nothing in me but pride and self. My soul groans earnestly to be renewed, to be delivered out of this cold, wintry state … I set resolutions, and say I will try and watch this day and keep my heart stayed upon God, but how vain are all my purposes! I cannot keep one good resolution, but am continually borne down by the current.[4]

1762

23 February

Alas, alas, how full of sin has this long space[1] been! The distress of my soul caused me to quit this exercise and, indeed, how should I pursue it seeing I am as miserable almost as I can be here? Fierce and frequent temptations and an indolent spirit have produced in me an hardness of heart ... that can neither feel the love of Jesus nor the threatenings of the Lord, nor even my own wretched, wretched state. Alas, alas! ... I had all that could make a created being happy. I had the favour of my God, and what could angels desire or wish for beside? But O, what words can describe my folly, my more than perverseness, my devilishness, thus to fool away the grace of God, to sell my Saviour for naught, to spend my thoughts and set my affections upon airy trifles, and neglect the only true good, the only comfort and support of an immortal soul! ... And now the thing which I greatly feared[2] is come upon me, and I, whither shall I turn? O my offended God, to thee I must come ... My necessities drive me to thee, and thy mercy invites me, notwithstanding the multitude of my sins ... I have sinned against heaven and in thy sight, and am no more worthy to be called thy child. O Lord, take me, even as one of thy hired servants.[3] Pardon my iniquity, for it is great, and restore my backsliding soul, I beseech thee, for Jesus' sake.

1763

23 May

Here has been a long space[1] filled up with sin and distress. I first quit this exercise by reason of the deadness and distress of my soul, of which I could not see the cause, but think I can see it clearly now. Thus, the Lord graciously discovered to me the depth of sin which lay hid in my heart, and gave me earnest desires and strong hopes of being delivered from it, and about the beginning of the year 1757 I was particularly stirred up to seek a total deliverance from all my inbred corruptions. Hearing that the Lord had cleansed the hearts of many in England and some in Ireland about this time, and some near me at Newmarket professing to have received this grace, and others earnestly pressing after it, my soul also was filled with earnest hungerings and thirstings after it.[2] Mr Olivers, who was then our stationed preacher, was also much stirred up to preach it, but few, very few, could receive it. There were two more and I earnestly thirsting after it, and often met together to confer about it, but were all very ignorant of the nature of the grace we wanted.[3] My soul was on the full stretch after it ... and I enjoyed much comfort and happiness in the expectation but, as in this I was singular, my friends in the society began to fear for me ... till they had partly reasoned and partly laughed me out of my earnestness. Thus was the fervour of my desires abated ... Yet even then the Lord did not suffer me to fall into outward sin, or to quit the means of grace but, having lost the presence of God and being truly sensible of my loss, I became completely miserable ... In this state I bore the weight of a band and class, the burden of which had almost sunk me into the earth. I made several applications to the preachers to take them from me but all refused, and I dare not obstinately give them up lest I should sin against God. It is, indeed, very remarkable that I seldom had either power or comfort in prayer except in my band and class, and seldom without it there ... Thus I continued till about a year ago, when Mr Wesley came here and again revived the doctrine of holiness of heart.[4] ... With this I found power to wrestle and strive, till in a few weeks the Lord did heal my backslidings and

151

gave me power to believe in him, and filled my soul with abundance of peace and love. Yet I could not rest here. I saw and felt the corruptions of my heart, and could not be content in less than a total deliverance. The Lord was now blessing many in this society, and this made me cry the more earnestly lest the shower should pass away and my soul remain unwatered ... The day that I first found this change in myself it was at prayer, earnestly wrestling for holiness of heart, when, coming from prayer and pursued by my enemy with doubts and fears, I took the Bible, begging of God to direct me to a text of scriptures on which I might lay hold. And I opened it on the 11 of Mark and the 24th verse.[5] This brought comfort to my soul ... but soon again shuffled aside by doubts and fears ... Some days after this, I was writing to a Christian friend, and the Lord did pour such a measure of his love into my heart as I was scarcely able to contain, and was constrained to quit my writing and go to prayer, and had then a strong testimony in my breast that the Lord had taken the bent of backsliding out of my heart, but this was followed by ... such strong fears of deceiving myself as made me cry out in an agony ... Thus agitated, I sat down to finish my letter, but could have no rest till I would open the Bible and see what God would have me to do. Then, taking the Bible, I opened it on the 10th of Romans and the 10th verse.[6] Here, surely, my request was answered ... but still the fear of deceiving myself made me ... determined not to receive this blessing whilst it was accompanied with doubts. Thus my ignorance blocked up my way, and by degrees I lost my fervour of spirit and the sweet communion I enjoyed with God, and again found the strength of my corruptions even as before ... During this time I was often drawn to resume this exercise, which I had often found a blessing to my soul,[7] but was hindered, I know not how. But, seeing the Lord has enlarged my heart and multiplied his blessings to my soul, why should I not record his goodness, and treasure up a testimony of his truth and faithfulness and the abundance of his mercy and love to a sinful, backsliding, perverse creature? ... Yesterday, being Whitsunday, my heart was drawn out in earnest expectations for some days before that God would then give me some blessing. I had hitherto denied myself the comfort of attending the sacrament in the Established Church lest I should give offence to others, but was now determined to do so no more, and accordingly waited upon the Lord in this means, having my heart earnestly drawn out in prayer for some days before that God would this day visit my soul and make it a Pentecost, indeed, to me.[8] In the morning, being kept from the preaching by the illness of one of my children and not having much leisure for prayer, my mind was in a hurried, forgetful frame going to church and drowsy under the sermon ... My soul was in deep distress, and my state appeared to me like that of blind Bartimeus, or the leper at the poolside[9] ... when these words of our Lord were cast into my mind: 'Believest thou that I am able to do this?' My soul immediately answered: 'Lord, I believe thou art able.' ... Thus I went to the table of the Lord, my soul still breathing out in earnest desires and expectations ... And in receiving the memorials,[10] my soul by a sudden act of faith cried out, 'Lord, I believe thou wilt save me from sin.' ... This brought comfort to my soul ... but all the day after Satan thrust sore at me ... Yet does the Lord condescend to bless my soul, and fill it with large expectations.

2 June
... This day a Christian friend coming in, we talked of the things of God, and he prayed. And my soul was much refreshed and humbled before the Lord, and filled with sweet and comfortable hopes and large expectations, and this night at private prayer my soul was much enlarged and brought near to God. Then I said in my heart, 'I will now pray to be delivered from my idols.' And whilst I sought for them they were gone, taken away in a moment, and my heart so filled with his love that there was no room left for anything beside ... I sought for my husband and children in my heart, but they were given up to God, and their place filled with the love of Christ ... Thus did my soul breathe after God, being wrapped up only in his love, and brought to a sweet nearness and union with him such as I never experienced before ...

9 June
Was hurried by company all this day so as not to have leisure for

much prayer or meditation, but when delivered from this at night, I found it sweet to return to my God in private, and thank him with a heart full of gratitude for not placing me in a high station of life, where a continual round of company, or even frequent visits, would intrude on my most delightful hours ... Blessed forever be my God for this distinguishing mark of his favour in not placing me amongst the multitude of whom he himself said, 'Not many shall be saved.'[11]

19 June
... I still find my husband and children and possessions which were my idols often presented before me, and would again strive to regain the place they have lost, but do find that, though they retain my affection, they do not engross that part that belongs to God. I know, and feel, that I love my husband and children with the most tender affection, and more so than I have ever felt before, but my heart is given to God. He is my desire and my delight, my portion and my choice. To him and for him I give all up, and take him for my all ...

23 June
... On the strictest examination into my state this day, I think the Lord my God is the only and ultimate end of my desires ... I find no idol in my heart, but know that my love is centred in him alone, and feel my will wholly lost in his. ... Fourteen years this day since the Lord first spoke peace to my soul ...[12]

5 July
... Being long desirous to lay my state before an experienced Christian, I this day opened my mind to that dear servant of God, John Dillon, telling him in what manner the Lord did work on my soul[13] ... and, upon the closest examination, I trust that though my grace be very small, as indeed it is, yet that it is of the right kind ...

13 July
I set this day apart for fasting and prayer, and a Christian friend desired I would permit him to do the same on my behalf. O, blessed be God for such a friend! ... We had for a time sweet

communion together, and the Lord was present with us all this day …

16 July
… O, blessed be God for a Christian friend … on whose heart thou hast laid the burden of my soul! … Establish his heart in thy love, and make him strong in the Lord, a father in thy church, a pillar in thy temple … I have been this day held up, as it were, by the chin by the prayers, entreaties and exhortations of my dear friend …

21 July
This day, on my husband's acting as I thought unreasonably and inconsistently, I found my spirit grieved and agitated, and in much love expostulated with him, but when this was over Satan did come in as a flood upon me, telling me that I was angry and, though I did not suffer it to appear outwardly, yet it was in my heart … Thus grievously afflicted was I when my dear friend came in, to whom I opened my state … I went to hear his word, my spirit being … quieted under the advice and prayers of my dear friend, but at the preaching the Lord revealed himself to me in such a manner as excluded all doubt …

22 July
… My spirit has been rejoicing and my soul sweetly lying at the feet of my dear Jesus all this day. My dear friend, who came to me yesterday in my great distress and whose words the Lord did bless to my soul, told me this day that he was so pressed in spirit to come to me at that time that he could have no rest till he came. This instance of the goodness and care of my God over me quite broke my heart …

28 July
… Some of my dear friends and I being in prayer for my husband, the Lord did refresh our souls abundantly, and did give us all a confident assurance that God would convert his soul …

29 July
… Satan … has stirred up some of my acquaintance to notice the

frequent visits I received from my dear Christian friends, and has endeavoured to prejudice my husband's mind about it … I spoke to my husband about it, declaring my willingness to deny myself of even this liberty (though very dear to me) rather than have his mind one moment disturbed about it, but … found his mind quiet from all suspicious thoughts and received a free consent to continue my custom of receiving and conversing with my Christian friends. O, blessed be my God for this …

30 July

… On meeting with some provocation this day, I found some agitation of spirit … A dear friend at the same time was pressed in spirit to come and see me and bring some letters with him which he had some time before received from Mr Wesley relative to the very thing that now distressed my mind … and when he came found me in the above state. He then read these letters which answered my doubts, and whilst he read them the Lord removed the distress from my mind, and banished all my fears …

3 August

… Had sweet access to God in prayer. Gave my husband, who is going a journey, into his keeping, believing he would preserve him. In conversing with a Christian friend afterward, my soul was abundantly blessed …

6 August

… Yesterday spent some time with a Christian friend, but was condemned for staying longer than might be profitable. I came home and went to prayer, and was grieved because of my trespass. But never did I see my God more loving. He did reprove me for my folly, but it was with caresses and endearments, the intercourse was open and I was brought, as it were, into his immediate presence, and my God did pour his blessings into my soul so that I was even overcome with a sense of his astonishing love … The light still shines clear on my heart these three days without intermission, and discovers no darkness or sin in it … After I had wrote the above, some Christian friends seemed to think it advisable that I should meet in the select band, to which, when I could not agree because of the littleness of my grace, my friend, willing to help me even against my will, brought the preacher to me, as it was necessary I should speak to him first[14] ... But, in talking with him concerning the work of God on the soul, he affirmed that, where sin was cast out, that soul should not feel any disturbance or agitation from temptation ... 'Then', thought I, 'if this be so, I am only deceived, for I have found temptations sharp and strong ...' ...The light which shone in my heart is withdrawn, and now I fear my heart is full of sin ... I being not desirous, my friend, still willing to press me to it, asked leave of the preacher that I should meet in the select band, but what shall I do there? Surely my friend is mistaken. O my God, direct me ...

7 August
By the persuasions and importunities of my friend, I went this morning with much reluctance to meet with the select band. The awe I had upon my spirit on going in amongst them made me tremble and hearing the preacher affirm the same thing in the band which he had before said to me, made me the readier to conclude that I had certainly deceived myself ... I know not what to do. I fear to quit, and fear to keep my hold, and in this my distress I fear to take, and fear to refuse the comforts that offer. O Lord, I leave my cause in thy hands ...

10 August
... Why did I doubt? Why did my foolish heart stand reasoning with my enemy? Now I see clearly it was all a storm raised by him in my soul to overwhelm me ... How scarcely have I escaped from being swallowed up in the deluge! O, may I here set up my ebenezer,[15] and say, 'Hitherto my God hath helped me. O Lord, in thee will I trust ...'

20 August
This space[16] has been filled up with grievous and sore trials ... Most grievous of all, Satan has stirred up some evil-minded person to sow discord between my husband and me, by insinuating that I had been unfaithful to him ... This I find a most grievous stroke. It is touching me in the most tender part, such a trial as I never looked for ... being, as I thought, secure in my conduct,

character and in my husband's affections ... Tongue cannot express what I have felt in this trial. My soul and body were pressed so sore that I think I could not live many days under the same exercise, but my God in pity to my weakness would not suffer me to be entirely overcome, but stepped in to my relief and calmed the mind of my husband, giving him to see it was the work of an enemy. In the midst of this trial, I have found the most tender affection for my husband. I do not know my enemy, but find a sincere desire for their conversion and power to pray for them without any grudge or ill-will to them ...

23 August

I find it harder to stand now than in the midst of my trial ... Satan has so far prevailed as to deprive me of much Christian conversation, and this I find grievous, very grievous to me. My soul mourns over the loss, and sorely feels the want of this help, but perhaps this may also be needful for me, perhaps I looked for too much from this means ...

25 August

... The remembrance of my trial is more and more grievous to me every day. It even presses down my body ... In this state I took the Bible, beseeching the Lord to direct me to a text whereon I might lean in this my distress, and opened it on these words: 'Come, take up the cross, and follow me.'[17] This calmed my spirit ...

26 August

Having some discourse with my husband concerning the cause of my present trouble, I had found the care of my God over me, being often resolved to resent the usage I had received and to speak my mind in sharp words. But now, when I did speak, I found my heart filled with the tenderest affection towards him, so that I could use no other language than the language of love, and found that by this means the Lord had wrought also on him, so that peace was made in both breasts and our hearts more closely united together. Lord ... increase and continue the peace thou hast made, and forgive my enemy, I beseech thee ...

10 September
My soul this morning in much heaviness, full of doubts and fears. A Christian friend coming in, we opened our state to each other and spent some time in converse and prayer together, and found my soul much relieved ... Had much power in praying for my husband and strong hopes for him ...

11 September
A blessed Sabbath ... and was much comforted by a letter from Mr Wesley ...[18]

25 September
The Lord did make his own day a day of blessings to my soul. Under the sermon this evening, whilst Mr Johnston[19] showed the insufficiency of our own righteousness and the extent of that mercy purchased by the blood of Christ, my soul was sunk into nothing ...

5 October
This day was visited by my dear friend, Mr Dillon, to whom I opened all my heart and told all my trouble, and ... found my burden entirely removed ...

26 October
My dear brother Dillon coming to converse with me, I laid open my state to him and he, as a friend, reproved me for trifling conversation. I was immediately convinced of this, and found my heart drawn out in thankfulness and gratitude for this reproof ... and my heart was closer than ever knit to my dear friend. O, blessed be God for this mercy – for a Christian friend, for that love which unites, for that openness of soul, that freedom of spirit, that expels both shyness and sin! And O my Lord, bless, abundantly bless my dear friend. Let his soul prosper, let the friendly reproofs and admonitions of thy good spirit follow him, to guide him into all truth and warn him of every error. Reward him sevenfold for his care over my soul, and O, stand by and preserve him in every hour of temptation and time of trial, that he may stand immovable in thy grace, and be profitable to thy church.

30 October

… This has been a Sabbath of rest, a day of blessings … My soul humbled to the dust, and my heart cleaving to my God, my spirit mourning over the ungodly and closely knit to the people of God and earnestly groaning for the salvation of all … O my God, my soul thirsts for thy full salvation. As the hart panteth after the water brooks, so doth my soul hunger and thirst after thee …[20]

16 November

My soul sweetly watered in conversing with a Christian friend, and we have agreed to meet each other at a certain hour every day at the throne of grace that, though absent in body, yet we may be present in spirit to ask a supply for all our wants, and particularly that God would bring in his sanctifying grace into our hearts … We began this day, and my soul was much blessed …[21]

20 November

This evening my husband being taken ill, Satan … did for a time bring much distress and heaviness on me, still casting it into my thoughts that his disorder was on his mind, and that my enemies had again stirred up evil in his breast against me … but, on speaking plainly to him, found my mistake …

11 December

Much refreshed in conversing with my dear friend and receiving his advice, which I found sweet to my soul … This day I have found the Lord very gracious. He has made it a Sabbath, indeed, to me …

17 December

This day Satan came with unusual force, endeavouring to raise resentment in my mind against the person who endeavoured to sow discord between my husband and me. The temptation was violent for a little time, but the Lord gave me power to examine and reject it …

19 December

Being much afflicted with a pain in my head and teeth these

many days, I found nothing contrary to an entire resignation of will, and always found thankfulness of heart that my pain was not exquisite, though continued. But now my pain being much greater than usual, Satan did thrust sore at me to raise dissatisfaction in my mind, but by looking to my Jesus ... my soul enjoyed an entire tranquillity ... being as perfectly resigned in the continuance of my pain as in the removal of it. But do find an earnest desire to know the will of God in this visitation ...

25 December

Had large expectations from the ordinances of this day ... but ... my pain being very great, it prevented my meeting this morning at four o'clock with the people of God. The Lord was pleased to give an abatement of it whilst I waited upon him at his table and at the preaching in the evening, but then increased and continued, so that I feared I should want patience under it. But, casting myself before the Lord ... received a fresh supply of strength, suitable to my need ...

27 December

My pain continual and sometimes exquisite but, blessed be my God, I find patience under it, though sometimes I think I escape only with the skin of my teeth. Yet find thankfulness that even thus I am preserved ...

1764

3 January

These few past days my pain has been great without intermission, and often exquisite, but find not my heart depart from God … This night … my dear friend, Brother Dillon, came to me and prayed for me, and as he prayed the Lord did give ease of my pain … Together with my pain of body, Satan did endeavour to distress my mind from different quarters, particularly to make me imagine my husband slighted me, and was for some time under this temptation before I could see it to be such, but the Lord my God did ease my pain and deliver me from this also …

16 January

This morning went to the early preaching for the first time since my illness … and was enabled there to make a solemn dedication of myself to be the Lord's, without any reserve … Having got cold by going out this morning, I was this evening taken very ill, and thought that perhaps the Lord was about to lay his hand on my body again, and found … such a sweet, thankful submission and springing forward in my whole soul to suffer his will as brought much comfort with it …

1 February

A house some distance from mine being burnt the last night, my heart overflowed with thankfulness and gratitude to my God for exempting me from this calamity, and for sparing the lives so that none were lost …

9 February

It has been often on my mind these some days past that my friend, Brother Dillon, has not dealt faithfully by me, that he has seen cause for reproof and has not given it and, on speaking my thoughts to him this day, found they were not groundless. He acknowledged he had seen me give way to laughter and suffered pain in his mind on my account, yet had not freedom to tell me of it. This breach of friendship in him grieved me to the quick, yet found it a wonderful blessing to my soul …

28 February
My dear Brother Dillon, having spoke to me this day that we should set apart a certain hour every day at which time we should endeavour to be punctual to meet each other at the throne of grace that, however distant our bodies might be separated, our prayers might then unite for each other, this raised thankfulness in my heart to my God for thus putting me ... on the heart of his dear servant ...

17 March
Being this day in great heaviness ... I opened my mind to my dear Christian friend, and found his counsels sweet and my soul much relieved. The Lord did bless both our souls in prayer, and gave us strong hopes for my husband ...

10 April
My mind hurried about temporal things ... but had much comfort at the meeting of the public bands this day. My friend, having acquainted me that he had proposed to the select band my meeting with them and that it was approved, I found my spirit seized with an awful dread ...

15 April
Went with awe and trembling to meet in the select band, and in much heaviness of spirit and distress of soul ... till the moment before I was spoke to, when a ray of light darted into my soul and gave me to see and rejoice in the Lord ... My soul was thus happy till I had done answering, when immediately again my mind was overspread with a thick mist, so that every grace was again hid from my eyes, and thus it has continued all this day ...[1]

22 April
... I waited upon the Lord at his table, and he did visit my soul with his love, and at the love feast my heart was sweetly given up to him, but particularly in meeting my class. At the sight of a backslider again returning to God, I felt such an overflow of love and joy and thankfulness as tongue cannot express. O, blessed forever be my God! He has made this a day of blessings to my

soul, though, indeed, my joy has been much damped by parting with my dear Christian friend.[2] I feel sensibly the sharp severe pangs of parting with such a friend, a friend nearer than a brother, a sympathising, praying friend, to whom I could lay open all my trials and temptations, and whose conversation and advice I have often found blessed to my soul. I feel parting with him to be a trial indeed, but am enabled to look to Christ and cast my soul simply on him …

25 April

I find the loss of my friend (though, indeed, a trial yet) has proved an unspeakable blessing to my soul. It has caused me to cleave so entirely to my dear Lord Jesus, and given me to feel such a sweet separation from every person and thing here below as tongue cannot express …

4 May

My spirit being grieved at the trials of some and the sins of others, I uttered a few words by way of reproof in a hasty manner, for which my soul has since been much weighted down …

15 May

This has been, indeed, a day of trial and sore distress from a quarter where I least of all expected it[3] … and were it not for the rest and consolation which my soul finds in Christ, I should certainly sink under my burden … O my God … be with me in the fire and O, take care of me there, that I lose nothing but dross …

19 May

I have been examining how I have hitherto gone through this trial … And, upon the strictest scrutiny, do not find that I have in any measure acted hastily, impatiently or inconsistent with the grace of God … I find much dissatisfaction at the hypocrisy and indiscretion of the person, mixed with the tenderest love. I find no resentment, nor have I used any correction upon the author of my trouble, though under my authority, and find much thankfulness to God for discovering the evil so soon and preventing much greater …

29 June

… It has been for some days strongly impressed upon my mind that some heavy trial is at hand. Whether this be a temptation or not, I cannot say, but am enabled to leave it to the Lord, and this day at prayer … I received this answer: 'I will never leave thee, nor forsake thee' …

22 July

Blessed be the God of my salvation. He bringeth down to the grave and bringeth up again, and I remain a monument of his sparing mercy to this day[4] … Though my pain was for a time very great, I found not the least degree of impatience, but an entire submission to the will of my God, and such a love to, and patience with every one around me as I never before felt in any sickness … I for a time did expect that the Lord was about to call me away, and found myself entirely disengaged from every earthly thing, having no desire either for life or death, but an entire willingness to either, as the Lord should choose … During my recovery, my soul was for some time under much heaviness, but enabled to trust in the Lord from a sense of his goodness to me …

10 August

This space[5] has been filled up with much pain of body, but blessed be my God, who enabled me … at all times to find my heart separated from the world and wholly, unreservedly given up to him …

12 August

Sabbath day. Having company to dine with me, I was condemned for sometimes joining with them in worldly conversation … Having occasion to reprove one of my children for a breach of the Sabbath and being strongly opposed by my husband, I found my spirit grieved very much, yet was enabled to leave it to the Lord without answering harshly …

17 August

Weighed down with bodily illness and heaviness of soul …

9 September

Sabbath day. Weak in body, but my confidence steadfast and my soul sweetly stayed upon Christ whilst I went to meet my class. Was hurried from it by a cry of fire in my house, one of the chimneys having taken fire, and was burning fiercely. I received the account without any hurry or disturbance of mind. The Lord kept my mind calm and gave me a strong confidence that no evil should happen ... and ... was not disappointed of my hope.

16 September

Sabbath day. Was confined from the word by the weakness of my body, but the Lord did bless my soul ...

23 September

Received a new ticket this day,[6] and found a solemn sense of God resting upon my mind, and much thankfulness for past and present mercies. Was asked by the preacher whether I found patience in all things, to which upon reflection, I was enabled to answer that I did ...[7]

9 October

... Met with the select band in the morning, with my own in the evening and with the public bands at night, and in all found my soul brought nigh to my Jesus and sweetly resting in him ... In all, my soul is convinced of its own weakness and, emptied of self, sinks down with all its weight on Christ, seeking him only as my portion and inheritance and resting sweetly in his all-sufficiency, and here I find solid footing, substantial happiness, peace and rest, such as can nowhere else be found. O my Jesus, in thee I have all and abound, and set to my soul that thou art true, that none ever sought thy face in vain.[8]

10 October

I find my soul happy, sweetly, confidently happy, in the love of my dear Jesus. I have not the testimony of his spirit that my heart is cleansed from sin – I see now that I have lost this by my unbelief, for which my soul is much grieved and cannot be satisfied till I find it again restored ... And yet my soul is happy, very happy. I find it continually lying low at the feet of my dear Redeemer and feel the sprinkling of his blood every moment. I see my continual need of this and my necessities drive me to this fountain and am never sent empty away ...

21 October
Sabbath day. My husband being taken suddenly ill this morning, I was thereby detained from the public worship all this day, and found my need of these blessed supplies which the public means affords ... I did not find my mind full of anxious fears and deep distress on my husband's illness as in time past ... and by looking to my Jesus still found my soul kept in sweet, calm serenity, free from the storms of grief and fear, which on the like occasion used to agitate my breast ... Yet do feel that this does not proceed from any abatement of my love to my husband. No, I find my love for him more tender than ever and, were it not so, I should immediately conclude that was not from God ...

23 October
... Met the select band in the morning, my own band in the evening and the public bands at night, and in all my soul was sweetly refreshed. The Lord has restored my husband's health, and for this I feel much thankfulness and gratitude of heart ...

30 October
Came with a heavy heart from the select band and in the same manner at night from the public bands by reason of the silence and shyness which has overspread the whole.[9] My mind was filled with fears on this head, but my soul was refreshed in laying them all before the Lord.

2 November
Meeting with some insolent behaviour from my servant this day, I found my breast agitated with dissatisfaction at her insolence and, she still persisting, I ... went out of the house with my spirit much grieved ...

6 November
My servant behaving this day in a very insolent manner, I found

much dissatisfaction and spoke sharply to her, and now I fear lest I should have sinned in this ...

16 November
One of my children being visited with sickness, I have had much fatigue of body attended with heaviness of soul ...

23 November
Blessed be my God, he has restored my child. But my ... spirit is borne down by the weakness and indisposition of my body so that I find a weariness and heaviness of flesh and spirit continually attending me ... Look upon me now, for I have need of thee, O my God.[10]

1765

12 January

... This space[1] has been filled up with a tedious and dangerous illness of body, with deadness and heaviness of soul ... The sufferings of my body were great but O, how insignificant in comparison of the sufferings of my mind ... I found temptations to the contrary of every grace – to impatience, to dissatisfaction with all around me and even with God, to self will, to love of life, love of the world, to jealousy with my husband and almost everything ... I am, indeed, at present surrounded with trials, both from without and from within ... Undertake for me, Lord. I ask not for outward things ... only I ask that sweet communication of thy grace which may bear me up above all earthly things and may enable me to say: in all, thy will be done ...

31 January

... This day I have lost a dear, a faithful, tender, loving, Christian friend and companion[2] ... I found the parting with her a severing stroke, yet felt a sweet and joyous satisfaction at her happy escape from all these things which I am still left to struggle with, and the thoughts of soon meeting her above allays my grief for my present loss ... My own weakness hindered my being often with my friend or staying long when I went, and by that means could not gather much of her experience, but what I could I shall here transcribe as I wrote it to a friend ...

January 25th 1765: I went to see Sister Moore and found her very weak in body, emaciated to a skeleton even beyond conception, but perfectly in her senses and happy in her soul ... She complained much of her weakness, and feared exceedingly lest her last struggle with death should be hard and her mind by this means drawn off from God, which made her pray earnestly for a safe and easy passage into eternity, and requested of her friends to do the same. ... When I came away she said, 'I believe Sister Bennis had a desire to receive the sacrament with me and I will gratify her', and accordingly she sent for me the next morning for that purpose. I found her pain of body much abated and her soul in perfect peace ... I asked her did she entertain any hopes of life from this sudden change. She answered, 'No, I have no thoughts of life. I desire to die that I may be with my Jesus. I have done with everything here below. I have given up my husband, children and mother without one uneasy thought or desire concerning them, even Betty, [meaning her eldest child and her idol indeed] who you know was so dear to me, I can and have given her up and have not seen her these three days, nor have I any desire to see her or any thought about her. And what but the mighty power of God could effect this? ... My poor husband seems to have some hopes of my recovery but I think he is mistaken though I would not grieve him by telling him so, nor do I feel any fear but that of a possibility of my recovery.' ... I did not see her the next day but ... the day following, which was Monday, I went again to see her and found her rejoicing in spirit ... She called her friends one by one as they came in and spoke to them as their several states required, pointing particularly at each person's besetting evils, and enforcing all by earnest prayer for them severally ... I asked her was her mind now perfectly easy. She answered, 'Yes, the Lord ... has answered all my requests, and am confident that he will not leave me till he has taken me to himself. I asked of him a resigned will for my mother, and my God has granted my request and gave her power last night to give me up, what she never could do till then, and I know he will enable my husband also to bear this trial with patience because I have asked it of the Lord ...' She spoke often of the unprofitableness of her past life ... and often praised God for this long and painful illness as a means of weaning her heart from the world ... Thus she continued till Wednesday morning ... I found her then very weak, cold and clammy and not able to speak much. She said, 'I have had hard work since I saw you.' I said, 'You have been fighting the Lord's battles, and are come off conqueror.' She answered, 'Yes, it would be bad to hold out till now and yield at the last ...' I asked, 'Do you feel any pain of body?' She answered, 'Heartbreaking pain, but it will soon be over ...' Thus she continued fighting and conquering till Friday morning when she sweetly and calmly breathed out her soul into the bosom of her Lord, being for some hours before delivered from every temptation and enabled to rejoice without any mixture of doubt.

15 February
… My time of trial being near, I find some distressing thoughts from that quarter. O Lord … undertake for me.

23 February
Weak in body and mind …[3]

14 March
Still I remain a monument of the free grace and mercy of my God … He has heard me in my distress, and made me the living mother of a living child … In my extremity, when my pangs came upon me, Satan laboured much to distress my mind … when these words were given me: 'Fear not, I am thy salvation.' This revived my drooping spirit and enabled me to stay my soul upon the Lord, and after my deliverance filled my heart with thankfulness and gratitude for his gracious, condescending love …

7 April
Went abroad for the first time and waited upon the Lord at his table. Found my heart thankful and my soul humbled in the dust before the Lord …

23 April
Being harried with company, I went to meet my band with a heavy heart, but my gracious Lord made it a blessed happy time to my soul …

8 May
Blessed be my God, he did enable me to speak for him and vindicate his cause … O Lord, let it not be in vain, for thou canst work by thy own mighty power, even with small and base instruments.

8 June
… Found much thankfulness of heart this day on seeing that

dear man of God, Mr John Wesley.[4] O, may his coming here be a blessing to my soul and to many more!

11 June

Waited upon Mr Wesley this day, and laid my whole experience before him and received his advice and direction, which was much blessed to my soul. It gave me to see more clearly into my own state, answered some objections and solved many difficulties ... The Lord did abundantly refresh me at the love feast and fed me with the bread of life ...

22 June

My mind hurried about temporal things, yet the Lord my God did sweetly refresh my soul whilst writing to a Christian friend,[5] and in prayer, and in looking over former experience ...

23 June

... My former state has been often this day brought to my view ... By looking back I am given to see more clearly what I now possess and great, unspeakably great indeed, are the mercies I have received ... O my gracious Lord, still keep me ever thine, bind my feeble soul to thee, nail my heart to the posts of thy door, deliver me from those things which still trouble me and save me into all thy great salvation ...[6]

9 September

Blessed be my God, he has again refreshed my soul and cheered my heart after much sorrow and distress ... O, thou great inexhaustible fountain of blessedness, author of all my mercies and end of all my hopes and desires, let this little spark which thou hast kindled in my breast become a great flame! O ... let not the fire ever go out, but let this as a continual sacrifice flame before thee and let the odour thereof arise as incense from the altar of my heart! O, let my soul in sweet and solemn silence wait upon thee amidst the bustle of a busy world, and feel continually that holy retirement, that sweet sequestration of spirit which my soul longeth after! ... Thou art my Lord and my only love ... I have taken thee for my portion and my inheritance and do renounce every other claim. I give up to thee my all of earthly good – my husband, my children, my friends, my family, my houses, lands, possessions and inheritance here below and do take thee, my Jesus, as my whole inheritance, my all in earth and heaven, my rock and my refuge, the desire of my soul and the joy of my heart. Thou knowest, thou knowest my whole soul acquiesces in this choice. O save me from apostasy, let me never recant, bind my soul to thee forever by indissoluble ties for in myself I am nothing, I can do nothing. O, bind me with the cords of thy love that my weakness may never yield!

16 September
My soul much blessed in the select band and afterward, meeting with a Christian man from Holland, I found much comfort in conversing with him about the things of God.[7] My soul rejoiced in the goodness of God and I found, indeed, that

> Names and sects and parties fall,
> Where Jesus Christ is all in all.[8]

18 September
… Was much refreshed in conversing with the above person, and in talking to him found my own judgement informed.

27 September
… My soul has been much and often refreshed in conversing with the aforementioned Hollander, and much stirred up to ask and wrestle for the witness of God's spirit to testify his own work …

30 September
Received a letter this day from a dear friend[9] which, whilst I was reading, I was struck with a sentence in it and enabled to believe, and in that moment found a clear testimony in my heart that the Lord had cleansed it from all sin, and was filled with comfort and joy. O my God … do thou sustain my feeble soul and enable me still to conquer through faith in thy blood![10]

9 October
The Lord does abundantly bless my soul … yet feel the weight of the church of God heavy on my heart. O Lord, bear thou the bur-

den of thy people and let not temporals weigh down the souls of those who have laid up their treasure above.[11]

16 October

My mind heavily weighed down because of the sins of others, yet sweetly refreshed in conversing with my friend the Hollander about the work of God on the heart. Indeed, the Lord has made this man a blessing to me ... I have often in conversing with him about holiness of heart found my own judgement informed. I have been at times called to defend the very points which were most doubtful to myself ... and in talking of, and defending it in these very points I have had such a light cast upon the matter and my understanding so cleared with regard to it as gave me much satisfaction ... My friend requested that I would give him my experience in writing, which after some considerations I was persuaded to do, and in this exercise my soul was unspeakably blessed. The looking back and reviewing and recounting the manifold mercies of God to my soul filled my heart with gratitude, love and praise to my gracious, loving Lord and, as a monument of his goodness which I may have recourse to in time of need, I shall here insert the same as I wrote it for my friend, that my God may have the glory.

I was very young when the spirit of God began to strive in me. In my childhood I had many drawings which then passed unheeded by me. When I was about ten or eleven years old, I threw aside the forms of prayer which I had learned and prayed extempore when alone ... I was fond, very fond of reading and would sometimes read books of divinity for want of others and would then observe the effect that these had upon my mind different from the others, yet could not confine myself to them. I was, I believe, about thirteen or fourteen years old when Mr Allen's *Alarm* came to my hands.[12] This was the first alarm my conscience got. When I had read but a part I began to fear exceedingly and resolved to read no more ... but I was immediately ... given to see that wilful ignorance was nothing less than wilful damnation, and that it was my duty to enquire and make all possible and diligent search after truth ... These thoughts made me take up the book again which I then read with much prayer, beseeching God to enlighten my understanding and to teach me his will. But, though I prayed for it, I was not attentive as I should to the teachings of his spirit, neither had I any other teacher to direct me what to do. I was for some few years thus tossed to and fro … I saw, indeed, in the scriptures that … whoever is saved, it must be through faith, but what this faith was I could not find out. I saw clearly that it must be more than a bare outward profession … but who to enquire of I knew not. Therefore I kept all these things to myself and … both my heart and life remained unchanged … Once, after much trouble of soul, the Lord did sweetly attract my heart and incline it to follow him, and in receiving the sacrament did enable me to take Christ, as it were, in my arms and offer him up to the Father as my propitiation. Here my burden fell off and my heart was filled with such love, joy and comfort as I never before experienced … For some little time I was very happy and, meeting with a covenant in Mr Allen's writings to which my whole soul acquiesced, I drew it out and entered into the same solemn covenant with God to which I sub-scribed my name, being determined to live wholly devoted to him.[13] But in a little time I again grew careless, though I had still many sweet and comfortable visits from God … I had many sweet, retired hours in the garden and in the fields, quite alone, where I found it sweet to read and pray and meditate, yet all this passed unknown to, and unheeded by any. I then often thought how comfortable a thing a Christian friend would be to whom I might declare all that passed in my heart, and would have prized such an one as my greatest treasure below, but did not then ever expect to meet with such. In a little time, my father died and I mar-ried.[14] I had still continual stings of conscience. I saw I was not right, yet saw that I was not as bad as many, and would often, with the proud Pharisee, thank God that I was not like such or such a person though, indeed, I was as bad as any.[15] … I looked for the church of Christ amongst the visible con-gregations, but could not find any body of people who I thought deserved the name. The body of people to which I belonged – viz the dissenters[16] – were now, as I thought, the most circumspect of all, yet could not see that even these could be called by this name, seeing many things in their common way of living which I thought must not be acceptable to God. Thus distressed and bewildered, I would cast myself before the Lord and beseech him if there was any other more perfect or acceptable way of serving him that he would make it known to me. This was my state when the Lord first sent Mr Wesley's preachers to Limerick. I saw Mr Swindells (who was the first of them that came here to preach) pass by my door with a great mob after him.[17] Upon my enquiring who he was, they told me he was one of the people called 'swaddlers',[18] of whom I had heard some random accounts, but had no desire or intent to hear him preach, being tenacious of my own church and her principles, though indeed I knew not what they were ... This was the 17th day of March 1749 and the first time that any of these preachers had come here, nor was he come to make any stay, only made it his way to Cork and was now going to stand up in a convenient part of the street to preach.[19] This was in the morning about ten o'clock. I did not go to hear him, nor would my pride suffer me to mix with such a rabble[20] but afterward, hearing a great account of the sermon, I resolved to go in the evening when I heard he was to preach again, which I did and was much affected, and was asked to spend the evening in company with him. My heart was much softened and affected by his preaching and conversation, and was determined I would not miss another sermon whilst he stayed in town, which was about three days ... In about a month after another preacher[21] came to town and, finding many here willing to receive the word, they soon established a society, of which I was determined to be one ... I was one of the first that joined. Indeed, I did it in much fear and trembling, being perplexed by various reports which were brought to my ears concerning the wickedness and cunning of these men, but I had set a resolution that I would not believe any report but would hear and see for myself ... I now felt my sins but did not see clearly where my remedy lay till one day the preacher was explaining these words: 'By grace ye are saved through faith, and that not of yourselves. It is the gift of God.'[22] ... and as he explained it, the spirit of God

... gave me both to see into the true nature of faith, and that I myself was wholly destitute of it ... In this manner I was till the 23rd when, conversing with the preacher about the state of my soul, the light broke in upon me in a moment and banished all the shades of darkness. All doubts were done away and I could now believe in, and lay hold of Christ as mine and appropriate his merit to my own soul ... Thus did the Lord create peace in my soul, bringing order out of confusion, and thus happily did I go on for about three months before my inbred corruption began to appear ... and not only so, but also the world up in arms against me ... I was as a sparrow upon the housetop, not one of my family or relatives seeing the necessity of being born again, therefore was obliged to suffer much on this account. ... I thought whilst I was seeking the Lord that if I could once get an interest in Christ I should have nothing to do afterward but sing and rejoice, but I now found that my faith was given me as a sword wherewith I must fight my way against the world, the flesh and the devil. Indeed, the strength of these my adversaries did often make me fear exceedingly ... but at every such time the Lord did sustain me and did wonderfully uphold me in the midst of a thousand trials and difficulties ... I began now to see the necessity of holiness ... I saw that the justification of my person would not do without the sanctification of my nature, but how this should be accomplished I was quite ignorant and had no hopes of being delivered till I came to die, which made me earnestly long to lay down my body that I might also lay down my sin ... Thus I continued sometimes mourning and sometimes rejoicing but continually bearing my burden, till about the beginning of the year 1757 ... As I found that God was now at this time blessing his people in a wonderful manner ... and had cleansed the hearts of many in England and some in Ireland about this time, and some in the country societies near Limerick professing to have received this blessing and others earnestly pressing after it, my soul also was filled with earnest hungerings and thirstings after it. Mr Olivers, who was then our stationed preacher, was also much stirred up to preach it and press it home upon the people, but there were but few, very few, who could receive his testimony – I think only two more and I and we three used to meet often to confer together and were all upon the full stretch after this blessing[23] ... But, as in this we were singular from all the society, which I believe consisted of about two hundred persons, my friends in the society began to fear for me lest I should go too far and, as they did not see either the probability or necessity of having their hearts cleansed from sin, they began to take some pains with me till they had partly reasoned and partly laughed me out of my earnestness. Thus was the fervour of my desires abated, and some of my friends rejoiced at my deliverance. Now was I more miserable than before. ... My unbelief brought on me unthankfulness and then hardness of heart till a kind of stupefaction had overspread my whole soul ... Yet even then the Lord did not suffer me to fall into outward sin or to quit his people or the means of grace but, having lost the presence of God and being truly sensible of my loss, I became completely miserable ... In this state I bore the weight of a band and class, the burden of which had almost sunk me into the earth. I made several applications to the preachers to take them from me but all refused and I dare not obstinately give them up lest in so doing I should sin against God. It is, indeed, remarkable that I seldom had either power or comfort in prayer during this state of deadness except in my band and class, and seldom without it there ... Thus I continued more miserable than words can express for near two years, till in the year 1762 Mr Wesley came to this town and again revived the doctrine of holiness of heart[24] ... I saw the desirableness of that happy state but, alas, it was far out of my reach ... till Mr Wesley in one of his sermons described my state much clearer than I could myself, and then encouraged such to seek the Lord, both for justification and sanctification, saying that God was able and could give two blessings at once ... These words came with power to my heart and I was determined to seek the Lord with all my might and never to rest till I had received some blessing from him ... The Lord had greatly revived his work amongst us at this time ... He had enabled some to testify that the blood of Christ cleanseth from all sin and others were earnestly seeking after it.[25] This made me cry the more mightily to God lest the shower should pass away and my soul remain unwatered … Thus I continued earnestly striving and my soul unspeakably happy, till the 22nd day of May 1763, being Whitsunday. My heart had been much drawn out in earnest and sweet expectation for some days before that God would this day visit my soul and make it a Pentecost indeed to me. Under these expectations I attended the Lord's table and, being on my knees before I went to the communion … these words of our Lord were spoke to my heart: 'Believest thou that I am able to do this?' My soul eagerly answered, 'Lord, I believe thou art able.' The word came again: 'Be it unto thee according to thy faith.' … And in receiving the memorials, my soul was enabled to lay hold on Christ for my complete salvation from all sin … Thus I continued grappling hard, sometimes up and sometimes down, till the 2nd day of June when, being at private prayer, I besought the Lord to deliver my soul from the power of my adversary … Whilst I thus prayed, the Lord did remove all my burden and enlarge my heart and admitted me to a closer communion with him than ever I had before. Then I said, I will now ask to have my idols taken out of my heart, but whilst I sought them they were gone, taken away in a moment, and their place so filled with God that there was no room for anything besides … I sought for my husband and children in my heart (that is, I examined whether my heart was in any degree so bound up in them as to separate any part of it from God), but they were given up to God and my heart so filled with his love that I was constrained to cry out, 'Lord Jesus, thou art the only object of my soul, thou hast taken possession of my heart and there is no room for any beside thyself' … Thus did the Lord bring me, worthless and unworthy, into the glorious liberty of his children, according to his promise made in the 36th chapter of Ezekiel and the 25th and following verses.[26] … Thus I continued, inexpressibly happy yet foolishly giving way to doubts and fears and continually questioning the work of God on my heart notwithstanding so many clear evidences, till I again lost this witness after having had it for about fifteen months[27] … Thus did I continue for about a year[28] … This was my state when you, my friend, requested that I would give you in writing an account of my experience. Your request made me cry the more earnestly to God for the witness of his spirit ... The want of this kept me back for some time from gratifying your request, till on the 30th day of September last 1765, as I was reading a letter which I had received from a Christian friend,[29] the light again broke in upon my heart and I was enabled to believe. This was accompanied with much peace and comfort and joy, and afterward it was (at prayer) made indisputably clear to me that God had taken possession of my heart and that it was now wholly given up to him ... I do not find, nor have not found since the Whitsunday before mentioned, anything in my heart contrary to pure love ... But, alas, I see I come short, far short ... in meekness, in patience, in longsuffering, in resignation, in humility, in love, indeed in every grace ... I see my continual need of the application of the blood of Christ to my soul ... and am enabled through grace to fly to it continually and to feel it applied to my heart and atoning for all my shortcomings ... Thus, my dear friend, I have, according to your request, given you a minute but imperfect account of the dealings of God with my soul ... In what I have here wrote, I have endeavoured to speak as clearly as I could so that I hope you will be able to read and understand it without an interpreter. Upon reading it over, I find many things in it which need mending but, as it would be too tedious to write it over again, must leave it as it is. I know it would not bear the eye of the curious or critic, but am not careful about this if in any degree it may be made a blessing to your soul, as the writing of it has been to mine. I am myself dissatisfied at the length of it, and yet I did not know which part of it I could leave out. But be it as it is, let it be a demand on you for your prayers. I have much need of them, and hope when you are in a distant kingdom the Lord will bring me to your mind, and trust I also shall remember you. I am, my dear friend, yours in our dear Lord Jesus, EB, Limerick, October 18th 1765.

27 October

I have been much hurried this week by the affairs of my family and have had less time for prayer, which ... together with the ill conduct of others, bears me down much ...

1 November
My husband being suddenly summoned to go to Dublin, the great inconvenience and hazard of his going now brought some vexation on my mind, but a word from a Christian friend roused me and I found immediately power to resign my will even in this to the will of my God, and ... thankfulness for a Christian friend and for a word in season ...

4 November
My husband set out for Dublin this morning, and I found my heart entirely resigned, and an entire trust in God for his protection ...

10 November
The Lord my God did make this a comfortable Sabbath to my soul, and did give me power to confess him before gainsayers. O my blessed Jesus, let me never deny thee ... and let my name be ever numbered with thy little despised flock!

15 November
The Lord has restored my husband to his family again in heath and safety, and for this I find my heart thankful ...

22 November
The Lord my God does keep my soul very happy, and gives me sweet, precious opportunities of Christian conversation ... At such times, the Lord does enlighten my understanding ... and by the experience and understanding of others my judgement is informed, my questions answered, my difficulties solved and my way made more clear, and in this exercise my soul is always happy. This makes me greedy of every such opportunity, and in this I have infinite reason to thank and praise my God, that he has of late indulged me with opportunities of this kind and with a place of retirement (such as I have not had before)[30] where I

may enjoy these opportunities … and find my heart in an extraordinary manner thankful for – yea, more than for all my possessions beside …

8 December
… Blessed be my God, my soul did enjoy much of his love all
this day, and was enabled to praise my God with my whole
heart for the teachings of his spirit and to prize it above much
learning and many attainments …[31]

28 December
… I have found this to be, indeed, a happy Christmas to my soul
such as I have never before felt, a time of feasting and rejoicing
and banqueting with my God. My soul has enjoyed in sweet,
calm, still silence what words cannot express …

1766

1 January

… My soul has been much refreshed in again being permitted to see a dear, dear Christian friend, and drawn out in thankfulness in God for giving us to see each other's faces again with joy and not with grief …[1] O my blessed, gracious Jesus, what hast thou done for such a poor insignificant reptile! … I remain to this hour a monument of thy grace, a barren tree whom thy love still spares, brought to the beginning of another year through the gracious intercession of my blessed advocate! …

10 January

… The enemy has strove hard to disturb my mind and raise jealousy against a dear Christian friend and in my friend's mind against me, but by opening our minds to each other the snare was broken and Satan disappointed, and our souls much refreshed in prayer together …

19 January

… I have found my heart this some time past drawn out in an extraordinary manner for my husband, and am enabled to pray for him in faith, having a constant and steadfast assurance that the Lord will convert him …

12 February

My soul has been much blessed these three days in conversing of the deep things of God, and I find in general that the Lord does make this the chief means of informing my judgement concerning his manner of working on the soul for, whilst I am employed either in maintaining his cause or enquiring concerning these matters, I find often a light cast upon my understanding and clear discoveries made to my mind concerning these particular points which before were dark to me …

26 February
My wish

Should God, indulgent, now but grant
My wish, and fill up every want,
Speak as to Solomon from heaven,
Ask what thou wilt, it shall be given.
Say, O my soul, what wouldst thou have?
Look round upon the rich and brave,
Examine well, look round again,
Nor throw thy wish away in vain …
I ask no portion here below,
Content with what my God bestow,
But should I ask, I saved would be
From riches, sin and poverty.
A middle state I'd choose where, free
From want, or popularity,
In frugal neatness I would live,
Possessing more than earth can give …
Few and select my friends should be,
Dear to my Jesus, and to me,
Whose holy converse still should prove
A furtherance to my faith and love.
But joined in holy friendship one –
I, like my Lord, would have my John,[2]
My chosen friend, my other part,
And next to Jesus in my heart,
Whose vigilant and impartial love
Should mark my faults and then reprove,
Should all my griefs and comforts share,
One heart, one mind, and one in prayer …
Thus happy in my God and friend,
I'd wait till life's short journey end.
Then with my friends above appear
To have my wish completed there.

28 February
Some disappointments and losses in the world have been laid in
my way these two days past[3] … Though the loss was considerable, I found in the midst of all … a sweet, submissive confidence in my God that what is best he will do …

2 March
Waited upon the Lord at his table where my soul was much refreshed, but ... when I came home found my husband preparing
for a Dublin journey, which was entirely unexpected by him or
me till now. Many things were in a moment presented to my
view, such as the season of the year, the length of the way, the
short time since he was there before on the like occasion, the
greatness of the expense which he has been put to by these frequent journeys, and the cause not his own, besides his late losses
and the present situation of his affairs, which makes his presence absolutely necessary at home. Yet in the midst of all this,
found such a sweet, calm resignation of soul as left me ... even
astonished at myself ...

3 March
My husband set off on his journey, and I was enabled to give
him up into the hands of my God with a sweet confidence in,
and an entire dependence on, his care ...

5 March
This has been a happy day, full of sweet consolation. In the
morning at prayer, the Lord my God did pour into my heart
such abundance of his love as almost overpowered me ... And
in the evening, whilst I was conversing with some friends about
the work of God on the hearts of his people, the Lord did open
my understanding, and give me to see more clearly into the nature
of the work in such a manner as was sweetly satisfying to me
and my friends, and made many things which before appeared
perfect inconsistencies to me appear now quite consistent ... It
appeared to me that sin is (either more or less) some degree of
rebellion in the will, and that where no degree of rebellion is in
the will, there can be no sin. But though there be no sin, yet there
may be many infirmities and imperfections, and must unavoid-
ably be so as a consequence of the fall ... These considerations
have brought much ease to my mind, and find my heart much
drawn out in thankfulness and gratitude to my gracious God for
this discovery, which my own ignorance could not see into but
by the light of his spirit.[4]

6 March
This day, in conversing with a person who I saw intended to do my husband an injury under a cloak of friendship, I was constrained to speak home and plain … I found distress of mind for being constrained to use sharp words … but … immediately the Lord did give me to see … that I had not sinned, and gave me sweet liberty of soul and peace of conscience …

15 March
Being obliged to act for my husband in his absence, I found my spirit a little hurried on being surrounded with clamorous and unreasonable men … My God … did preserve me from anger, and gave me a watchful spirit, yet found grief and pain of mind at their unreasonable and wicked conduct …

16 March
The Lord my God has graciously restored me my husband in health and safety … This has been a comfortable Sabbath to my soul but, my husband coming home this night, I brought condemnation on myself for speaking to him about temporal things which I might have omitted, and on account of this, my soul is grievously distressed …

30 March
This being the anniversary of our Lord's resurrection, I found not my heart so lively as I would desire in commemorating so glorious an event.[5] At the sacrament and love feast and in every ordinance of this day, I found a languor of spirit which has been very grievous to me. Yet the Lord my God does refresh my soul, and enables me to see clearly his work on my heart and to know that it is cleansed from sin, though meeting with much opposition to this work, even from some of the people of God …

4 April
I find my mind often pained under the thought of parting with a dear Christian friend whose conversation the Lord has made abundantly profitable to me, and as the time of parting draws near, the prospect becomes still more painful, yet find that even in this my will is resigned …[6]

8 April
I found it painful to part with a dear Christian friend ... But, by looking to the Lord, my burden was in a moment removed and my whole soul filled with the love of God ... Now, O my Lord, magnify thy grace still more, and bring my husband to the knowledge of thy truth. Thou knowest his soul is dear to me ...

10 April
... I do find that distance cannot separate two hearts whom Christ has united in one spirit with himself in the bonds of pure and holy love, surpassing the strongest ties of nature.[7] O my Lord, how sweet, how cementing, is that love which thou dost shed abroad in the hearts of thy own people!

12 April
My spirit grieved and pressed down under the sins of another, but ... very happy in my God. My heart this night drawn out in prayer for my husband in an extraordinary manner and filled with strong and confident hopes of his conversion ...

19 April
... Two of my children being taken ill, I found many distressing thoughts and fears cast into my mind ...

23 April
My children being much worse ... my spirit is grievously pressed down. I find I have not now that strength which I shall have need of if the Lord shall see fit to try me by taking one, or both of my children ... Thou hast been with me in six troubles, and wilt stand to me in the seventh also.[8] O, pardon my unbelief, and help me to trust in thee ...

24 April
One of my children being much worse, I found nature again giving way ...

30 April
The Lord hath graciously restored me my children ... O my God, I desire to praise thy name for this, with every power of my

soul ... O, make me more simply faithful to thee, my God and my all, nor suffer me by unbelief ever to grieve thy spirit more ...

3 May

... This day I brought distress on my mind by needlessly sauntering away the eleven o'clock hour, which I ought to have given to prayer.[9] I was convinced firstly, of misspending my time; secondly, of unfaithfulness to my friends, whom by engagement I ought to meet at that hour at the throne of grace; thirdly, of omission of my duty to God, having dedicated that particular time of every day to him, when not hindered by necessary occasions. O Lord, pardon ...

14 June

Much hurried this week past by my temporal affairs, and found the want of retirement and recollection. This brought thankfulness into my heart for my situation in life, which does not often demand my entire attention, and made me often ashamed before the Lord of my unsteadiness, and liableness to be diverted from the main point by earthly objects, however lawful in themselves ...

2 July

I find it hard to keep my thoughts stayed upon God through a multiplicity of worldly employments. My thoughts wander and gad abroad, and bring home nought but distress ... O, when shall this be at an end? ...

21 July

Had some sweet considerations and meditations on death occasioned by some little indispositions of body, and found the thoughts and prospect of death sweet and salutary to my soul ... This day, in meeting my band, I was so overpowered with the love of God that I could scarce contain, my heart did almost run over, and my soul lay happy at his feet ...

6 August

... Went this day to the country to view part of my earthly possessions[10] and, as my husband showed me every part, I felt my heart thankful to the Lord for his gracious dealings towards me in these things, but found ... a giving up of all my earthly inheritance, and a grasping of my Jesus as my only portion in such a manner as threw contempt on everything beside ...

16 August
... Having a large company at tea this evening, I was so overcome with shame, and so many reasons brought to my mind, that I did not ask a blessing on the tea, for which I was afterward brought into much distress ...

18 August
... A person in my band being offended with my dealing plainly and honestly with her, I found much grief of heart, she being very dear to me, but found it otherwise a great blessing to me, in driving me closer to my Jesus as my only friend ...

13 September
One of my sons being taken ill, I found much trouble of mind ...

14 September
My daughter being taken ill, I have found my distress redoubled and my heart so loaded with grief that I have been scarce able to bear up under it. Her case is still set before me in the worst light, and haunts me continually ... Through all do find my heart cleaving to God, but find the powers of darkness ... endeavouring to work unbelief in my heart, and a want of resignation in my will ...

18 September
The illness of my children has been a continual exercise to my mind, notwithstanding all my endeavours, and this day I met with another trial on the back of all the rest: one whom I loved much has turned out of the right way and grown weary of serving the Lord. This has brought much grief on my heart yet, in the midst of my trouble for her, I found my soul even overpowered with love and gratitude to my God for preserving me from the like condemnation ...

21 September
… My children are better … O Lord, help me to praise thy name!

14 October
… This, like the few weeks past, has been thick strewn with temptations, and through all I have found much comfort and support in Christian conversation. This has been to me through my pilgrimage one of the greatest blessings in life, and as such I have prized it and loved it and coveted it, and have rejoiced in the liberty I enjoyed of late with my Christian friends more than in the increase of houses or lands. But now Satan has again endeavoured to rob me of this privilege, which has brought much grief and trouble on my heart. Indeed, I find that this is touching me in the tenderest part, yet if it be the will of my God to try me here, I find no opposition in my soul …

2 November
Another trial … But, blessed be my God who does stand by and support me in every time of need, in this trial I was conscious of the wrong done me, and found it grievous to have all my words and actions taken in a wrong light, misconstrued and misrepresented, and that by the very person who should rather cover my defects. But found my heart sorely pained for the person, and a disposition of soul that would be willing to stoop to anything to convince them of my love to them. But, as I could not, without wounding my conscience, make any concession that would satisfy, I gave it up to the Lord, being determined by his grace to continue in his ways, and let him take care for me …[11]

10 November
More trials still. Satan seems resolved to distress, since he cannot hinder me in my spiritual progress. The oppositions I meet with from without are, indeed, very grievous to me … But through all, find a firmness of soul that is resolved not to yield, let the consequence be what it will and, though my liberty be invaded and I be deprived of outward helps, yet my trust is in the Lord

that he will make me more than amends … if I lie patient, passive and resigned in his hands …

14 November
… I find it very grievous to be debarred the company and conversation of my Christian friends, and cannot help looking back and reflecting with grief on the many happy, blessed opportunities I have had of this kind, which by being so loved and prized make their loss the more regretted and more sensibly felt.[12] But … perhaps the Lord has done this … for my good, that I may the more closely cleave to him as my only friend … or perhaps he has done this to try my love, whether I can part with all when he commands. And when I consider it in this light, I do not find one negative in my whole soul, but rather a continual offering up of this and all to him, as a whole sacrifice and a steadfast resolution to be forever his.

22 November
Blessed be my God, a sense of his goodness and care over me and mine does fill my heart with gratitude, and in prayer for my husband my hopes are often strong and my heart drawn out in sweet expectation, but often tempted to impatience at the delay of the blessing …

30 November
The Lord my God has made this a blessed Sabbath to my soul. I am nothing, I have nothing, I can do nothing, but in my Jesus. I have all things, and am wholly his. I would do nothing to displease him, nor can do nothing to please myself. My Jesus is my all, and my soul desires no other, but rejoices in his suitableness to my vast necessities. O blessed, blessed forever be my dear Lord God almighty for such a saviour, and for such a gracious, glorious method of salvation![13]

17 December
My husband being taken ill, I find sometimes uneasy forebodings and fears of things to come, but am enabled to trust in the Lord and look for every help from him …

20 December

… This night, being in much heaviness and trouble of soul, I cast myself before the Lord, opening my distress and spreading my case before him, and found a steadfast assurance in my heart that my husband would recover … In a few hours after this, the candle which was burning in the room suddenly quenched of its own accord. Then said Satan, 'Will you now believe that he shall recover?' 'Yes', said I, 'I will still believe, for God hath promised.' O Lord, let not my faith fail …

25 December

Blessed forever be the God of my salvation, he has answered my request and filled my heart with thankfulness for his mercy: my husband is recovering … Yet, notwithstanding the mercies of God being so singular to me, I find myself more than ever unworthy of his grace. The illness of my husband, together with my other domestic affairs and other necessary business, has kept my time and thoughts employed, and left very little for retirement or recollection … I do not find the sweet, profitable reflections and meditations which used to accompany this season, but rather much emptiness and heaviness of soul … Behold the earnest longings of my soul and have pity on me, gracious Lord, for thy own name's sake.

1767

1 January

O Lord, I thank thee with all the power I have for giving me to see the light of this day ... I know not where to begin, thy blessings crowd so thick upon my mind – life, health, friends, prosperity, the life and health of my children and, what is yet more to me than all these, the recovery of my husband ... How many calamities have surrounded me the year past, but thou hast graciously turned them all from my door ... Thou hast given me plentifully of the good things of this life, and hast enabled me to contribute to the necessities of others more worthy than me. And how is this? Why is not my hand stretched out to receive rather than to give? Why have I a comfortable habitation and everything needful, whilst other dear children of God feel cold and hunger and pinching necessities? ... Why did not that bell yesterday toll to my distress and usher in my trouble with the new year? The news which I heard of a neighbour's daughter breaking her leg, and the son of another his arm – why was not this calamity mine? Why was my family kept mercifully preserved from this? How numberless are the instances of thy love which I could recount! ... Lord, let this be the year, the season of thy grace, when my soul shall be sweetly guided and actuated by thy blessed spirit alone ...

19 January

More trials still, sharp and in the tenderest part, but ... find an entire willingness to suffer all the will of my God. And, indeed, it appears that I must suffer, and continue to suffer, such things as God only knows, and love and discretion obliges me to keep concealed. At some times the prospect appears gloomy ... but when I am enabled to look to the Lord and give up my cause to him, I find strength of soul and quietness of mind. I find it grievous, very grievous to flesh and blood, being conscious of my own innocence, and find deep distress of soul which even affects my body, yet the Lord does enable me to bear all without complaining, or letting the grief of my heart be seen in my countenance ...[1]

23 January

… This morning I dreamed that, passing through a long entry, I saw coming towards me from the other end a woman dressed in white, and her face of a death paleness … I said in my mind, 'This is Death' … We both went forward and met each other, and she in a sprightly manner took my hand in hers (which was cold and stiff like the hand of a corpse) and said, 'I was sent for you.' … 'And', said I, 'who sent you for me?' 'Why', said she, 'God sent me.' All this time she held my hand and seemed inclined to kiss me, which I would rather have declined, but she kept my hand and drew near and kissed me. Her mouth and face had such a death-coldness and clamminess as made my nature shrink and woke me … But, blessed be my God, he … gives me to see death as a messenger of peace, sent from a friend and bringing glad tidings …

8 February

In reviewing my state this day, I see that I have lost much of the life and fervour which I had … My soul is like the spouse in the canticles, roving about in every means, crying, 'Saw ye him whom my soul loveth?'[2] and cannot be satisfied till he appear …

11 February

… When I first set about putting my house in order and moving my family into it, I feared lest it should engross too much of my time and thoughts[3] … Through the whole I … have often found my thoughts more engaged than I would have them, in contriving, managing and forwarding the business. This, with the loss of Christian conversation and want of retirement, has brought a leanness into my soul, and at times have had many fears lest this house had drawn my heart in any degree from God. But yesterday, at prayer, the Lord did enlarge my desires, and gave me to see clearly that my heart was wholly given to him, and enabled me to give up houses and lands and every earthly possession to him, desiring and requesting of him that he would not suffer me to go into it without his gracious presence accompanying me, and do still find that, notwithstanding all my trouble and expense in fitting it according to my own desire, yet am willing, nay desirous, never to go into it if the Lord sees it best for me …

12 February

My heart much grieved at the death of a dear child of God and friend to his people, yet found his death a great blessing to my soul.[4] It wrought gratitude and joy in my heart for his happy, victorious, triumphant exit …

9 April

… Found earnest desires to do something for God who had done so much for me, yet could not help refusing a class (which was pressed upon me) from many considerations, but chiefly that of my own unfitness … Thou, Lord, knowest … my blindness, ignorance, slackness, stupidity, instability and all my proneness to errors and mistakes … Teach me, lead me, by whom thou wilt, for what am I that I should go forward amongst thy people?

11 May

Sabbath day. Found the word sweet and my soul mourning after a closer union with God, and filled with thankfulness and joy at the sight of his dear messenger, Mr Wesley. O my God … make him a messenger of peace to my soul, and to thy church in general.[5]

16 May

The Lord does bless the word of his servant, and sends it with power to my soul, and do find a revival of his work in my heart, yet cannot be satisfied till the mist is withdrawn …

24 May

… On hearing myself named as leader of a class, I found myself much cast down under a sense of my own inabilities and unfitness for this office in every respect yet, looking upon it as the will of God, found no resistance in my whole soul, but a sweet springing forward to take up this cross (though heavy) and abandoning myself into the hands of the Lord …

25 May

Blessed be God, his messenger has not come here in vain to me. I do find my soul quickened and am given to see his work more clearly on my heart. O Lord, let thy word have an abidance in me, and let thy light in my heart shine clearer and clearer to the perfect day … Prosper the way of this thy servant to the other parts of thy vineyard[6] … Strengthen, support and instruct him continually, give him bread to eat and bread to distribute, and let him see Zion prosper in spite of all the force of hell …

31 May
Met my class for the first time, and found the Lord with me …

23 June
… The remembrance of former mercies and the enjoyment of present ones, and the return of this day, the anniversary of my deliverance from the guilt and power of sin,[7] afford much comfort and sweetness of soul …

20 July
My littleness of faith, of love and of every grace does often burden my soul and causes me much grief of heart, but my dear Jesus is my strong tower and my hiding place, my rock and my refuge …[8]

26 July
Sabbath day. Have been more than ordinary harried this last week preparing my new habitation … But … in the midst of my hurry about temporal things, do find sweet moments of recollection and retirement with my God, and do find him more precious than houses and lands, and the expectation of enjoying him forever is more to me than all earth and heaven. And, though my heart is at times overwhelmed with thankfulness for temporal mercies, yet find often a weariness at being detained by these, and a rejoicing in spirit at the expectation and prospect of a deliverance from all these temporal things … that now take my thoughts and attention from the things of eternity.

1 August
Have been much taken up with temporal things these few days past, and one of my children sick, but through the whole … have found sweet composure and calmness of spirit and an entire resignation of will to the will of my God …

6 August
My thoughts and attention much taken up with temporal things, contriving and adjusting ... One of my children being taken ill and, having some apprehensions that perhaps the Lord was about to remove her and finding in myself no strength or power to stand in this trial, I applied to the Lord by prayer ... and found power to give up my all to him with such an entire resignation of soul as satisfied me ...

14 August
The Lord has restored to me my child, and has laid his afflicting hand on another of my children ... I have found my spirit much bowed down under their sufferings and the apprehensions of their death ... but through all could not find any ... tendency to murmur or complain ... but an earnest groaning in my soul to be, do and suffer all his will, and a sweet giving up of all I have and am into his hands ...

19 August
Blessed be my God, he has restored me my other child and has laid his hand on my maidservant ...

30 August
... My maidservant is again restored. O, may I be thankful. This day I began to move my family, and consecrated my new house with a few Christian friends by prayer ...

1 October
Since my removal[9] I have been more constantly taken up about temporal things and have had but little leisure and few opportunities for retirement ... so that at present my soul is much weighed down ...

25 November
During this space of time,[10] I have been so exercised with sickness, business and country friends who have made some stay with me as has left but very little time for this exercise, for retire-

ment or recollection … I see I have suffered loss, and feel continual distress on that account and an earnest desire to cleave close to the Lord to recover what I have lost …

6 December
I have been this some time past much hurried fitting up a room for myself, convenient and retired from the rest of the apartments of the house, where I may have the opportunity of being alone at any time.[11] The want of such a place has often grieved me since I came to this house, and when I have found heaviness and leanness of soul I have imputed it in part to the want of retirement. But now that I have got my room finished and my hurry over, I find the want of a disposition of soul for this exercise, so that when I do retire I can only grieve and mourn and weep over my loss …

25 December
This fortnight past I have suffered much indisposition both of body and mind … This, with the constant and sometimes extreme pains in my head,[12] bore me down, so that at times I was scarce able to look up. I bore it, indeed, as a chastisement for my continual disobedience, and upon the strictest examination could not find any desire to have my pain abated contrary to the will of my God, but found through the whole a sweet submission to his will and an earnest desire that this visitation might not pass away without some fruit …

1768

6 January

I have ever found the world an enemy to God and find it the hardest thing in the world to preserve a stayed mind amidst the hurries and bustles of life. My situation these few months has brought many trials of this kind in my way. One hurry after another ... has left me less time or opportunity for retirement, and has almost entirely deprived me of that blessed means of Christian conversation which above all other has ever been most profitable and delightful to me. The want of these has brought leanness into my soul, and my constant attention to outward things has left me less fit for spiritual exercises ... but blessed forever be my God, who does not suffer my heart to depart from himself ...

27 January

... This day one of my little children being sent on an errand, and a guide with him, a little way into the street and, not getting their errand there, went further, when the other person going away left the child standing in the street who, not knowing where he was or how to get home, wandered still further, weeping and in great distress, till he was taken notice of and brought back ... I thought, thus it is oft times with the children of God: this little one went about his lawful occasions and by his father's commands and under the inspection of a guide, yet had like to suffer by going too far. And thus the child of God, when lawfully and necessarily employed, may apprehend no danger because he acts by the command and in things agreeable to the will of his heavenly Father yet, if he suffer his attention to stray and lead him beyond his proper bounds and out of the sight of his father's house, he is not safe but will find himself bewildered and distressed, not knowing where he is and, like this child, will make him cry for home when he perceives he has lost his way ... And as I looked on the child who, though rejoiced to see himself at home, yet could not help weeping at the remembrance of what he had suffered in his mind whilst out of sight of home, and finding my heart pained and yearn over the child, I thought what yearnings are there in the heart of God over the dear child of his who, not wilfully but childishly or ignorantly, strays … From what I then felt toward my child, I had some faint idea of the tenderness of God towards his, and how often I had grieved his spirit by such strayings as these.[1]

1 March

The Lord has visited me this week past with a slight indisposition of body and, though I was confined from the outward means, I found the Lord Jesus more than means or health or life to me …

8 March

… This day a poor brother labouring under difficulties applied to me to lend him as much as would extricate him from his present distress. Having met with some disappointments from him and others in such cases before, I stopped to consider what I should do, my heart being pained for his distress, when these words were immediately brought to my mind: 'Be not weary in well-doing'[2] … And my heart was filled with thankfulness and love to God for thus showing me what he would have me to do, and with pity and yearnings over his poor member whom he had put in my way to relieve …

16 April

When I think my hurry of temporals is over and now I shall have leisure of body and mind for retirement and waiting upon God, then another hindrance is cast in my way, and after that another, so that I have been, as it were, immersed in the little domestic affairs of life, and my attention so taken up with them as to leave but little time or attention for the things of God, and this I sorely feel the want of …

10 May

… I find myself weary of the world and yet more encumbered with it than ever, and many fears arising from that quarter which I am obliged to lay at the feet of Jesus, casting my whole care upon him. I … call to mind that I have given myself into his care and am now just in that situation in life where he has placed me and, though my encumbrances and interruptions are many, yet, considering them all as the will of my God, I cannot be dissatisfied, but am enabled to thank my God that my hindrances are not more, or of another nature, and to cast my soul with all its weight on him who ... has hitherto helped me through every labyrinth and restored me after a thousand falls ...

22 May
My company being gone, I have these three days had a little time for retirement and recollection and ... do find a degree of thankfulness for this little breathing time, and earnestness after God, and sweetness and confidence in his love ...

23 May
My whole life long is only a register of the goodness and mercy of God! The last night a fire broke out in a house joining five of mine,[3] which seemed to threaten great danger, but the Lord stood by and rebuked the flames so that they spread no farther ...

20 July
My spirit much grieved with my own imperfections and with the sins of others. One whom I believed to be sincere at heart, having proved herself a hypocrite, has given me much trouble. I wonder at my liableness to be deceived, but my ignorance is the cause. O Lord, pardon, and above all keep my heart right with thee, that I be not a cause of grief to any of thy dear children ...

22 August
I do find my Lord very gracious. He has, indeed, gladdened my heart by graciously drawing a soul after him for whom I prayed. This has been matter of rejoicing and of thankfulness to me, but ... I find much need to pray for wisdom and grace that I may be enabled to help this soul forward ...

8 September
... My friend's soul prospers, and for this I find my heart thankful.

26 September
... I do find my mind much encumbered about a particular temporal affair which I have laid before the Lord, desiring to be directed by him and beseeching his gracious interposition either to forward or frustrate it as he shall see best.[4] I endeavour to leave the matter with him and to disengage my mind from it, but it still follows me, even into my most solemn duties, and one circumstance or other concerning it is constantly placed before me, and my mind so harassed that my soul is often distressed by reason of it ...

4 October
Blessed be my God ... he has freed my mind, has enabled me to leave this matter in his hands with an entire dependence on him that what is best he will do, and has set up an earnest cry in my soul after a nearer union with himself ...

17 October
... Thou art my father and my God. Give me counsel and direction in the affair which I have put into thy hands ... O, let it be as seemeth best in thy sight.

25 November
This space[5] has been filled up with fears, distress, anxious cares, paternal conflicts and domestic trials and, though I have much cause to praise my God for his constant care over me, yet I find much cause also for shame and self-reproach every day ... Indeed, I often think I am not fit to transact any affair in life because, however lawful it may be, I fear it becomes unlawful to me by taking up too much of my attention, and in this sense temporal things generally prove hindrances to me, though I know they need not and should not, but my spirit is such that I have need of a double guard over it. I know it was lawful for me to marry my daughter, and was enabled through the whole of this affair to submit it entirely to the Lord, beseeching him if it was not agreeable to his will that he would frustrate it, and in all my transactions about it have endeavoured to act agreeable to my profession and with an eye to the will and glory of God, yet could not help a constant agitation of mind, even so as to affect

my body and take away the power of sleep and desire of food, till I was even borne down with it. I could not see the cause: everything was done quite agreeable to my mind, and think the Lord interposed and helped me to have it done in such a manner as was most suitable and agreeable to me.[6] Yet could not get from under a constant load of distress and encumbrance of mind, which followed me into my most solemn duties and left me less fit for spiritual exercises so that I found need continually to cry to the Lord for help and succour ...

7 December
The Lord has given me a little respite from the hurry of my family affairs and find it sweet to retire into and converse with my God, but my soul thirsts for a closer union and more intimate communion ...

25 December
This that should be a solemn season to every soul, a time of thanksgiving and holy rejoicing, is likely to be to me a time of dissipation and heaviness, as being a time of feasting and company-keeping and as such I dread it, for indeed I feel the truth of Bishop Beveridge's observation on himself that he never went into company but he came out less a man than he went in[7] ... This day found much heaviness at the sacrament and in every duty. O, how happy for me that my own fitness is not the condition of my salvation! ...

1769

1 January

... I have this year enlarged my house, increased my possessions, married my daughter, enjoyed my family in health and
safety. But how have I prospered in soul? Alas, what slackness,
what deadness, what blindness, what cause for shame and self-
reproach! ... O, let this be a year of restoration, of growing in
grace, a season wherein thou wilt bless my soul with increase of
grace ...

9 January

This day parted with my daughter[1] and, though I found my
heart thankful to the Lord for providing comfortably for her in
the world, yet could not help the feelings of nature which at
times bore me down ... but find my soul wholly cast upon the
Lord, being enabled to put my child entirely into his hands and
in some degree confident of his care over her.

23 January

The Lord has put in my way a soul under convictions, darkly
feeling after God but willing to be instructed and capable of instruction.[2] ... I have been much blessed in talking to him and
praying with and for him ...

26 January

I find it good, indeed, to be engaged in the Lord's work. My soul
travails in birth for this man's soul and find much happiness in
praying for him and, whilst speaking to him, the Lord does
abundantly refresh and strengthen my own faith ...

28 January

The Lord has set the soul of my friend at liberty and abundantly
blessed my own ... O, that from henceforth I might live entirely
to his glory! ...

1 February

... Already the storm is raised and hindrances put in the way of
this soul, who is as yet but in his infant state, sweetly reclining

on the bosom of Jesus and wholly unsuspicious of any danger. Satan has employed his loving, tender wife, who is dearer to him than his own life, by soothing arts to draw him from God, and that too under a show of religion ... My soul is grievously distressed on his account, but can only pray for him, as they will not now allow him to converse with me ...

3 February

My soul has been grievously weighed down for the above person lest he should be drawn away from God, which I fear will be the case, his wife and her family being all strangers to inward religion except one, who they will not allow to converse with him on that head. They would have him outwardly moral but not conscientiously so, not singular for piety lest he should be ungenteel, but above all not a Methodist, therefore must shun their company as infectious, representing them as the vilest hypocrites and repeating all the base, lying tales that might prove them such. But as he was to leave the town, good manners obliged him to take leave of me. His wife, having almost brought him over to her own mind, would not suffer him to come alone but came as guard on us both. Seeing I was not likely to meet with any other opportunity, I spoke plainly to them both concerning their immortal state, and endeavoured to deliver my own soul, though I saw it was not pleasing to her, yet was enabled to act by them as in the presence of God, pressing plain truths upon them, and was comforted to find his soul very happy in the Lord but, from a certain sweetness and pliableness of disposition, liable to be misled. My heart yearned over him and longed to warn him of many devices of the enemy which I would have him guard against, and to exhort him to some duties which might keep his soul alive. This I could not do whilst she was present, therefore determined to write to him. This I did, and sent it by a person, who met him on the road a little distance from the town and gave it to him, he being so closely watched that he could not get it otherwise ... I am sensible that in acting as I have done in this matter, I have laid myself open to much censure, and am willing to suffer it if I might in any wise be helpful to his soul – indeed, I could not act otherwise, for I found his soul so pressed upon my heart that I could not be clear in my own conscience if I had left anything in my power undone ... As in this matter I have need to act cautiously (for already the cry is raised against me) I have here taken a copy of the letter I sent:

My dear friend, Love to your soul obliges me to undertake a task which even you, perhaps, may be tempted to think officious and needless, but I know too well the devices of Satan ... not to have a thousand fears for you ... The Lord has done great things for you in a short time: be thankful and never forget such mercy. Let your soul lie humble at the feet of Christ, continually renouncing your own wisdom and submitting yourself to the teachings of his spirit. And don't imagine that you are now able to stand alone, that you are strong enough and happy enough and that now you will keep the matter wholly between God and you, having no need of any outward help ... The strongest Christians find they cannot stand alone, and do still learn from and are helped by the very weakest ... Remember the helps that God provided for you when your soul was in distress, remember how these were blessed to you and think what would be your case if you had not happened into such hands ... I charge you, therefore, at the peril of your soul, that you associate with these wherever they can be met with in your travels, and that you be diligent in hearing the preaching wherever you can. ... Be much in prayer and reading the scriptures and self-examination ... Be punctual to the hour of eleven o'clock: count it your privilege to meet then with your friends before the throne of grace, and let our joint petitions go up as incense before the Lord. At this hour we pray earnestly for each other, for our families, for the children of God everywhere, and for the world in general.[3] And be thankful to God for even these little few: among them you may experience the communion of saints, and be assured they will bear you upon their hearts continually ... I would also propose another thing to you, which is this: you are much indebted to the Lord for his gracious dealings towards you. I would then advise you to set apart a day of fasting and prayer wherein you should humble yourself before the Lord ... I think Friday the tenth of February would be a proper day for this, as you will be then settled at home, and I also am determined to fast and pray with you on that day, and will engage a few more to bear us company on your behalf, and if you will not bear us company we will fast and pray for you. But I hope you will make one amongst us, and in so doing make a solemn surrender of yourself to the Lord … I hope by this time my friend does not think I have said too much … Indeed, it is love for your soul which obliges me to it, as having myself found mercy of the Lord and knowing the human heart and the subtlety of the enemy of souls. You have promised to write to me which promise I insist on. Direct it to Mrs Elizabeth Bennis, opposite Bow Lane, Limerick. I do not want a complimentary epistle, but a minute account of your state and the dealings of God with you and, after you have perused this paper often, I request you may frankly and freely write your thoughts on what I have said, and your objections if any you have, without the least reserve, and if you choose to receive another from me, let me know how to direct to you … Be assured that I shall pray for you, and hope if you love my soul that you also will pray for me. And now may the Lord Jesus … keep, sustain, uphold and preserve you, and bring you at last to his everlasting kingdom and glory, is the earnest prayer of your affectionate friend, EB

10 February
Kept this day with a few friends whom I had engaged in fasting and prayer for my friend according to appointment and, blessed forever be my God, he made it a good and a happy day …

20 February
Received a letter in answer to mine from the above person, brought to me by his wife who received it unsealed, enclosed in hers. This discovered to me enough to make me cease from writing, and by his letter I see his soul is in danger for want of instruction … Already the storm is raised against me, and I suffer the reproach of the ungodly, yet would I bear this willingly if I could help this soul forward, but my way is blocked up and my heart is pained for him. I can only pray for, and give him up to the Lord …

26 March

This was a solemn season, the anniversary of our Lord's resurrection.[4] It seemed to me as a day of jubilee on which the Lord would delight to bestow blessings, and from this consideration was encouraged to ask and strive and importune the Lord, and received from him an answer: 'I am thy salvation' …

7 April

… I found some grief of heart on being made a cause of offence to any of the people of God but, being enabled to appeal to the Lord in my own behalf, my soul rested sweetly in him …

12 May

… This morning, being much weighed down, I opened the Bible, beseeching the Lord to show me his will concerning me and to give me a word on which I might trust, and opened it on the 2nd chapter of Joel beginning at the 23rd verse.[5] Blessed be God for such great and precious promises.

14 May

Found much thankfulness of heart on seeing that eminent servant of God, Mr John Wesley, yet felt shame and self-reproach from a sense of my unfaithfulness to the grace of God and the loss my soul has sustained since I saw him last. I this day found his word profitable, and felt much brokenness of heart and an earnest labouring of soul after God …[6]

23 May

Found much grief of heart at parting with my dear Mr Wesley, to whom I find my heart more than ever united. I have found him a messenger of peace to my soul, and have had many fears lest I should again grow slack after his departure. … O my God, hasten thy coming lest I grow weary and faint in my mind …[7]

1 June

Was much refreshed this day by a letter from Mr Wesley. Blessed be my God for this and every help …[8]

5 June

Thankful for again unexpectedly seeing Mr Wesley[9] and my soul much stirred up and sweetly comforted by his word …

7 June

Delivered up my papers to Mr Wesley at his request. Alas, what … a true picture of my unsteady mind, an imperfect history of my many revoltings from, and rebellions against my gracious God! … When he asked for my papers, I found no unwillingness but gave them immediately, but have since then been much exercised about it.[10]

8 June

On parting this day with Mr Wesley, I found I had need to look quickly to the Lord Jesus and seek that help from him which can nowhere else be found … My soul has been blessed by his ministry and much stirred up to ask greater blessings …

20 June

This evening was constrained to testify of the goodness of God before his people and, though I found it exceeding hard to accomplish, yet found my mind much eased by it. Indeed, I do find the Lord exceeding gracious, and he does give me blessed opportunities of Christian conversation with a dear child of God to whom I find my spirit closely united.[11] I have been preparing for a journey to Waterford to see my daughter but, as I desire not to go over the threshold of my own house without the leave of my heavenly father, I have been asking counsel and begging direction of him. I find at times longing desires to see my child, yet a sweet passiveness in the hands of my God.

23 June

… The present opportunities of conversing about the things of God which I enjoy are so precious and are made such a blessing to me, that I could wish to be detained a while from my journey so long as these opportunities may last. I do not expect such opportunities there, and dread having my soul disturbed out of its present happy state, but I leave the whole to my gracious God …

24 June

My last night's conversation has left such a sweetness of soul and delight in the Lord as cannot be expressed. I have been very happy all this day, and my friend, whom I left struggling into the glorious liberty of perfect love, has been close impressed on my heart ... and this evening also was sweetly refreshed in conversing and pressing him forward. My soul labours with God for him, and am at times distressed at the thought of leaving him before I see him made perfect in love. I have prayed the Lord if he sees fit to put off my journey a little, but am in this passive in his hand ...

25 June

O, the blessings of this day! My soul was all praise, all prayer, all importunity for my friend, and in asking for him the Lord did abundantly bless my own soul and gave him a seal to his ministry, and afterward as we conversed together did enable him to lay hold on the promise of sanctification and to stand by faith. My soul travailed in birth for him, and rejoices in his deliverance with joy unspeakable. My journey also is put off for a little time. The opportunities I enjoy at present of Christian conversation are exceeding profitable and precious to me. These are not likely to be continued long to me, therefore had a desire to enjoy them whilst the opportunity should last, therefore am thankful to my God that my journey is deferred, and cannot but wonder at the gracious care and interposition of God in all my affairs ... O, let me be ever thine, and let this my friend live before thee. Let him stand fast in the glorious liberty and boldly testify to all that thy blood cleanseth from all sin and, O my God, remember me, a tender, feeble shrub, unworthy to wipe the feet of the servants of my Lord. O, how is it that thou dost enable me at all to speak for thee? ...

26 June

Blessed forever be my God, my friend stands by faith and my soul rejoices in the Lord on his behalf ... This night one of my children was taken ill. I found much distress of mind, but my soul was sweetly cast upon the Lord ...

29 June
Blessed be my God, my child is better, and the soul of my friend prospers, and my whole heart is thankfulness and praise.

6 July
Since my giving my papers to Mr Wesley, I have been closely exercised, tempted from every quarter and often distressed and cast down through the violence of temptations, and ready to wish that I had burned them first ...

8 July
My eldest son being taken ill, I found my spirit weighed down and many foreboding fears coming in upon me ...

11 July
My child continues ill and I find the feelings of nature very strong, but am enabled to hang upon my God, being fully assured that what is best he will do ...

12 July
My husband being this day in a passion, I thought him unreasonable and answered him with hastiness of spirit, for which I was immediately distressed. Though I could not accuse myself for the words I spoke, yet was grievously weighed down on account of the spirit in which I spoke ... I wept out my complaint to the Lord ... and as I prayed the Lord said, 'Go in peace and sin no more.' This humbled me in the dust and filled my soul with gratitude and love at the feet of my dear Redeemer ...[12]

20 July
Blessed be my God, my child is better. O, may I be thankful! ...

17 August
... Was much blessed this day in conversing with a young person for whom my heart has been drawn out in prayer for some time past without knowing the reason why, but now found that the Lord had made him partaker of like precious faith, and my soul rejoiced in his behalf.

12 September
I find often an eagerness of desire to see my daughter, and if I did not every moment watch over my own spirit I see it would rise even to impatience. Thus, even lawful things would prove a snare to me did I not every moment lay them all at the feet of my dear Redeemer. I know it is lawful for me to desire to see my child, and nature often cries out for this indulgence and at times I find it difficult to quiet it, but I have submitted it to the Lord and desire not to go out of the door of my house contrary to his will ...

18 September
I see continual need to watch over myself lest my love for even the people of God should draw away any part of my heart from him. They are to me, indeed, even as my own soul and I have ever thought a Christian friend a precious gift, but I would have my heart entire devoted to God ... Had an opportunity of conversing with the young man mentioned the 17th of August last and found him happy in the love of God ... and in praying with him was much blessed.

30 September
... I have been asking of the Lord if it be his will to suffer me to go see my daughter. My heart yearns after her and longs for this indulgence, but I am enabled to submit it to my God, desiring to be led and conducted by him only ...

1 October
Had a happy time with my God this day. I found it sweet to turn from every outward thing and rest wholly in himself, and my whole soul was thankful for his own sent messengers[13] and for a pure gospel. O, the privileges of the people of God! ...

5 October
Went yesterday to see a poor, sick woman, rejoicing in the Lord, happy in the midst of extreme poverty, having nothing but what she receives in charity, yet praising the Lord continually for his bounty ... I was filled with astonishment at the goodness of God to me and could not see the reason why I was not in her place,

reaching my hand to receive the bounty of others ... Had a happy time with my young friend. My soul rejoiced over him and found much liberty in speaking to, and praying with him ...

16 October

Had a visit this day from my friend, the master of the king's ship, mentioned the 3rd of February last. On his coming again to town, good manners brought him to see me. I spoke some plain truths to him and his wife who came with him, but could not say all that was in my heart lest she should oppose. My heart is pained for him and cannot think of giving him up. O Lord, do thou pursue after him and teach him thy will and make him a little child before thee.

20 October

Had another visit from the above person, who came alone and by stealth. I spoke all that was in my heart to him and found him to some degree happy in soul, but I fear in much danger of not continuing long so. He has got into a certain system of religion of his own contriving, or rather such as others have contrived for him, which exempts him from many duties and points out a smooth, easy, convenient way of serving God. I endeavoured to show him the evil of this and the necessity of Christian diligence. The Lord gave me arguments, he acknowledged himself confuted, yet after an hour's conversation I fear I left him as I found him ... O, that the Lord would set him right! ...

25 October

... This day, in wrestling with God for my husband, I received an assurance that the Lord would convert him and was enabled to thank the Lord in his behalf. Indeed, my soul is often distressed for him and I am ready to conclude at times that it is my fault, and surely if my life and example was such as it should be, I think some of my family would be convinced. O Lord, pardon my omissions and negligences, for Jesus' sake.

1 November

... This day received much insolent behaviour from my servant, which I found very grievous and hard to be borne ...

3 November
The time for my going to Waterford being now fixed, I find my heart strangely divided between paternal affection and Christian love. Already I anticipate the pleasure of seeing my child, and the pain of parting with my friends. O my God ... make thyself precious to my soul and be to me instead of all ...

7 November
I have been busy these two days packing up for my journey and my thoughts and attention taken up about my temporal affairs, but find myself through divine grace enabled to give them all up to the Lord, and am content if he should never permit me to see my own house again ...

11 November
Waterford. Blessed be my God, thus far hath his mercy brought me. We arrived here last night after a very fatiguing journey. During the three days we were on the road, my soul was at times very happy, particularly at the 11 o'clock hour when methought I met my dear, dear friends in Limerick at the throne of grace. When I came here I found my daughter and friends in health and blessed with the conveniencies and comforts of life. ... This day was visited by an old acquaintance, who was once very happy in the Lord. My soul rejoiced to find that the fire was not entirely quenched. I saw that diligence was wanting here, and hope it was not in vain to press him forward. Went with him to the preaching, and heard an excellent exhortation on the advantage of Christian diligence ... Spent a few minutes with the preacher afterward and found, indeed, the cementing power of the spirit of God ...

12 November
... Went to the morning preaching and heard a good sermon from Captain Taylor, a master of a vessel now lying here, from these words: 'Come see a man who told me all that ever I did.'[14] ... In the evening did not receive much benefit from the sermon, being over-fatigued from standing all the time, the room being crowded, yet my heart rejoiced to see sinners flock to hear the word. The preacher, Mr Saunderson, requested I would spend a little time with him tomorrow ...[15]

13 November
Sat an hour with the preacher and it was a happy time to us both. He is simple and childlike and seems to have only the glory of God in view. I feel my heart united to him, and think it a special providence of God in my favour to send him here just as I came to the town ...

14 November
Rode out this morning to see Passage, a curious, romantic place about five miles from Waterford,[16] and had company to dine with us. This day was all dissipation. I would rather have stayed at home to converse about the goodness of God with my friend, Mr Saunderson, but this could not be. Was very drowsy at the preaching and dissatisfied with myself ...

20 November
This day the preacher left this town to go into the round.[17] I had an opportunity of conversing a little with him and the Lord was with us. This morning parted with my husband and sister, who went home to leave me here for a time.[18] At parting with them, found my spirits sunk, but was enabled to give myself up into the hands of my God, desiring only to be and do as he would have me. Was hindered from prayer at my usual hour this day by friendly visits, which grieved me much. Indeed, I find thankfulness to them for their love, but when I think my dear, dear friends are assembled at the footstool of my Lord according to appointment and expect to meet me there, my heart feels pain at being disappointed. Heard a good exhortation this night from John Christian, a leader[19] ... I find my heart much drawn out in desire that the Lord would revive his work in this place.

26 November
... Heard a good sermon this morning and another this evening from the captain,[20] and my soul was blessed under both ...

1 December
Set this day apart for abstinence and prayer ... At the hour of eleven I retired to meet my absent friends at the throne of grace and the Lord did give me to meet them, and he himself was in

the midst ... I know not whether it be the work of the enemy or not, but it is strongly impressed on my mind that some heavy trial is near. O Lord, prepare me for it.

5 December

Had a comfortable hour of conversation and prayer with two women of the society, precious souls. Their station in life was no bar. I found them dear to me as my own soul and their burdens laid on my heart ... In conversing with these, I was cut to the heart because of my great unfaithfulness to the grace of God ... I saw something so amiable, so noble and so much easier for the grace of God to work upon than what I find in myself, that my soul was brought low before the Lord, yet full of thankfulness on their account. This evening I put myself in the way to speak to a person who I feared had substituted his opinions in the room of Christ, but was grieved to find I could do him no good. His head and heart is so full of prejudice and predestination as leaves no room either for the knowledge of himself or Christ ... My soul was grieved for him and my heart much drawn out in prayer for him afterward ...[21]

8 December

... My heart is much drawn out to God for a revival of his work in this place. The cause and people of God here are very dear to me, though acquainted with but few. But, blessed be God, his love is the same uniting, cementing principle everywhere.

10 December

The Lord did make this a good Sabbath to me. In the morning heard a sweet and useful discourse from the Captain on these words: 'Man liveth not by bread alone'[22] ... I came home refreshed, retired to prayer where all my soul was love, desire and enjoyment, then sat down to write of my happiness to a dear friend in Limerick, and in this and in prayer was much blessed ... Throughout the whole day the Lord did keep my soul in awful, rapturous delight before him, and gave me also a happy meeting with his people at the love feast.

13 December

Received letters from my family and from my Christian friends in Limerick ... and was much blessed in conversing with a Christian woman. She complained that the witness of her sanctification had been for some time clouded, but whilst we conversed she found it again, clear and satisfying, and went away rejoicing. ... It is strongly pressed on my mind that the Lord is preparing me for some heavy trial. O Lord, make me patient and submissive in thy hand.

18 December

The Lord my God does keep my soul happy in his love ... How did he feed my soul in conversing with some of his poor followers this day! ... O, blessed be God for his poor, little, despised flock, and for the blessed privilege of conversing with these, and learning from them more than all the wisdom of the ancients.

19 December

I spent this evening with a lady who I had never seen before but had sent to request my company on Mr Wesley's character of me, as I am told ... The most part of the time passed without any opportunity of speaking for God and found my spirit grieved, but afterwards there was an opportunity and the Lord gave me something to say and my soul was much refreshed, but troubled to see that pride and love of the world had shut out God from the hearts of this lady and her husband, notwithstanding the many strivings of God's spirit with them, breathing desires in their hearts after him. O, that they would seek that honour and riches which cometh from God. Still, I think some trial is near. O Lord, thy will be done.

28 December

... Was much blessed in speaking to the person mentioned in the 5th of this month whose prejudice and opinions had then closed his heart, but now sees that he needs a better righteousness. ... Had good accounts from my friends and family for which I thank my God, the giver of all my mercies.

30 December

The Lord my God has graciously brought me to the close of another year and O ... how wonderfully has my good Lord dealt with me! Life, health, friends, family, substance have all been preserved and continued with peace and quietness ... He has not only preserved to me life and health, but what is dearer than both, my husband and children, and what is dearer than all ... a joy unspeakable and full of glory, a sweet, refreshing confidence that he is mine, and that my whole heart is his ... But something whispers, a heavy trial nears.[23]

1770

1 January
Thus far hath my God brought me, and here do I bear my record and witness that the Lord my God is gracious and merciful, abundant in goodness and mercy and truth, and do now with the new year devote myself anew to be the Lord's, all I have and all I am, desiring and purposing to be wholly and forever his ... And now, O Lord, I beseech thee, give me a suffering grace for suffering times. Whatever trial thou art preparing for me, give me grace patiently to endure and meekly suffer thy whole will, and let it answer thy gracious intent to my soul.

3 January
... As I expected my husband to come for me and had an account of his setting out from Limerick, I was under some uneasiness at his delay, but this day the Lord has given me to see him safe and well, for which I thank my good God, and for satisfactory accounts from my family and friends ...

9 January
This day hurried, packing up and preparing for my journey to Limerick early in the morning ... O Lord, help me and take me and mine now into thy care ...

24 January
Limerick. Blessed be my God, thus far hath he brought me through much sorrow and distress ... We left Waterford the 11th and in our first day's journey, the frost being very hard, my husband's horse stumbled and he fell, and some of his ribs broke and his head and hand cut. The Lord only knows my distress in that hour: on the high road, in a strange place, and my husband to all appearance dead, struck speechless by the fall. I cried to the Lord, and he heard the voice of my distress and restored life to him who was dearer to me than my own life. I had him taken to the next town to an inn, where he lay under the care of a physician till the 15th. From thence I brought him by slow stages till we arrived safe home the 19th ... I could see that what I suf-

fered was but a small part of my deserts, and wondered at the gracious dealings of the Lord with me. In the midst of my trouble, I saw myself surrounded with mercies: having my son-in-law in company, who came to escort us, and its happening within a mile and half of a town where the help of a physician was to be had; the hurt happening to his ribs, which were the bones of least danger and soonest healed, and no fever ensuing ... Also, what cause of thankfulness that I was with him, that it did not happen in his way to Waterford when he had only an ignorant servant with him! ... The terror of this shock has so overpowered my spirits and sank me so low that I cannot get from under it, but my soul is wholly cast upon my God.

28 January
The Lord is graciously restoring my husband to health, for which I feel my heart thankful, but cannot help being distressed at seeing that this visitation has brought forth no fruit to his soul's advantage, but am enabled to trust the Lord for this also, seeing all power belongeth to him. Lord, it is thou alone that canst break the rocky heart and manifest thyself to the stubborn soul ...

23 February
Another instance of the goodness of God to me and mine: the chimney of a house belonging to me took fire last night, raged violently and threatened danger, but the Lord my God interposed and quenched the violence of the fire and prevented any further evil, and for this I thank thee, my gracious God ...

25 March
Busied preparing for my journey to Waterford, to attend my daughter's lying-in. I find many fears involuntarily pressing in upon me but find my God my all ... I find his people very dear to me and am thankful for their love but O, I feel I am a poor, worthless creature!

27 March
Busy packing up for to begin my journey tomorrow ... I often

find foreboding fears concerning my daughter, but in this also am enabled to cast my care upon the Lord and desire that his will may be done, knowing that it is good and best for me ...

31 March
Waterford. Blessed be my God, hitherto hath his mercy brought me, hath preserved both man and beast, and hath given me to see my daughter and her husband in health and comfort ...

4 April
Having observed some change in my brother-in-law for some days before I left home, and hoping from a few moments' conversation I had then with him that his prejudice against the Methodists is removed and that the Lord is in some degree opening his eyes, I have ventured to write to him this day ... I have in my letter spoke freely all my mind, leaving the event to God, who alone can send it with power and give it his blessing ...[1]

6 April
... Here I met with the *Letters* of Mrs L-, breathing a truly Christian spirit, the picture of a soul wholly devoted to God.[2] O, how did these break my heart, by showing me what I might and should be, and by showing me what a poor, little, insignificant dwarf I am ...

11 April
The Lord my God has afforded me satisfactory accounts from my friends and family in Limerick, and has rejoiced my heart by a letter from my brother-in-law, who is earnestly crying out for God, having no rest in his bones by reason of his sins, and determined never to take rest till he finds it in the Lord Jesus ...

12 April
The sense of the mercy and goodness of God to my brother-in-law fills my heart with gratitude and love. Wrote largely to him according to his request, and appointed him a day of fasting and prayer to humble himself before the Lord and implore his mercy, in which I have engaged to bear him company, with two

more in Limerick whom I have wrote to, and also to meet him next Sabbath at the sacrament ...

15 April
Waited upon the Lord at his table, and my heart was deeply engaged for my brother-in-law and for one in this town, with whom I engaged to meet in spirit at the Lord's table, and found that distance does not separate ...[3]

18 April
This being the day appointed to fast and pray in behalf of my brother-in-law, I found it a solemn time. A sense of the presence of God all the day, and my heart in a praying frame and much drawn out in behalf of my friends and in particular in behalf of my brother-in-law. Found my friends near and present in spirit in a particular manner, and the Lord did add to my comfort by affording me satisfactory letters from my friends and family, and find my heart thankful that the Lord is deepening convictions in the heart of my brother ... Spent the evening in company with some of the people of God here, and my soul was blessed amongst them ...

14 April
The Lord has afforded me some blessed opportunities in this place.[4] O, that through these my soul may be brought nearer to him! ...

30 April
... My spirit agitated against my little child[5] which ... weighs me down to the dust ...

2 May
Blessed forever be my God, he has afforded me satisfactory accounts from my family and particularly from my brother-in-law, who can now rejoice in the Lord from a steadfast assurance of the pardon of all his sins. This work the Lord wrought on the last day which we kept as a day of abstinence and prayer for him ... He has, indeed, refreshed my soul and revived my hopes concerning my husband. O blessed Jesus, welcome, welcome to my

house! … Let this be the earnest of a further work, and let me see the happy period when I and my house shall serve the Lord …

9 May

The Lord has graciously refreshed my spirit by satisfactory letters from my friends and family and, though my spirit is much weighed down, does enable me to rejoice in the happiness of my brother-in-law, and trust in the Lord for the conversion of my husband also. I find at times many foreboding fears concerning my daughter, but am enabled to cast my care entirely on the Lord, desiring that his will may be done.

11 May

… This day the Lord did hear and answer and deliver, and made my daughter the living mother of a living child.[6] O gracious author of all my blessings, how am I surrounded with thy mercy and how does thy goodness reprove my unbelief! …

16 May

Blessed be my God, his mercies are new to me every morning. He has afforded me satisfactory accounts from my family and friends in Limerick, and a letter from his dear servant, Mr Wesley, which has refreshed my soul.[7] Received an account of the death of Brother Dillon, a dear and faithful friend, which affected me exceedingly.[8] I found my heart thankful for his happy release from a world of pain and sorrow, though sensibly affected for the loss of so dear a friend, and could not but wonder at the unaccountable dealings of God. Here was a useful instrument, wise, faithful, diligent, humble, zealous and successful in his labours, called away at a time when the church needed such, and me, a poor, insignificant, worthless blank, left behind: a barren tree spared, and a fruitful, flourishing one cut down! O my God, who can fathom the depths of thy counsels, but in wisdom thou orderest all.

20 May

This day one came to me in the street, being at the same time under much heaviness of soul, and said, 'Madam, I have a message from God to you.' I said, 'Say on.' He said, 'I have taken notice of you and have bore you on my heart before the Lord and, as I was pleading for you with the Lord, he said to me "She is beloved".' However singular this might appear, it proved a great blessing to my soul. I wondered at the goodness of my God in thus laying me on the hearts of his people, even in a strange place, and was sunk into thankfulness and gratitude before him. We engaged still to pray for each other. Lord, help me to be faithful to this our engagement.[9]

23 May

My help being required to bring a matrimonial affair to a conclusion between a friend in Clonmel and a friend in Limerick, I appointed this day as a day of fasting and prayer for them both and a few more on their behalf, that we might jointly lay the matter before the Lord and ask counsel and direction from him. My heart was earnest and importunate with the Lord that he would interpose, either to forward or frustrate it as he sees most for his glory and their good[10] ...

3 June

As the Lord has graciously given me my errand here, I am now preparing to return home to Limerick, and find many fears proceeding from a sense of my own imperfections lest I should not be profitable to my family and friends ... O thou from whom alone our every comfort flows, bless, I beseech thee, thy little ones and let our coming together be for the mutual comfort of each. O, teach us how to be helpful to each other that we may love as brethren and in all things seek thy glory.

5 June

The Lord has graciously brought me again to my own house in peace and safety, and has given me to find my family in health and satisfaction ...

12 June

Have been much hurried since I came home about a temporal affair, mentioned in the 23rd of last month, but, as I have acted in it with an eye to the glory of God and the good of others, the

Lord has been pleased to keep my mind peaceful and calm, and find a degree of thankfulness for the success he has given ...

25 June

This day was appointed by the select band as a day of fasting, humiliation and prayer, to implore the Lord for a revival of his work in this place[11] ... The Lord did bless us together and gave me strong hopes in praying for my husband.

4 July

Walked out to the country with a few friends ... We talked of the love of Jesus from heartfelt experience, and everything around contributed to the sweet enjoyment. Spoke plain and home to one I love concerning some things which I fear will hurt his soul.[12] My heart was pained to see he took it ill yet I did deliver my own soul, leaving the event to God and earnestly beseeching him for a blessing on it ...

8 July

... My trials are many, and at times find it very grievous that my heaviest trials should come from those I love best in the world. I find in my heart the tenderest affection for my husband and have no doubt of his love to me, yet his manner of conducting his affairs is a continual cause of distress to me. At present his resolution of embarking in an affair which I see will be the ruin of him and his family gives me much pain, but the Lord ... enables me to cast my care on him.

11 July

Spent the last two days in the country and made his friend acquainted with my husband's intentions, who endeavoured to dissuade him from it, but after coming home found him as determined as ever ... I have thought that perhaps now the Lord is about to try me with the loss of every worldly good, and find a sweet resting of my soul on him and dependence on his love that he will give me suffering grace for suffering times.

22 July

... After using every argument to dissuade my husband from his purpose and seeing him after all determined on the affair, my heart sunk with trouble. This day was the time he was to meet upon it. I saw every argument was in vain and resolved to say no more to him but, turning to the Lord, I told him freely all my trouble, and besought him to frustrate my husband's intentions and turn his mind from this present affair ... and in a little time my husband came in and told me that he had put it out of his thoughts, and was resolved to have nothing to do with it. O my God, I thank thee ...

25 July
... My spirit is often grieved on account of temporal things, having of late suffered much from the indolence and obstinacy of my dear husband and, as our interests are one, I cannot help being dissatisfied with it. O Lord, lay it not to my charge ...

5 August
This Sabbath began heavily ... but in the evening the Lord made me amends, did sweetly refresh my soul with his love and with a letter from Mr Wesley ...[13]

10 August
... I find many things from without to disturb and perplex me, and am often constrained to act a part which does not belong to me and which is, indeed, very grievous to me. I am often doubtful whether this is my duty, and have submitted it to the Lord in prayer. I desire to be as helpful to my family as I can, both from inclination and duty, and if I would be so I must come out of my place and take many things upon me which otherwise would be neglected. This is, indeed, a great cross to me, but am enabled to do it, I trust, in a Christian spirit, though often with fear and trembling ...

18 August
I have suffered much uneasiness of mind these two years from my husband's obstinately persisting in a branch of business which has all along, and now appears to be a considerable loss to him. This has been a constant trial to me, and found it very grievous this day to receive ungrateful and unreasonable lang-

uage from those who were the cause of it, who had sorely injured me and received much friendship from me ...

25 August
I find my mind much exercised about the loss of so much of my substance, and find often much dissatisfaction at my husband on account of it and other things of a like nature.[14] Indeed, I am distressed from many quarters: my youngest child being taken ill is also a further trial ...[15]

2 September
... The Lord is graciously restoring my child: O, may I be thankful!

4 September
I think trials of any kind seldom come alone: a loss of £650 has now come on the back of the former £1,500. I am not enough dead to the world not to feel this heavy double loss and to be in some measure affected with it. Yet, blessed be my God, I feel much reason to be thankful ...

7 September
... My child again taken very ill. O Lord, let thy will be done.

19 September
This time[16] has been taken up tending my child, who has been often to all appearance near death. I found it, indeed, a time of sore distress and a variety of outward trials made the present more grievous ...

25 September
The illness of my child continues, and many other trials call for suffering grace. These occasion me often to examine my heart and find cause for self-reproach and humiliation every moment; yet ... upon the strictest examination, I have not found either impatience or dissatisfaction at the dealings of God with me, but an entire submission to his will, even when under the tenderest feelings and inexpressible rendings of heart at the prospect of my child's death. I could not, nor cannot ask her life lest I should

ask contrary to his will, but was enabled to present myself and child at his feet as a sacrifice to his will, beseeching him that his whole will might be done on me and mine, though it should cost my heart's last drop of blood, and still I think this is the desire of my soul. Blessed forever be my God: he is restoring my child.[17]

10 November

It has seemed good to the Lord that my sufferings should continue ... My child has again relapsed and has been very ill – perhaps an innocent sufferer for my guilt. The Lord has been pleased again to restore her: may I be thankful. This has been a time of much heaviness, and exercise of body and mind, my attention taken up with outward things and my mind wandering and unsteady ...

17 December

The illness of my child and a multiplicity of outward domestic affairs has broke in upon my private opportunities of retirement for some time past.[18] I feel the loss and often mourn after these happy moments. I find the Lord is my portion and am enabled to cleave to him; I consider myself as in his hands and just where he has placed me, and am willing to give up to him every enjoyment he shall call for, whether spiritual or temporal, only desiring that he would keep my soul close to himself ...

1771

11 January
Set this day apart as a day of fasting, prayer and thanksgiving to the Lord for his great mercy to me on this day the last year, in restoring and preserving the life of my husband when he fell from his horse on our return from Waterford.[1] Indeed, I desire never to forget this signal act of his favour, and hope I shall ever be thankful for it …

22 January
Being grievously distressed in mind, weighed down by trials from without and temptations from within, I laid my cause before the Lord … beseeching him to speak to me by his word, and opened the Bible to the first chapter of Nahum and seventh verse: 'The Lord is good, a stronghold in the time of trouble, and he knoweth them that trust in him.' …

20 February
My trials continue and are of an uncommon nature, and the conflicts of my mind are very great[2] … My spirit is often much bowed down, even so as to affect my body, but in some way or other the Lord does still deliver and saves me from sin. Being for some time much borne down on account of the soul of my dear husband and grievously distressed at seeing no likelihood of any change of heart in him, I thought the enemy mocked at me … This made me cry the more earnestly to the Lord from the depth of my distress, who answered, 'I have found a ransom.' …

28 February
… My enemy does continually provide fresh trials for me and suits them so to my natural temper and disposition as makes them the more grievous; and indeed I find it very distressing that my heaviest trials should come from the person who I love best in the world. But through the whole the Lord is my God, and my soul does cleave to him and desires my all from him alone …

3 March

… The Lord does give me patience under acute pain and an entire resignation to his will and a love to the hand that holds the rod … Indeed, his mercies are so very singular to me that they demand all my love: about two days ago my little daughter was taken suddenly very ill. I was grievously distressed, having had her so long ill so lately and not well recovered yet, but I thought, 'Vain is the help of man. I will commit my cause to the Lord as my only helper and physician.' And whilst I prayed I received a confident assurance that she should be spared, and when I came from prayer found the cause removed and the child well and has continued so since …

1 April
For the most part of the past month, I have been labouring under pains in my head and teeth, together with much deadness and heaviness of soul …

9 April
The Lord has thought fit to visit my eldest son with a fever. This, with all its train of fears and forebodings, increased by the tenderest feelings of paternal affection for a good and a beloved child, has borne heavy on me at times … The thought of having my dear child taken from me is as a dagger to my heart, yet cannot pray for his life, only with submission to the will of my heavenly Father … My heart is rent with yearnings over him, yet would not desire to have him back on any other condition than that he might live to the glory of God …

17 April
My son's disorder has turned out an ague and the Lord has been pleased to bless the means to his recovery … Since then the Lord has so graciously ordered matters in other affairs of mine, which seemed very intricate and often gave me much exercise of mind, as to give us the victory over those who would hurt us … As the Lord has restored my son, I am now preparing for a journey to Waterford to my daughter's lying-in …

25 April

Waterford. The Lord has brought me here in safety, has preserved both man and beast, and has given me the comfort of meeting my child and her family in health and safety ... I have made my journey here sooner than I need that I might have the advantage of meeting Mr Wesley here.[3] He is come, and I expect to hear him this evening ...

29 April
This day parted with Mr Wesley, and was enabled to look to the Lord and God alone for that help which none but he can give on his appointing me leader of a band ... I see I am not at all equal to it. O Lord, maintain thy own cause and let me not come from far to injure the least of thy little ones, but if thou wilt use even me, thy will be done ...

2 May
Met the band ... I found them a poor, afflicted, sincere, happy few, and find my heart closely united to them ...[4]

6 May
... I this day ... corrected my child hastily, my spirit being agitated and angry at the child ... I was grieved and distressed beyond measure ... In this state, I cast myself before the Lord and acknowledged my transgressions in much deadness and heaviness ... and the Lord did pour into my heart the sweet refreshings of his love, saying, 'Neither do I condemn thee. Go in peace'[5] ...

12 May
Since I came to this place, I have suffered much distress on account of one of this society, who was also a preacher but is now fallen into sin.[6] On seeing some marks of repentance in him, I have found my heart earnest with the Lord on his behalf ...

18 May
Received a satisfactory letter from Mr Wesley.[7] Blessed be God for these helps ...

20 May

Met the women's band and my soul was refreshed with them. I find my heart much united to the poor people of this place. Spent some time with John Swift, mentioned in the 20th of May 1770, the happiest soul, though the greatest enthusiast, I ever saw. Yet who that loves God would not wish to be in some things like him! ... O my God, make me thy own fool.

25 May
Received a large bundle of papers sent me by John Swift, being his experience for several years past, wherein is, I think, a great deal of wildness and nonsense and much attention paid to trifles and the mere workings of imagination, but through the whole discovers a heart truly devoted to God ...

30 May
A young man in this town, an acquaintance of mine, was a few days ago suddenly seized with a pain in one leg and at the same time with deep convictions. He was obliged to be laid in bed, and remained without tasting any food, in violent pain of body and mind. He is visited by a Christian man, but all about him look upon him to be out of his senses ... O Lord, be jealous for thine honour, and pluck this brand from the burning.[8] Received satisfactory accounts from my friends and family in Limerick ...

3 June
Had a visit from my brother Swift, who told me he has laid my children before the Lord in prayer and received a promise of their conversion. My soul was exceeding happy in conversing with him, and in the evening had an opportunity of speaking for God ...

12 June
... I have had much sorrow of heart on account of the above young man, mentioned the 30th of last month, who was under deep convictions and earnestly crying for mercy, but has suffered himself to be reasoned out of it all and, as the Lord has been gradually restoring his health, so his heart has gradually departed from God till he has got almost as far from him as he was before. O, the danger of trifling with God! ...
17 June

The Lord has refreshed my spirit and does sweetly draw my heart after himself. Was grieved at a sermon I heard yesterday and this day spoke to the person concerning it ...[9]

23 June

... It is now twenty-two years since my soul first tasted his pardoning grace[10] and, when I look back on that period, what scenes are opened to my view: scenes of love, mercy, forbearance, long-suffering! ... O, let me resound thy praise in accents such as angels use, when they record thy mighty deeds above. I would spread thy fame and sing the victories of thy cross, and make hell tremble at my song ...

27 June

... I find at times earnest desires to be back again with my family, yet I dread it. Since I came here, the Lord has been very gracious to me, and has afforded me some sweet opportunities of conversing with gracious souls, and I have my beloved retirement without the hurry or bustle of worldly affairs or family calls to hinder. This is what always suited me best. I long to be at home, yet dread coming down again into the affairs of life. My spirit is so active, and so apt to mix with the spirits of those who I converse with, and so apt to be detained with the things which immediately employ my time or call for my attention, that I think I have need of a superior degree of grace to keep me in any way steady in following the Lord. But he is my God and I will trust him ...

8 July

... Yesterday had a happy time at the sacrament ... and this day, though I have been hurried packing up to set out for Limerick tomorrow, have had much of the presence of God with me.[11] Finding the young man mentioned the 30th of May much laid on my mind, I this day made time to go see him ... I made an errand to the house, and the Lord gave me a fair opportunity and power to speak freely ... O my God, let it not be in vain, and whilst I press others forward, O let me not delay behind.

12 July
All glory to my gracious Lord, he has given me again to see my own house and family and friends in health and peace, and made my journey home comfortable with his own presence ...

30 August
Having brought my daughter home with me and her husband being now come for her, the friends of both have kept me in a constant round of visits and entertainments so that I have very little time for retirement, and the want of this, with the constant dissipation of spirit and the attention I am obliged to give to other things, has left such a want in my soul that I find myself as a fish on dry land, panting for my native element. I find the thoughts of parting with my daughter very grievous to me: these, with some trials from the world, weigh me down very much. This morning laid all before the Lord and found freedom so to do and my heart much enlarged but, finding some outward things bore heavy on me, I went to the Bible, beseeching the Lord to direct me, and opened on these words: 'If thou wouldst be perfect, sell all and take up thy cross and follow me.'[12] By this, I did believe there was still a more heavy trial near. I besought the Lord to stand by me and enable me to leave the world behind and cleave to him alone ... In a few hours came a heavier trial than before, seconded by another, so that my spirit was even borne down and distressed on every side ... But was enabled to lay all my case before him, beseeching him to take all these my affairs into his own hand, and to interpose in this present exigency and to overrule my husband's spirit in some cases where none else could. I then took the Bible to read on my knees, and opened it on the deliverance of the three Hebrew children out of the fiery furnace.[13] This portion of scripture came with power and much encouragement, and found my soul strengthened and enabled to depend on the power and love of my God, and I was not disappointed ...

6 September
Parted with my daughter. Recommended her and her family into the hands of my God, who has ever been the gracious preserver of me and mine ... Nature felt the pain of parting but was

enabled to cast myself simply on the Lord Jesus and take him for my all.

17 September

This has been a week of much dissipation. My head and hands busily employed, and my heart sore for want of closer communion with God, and grieved for speaking inconsiderately ... The Lord has afforded me good accounts from my daughter, blessed be his name.

13 October

The world is running mad after amusements at this time. This whole town is in a perfect uproar: horse racing by day and balls, plays, assemblies and taverns by night[14] ... O, how deluded, how more than mad are the children of men and how wonderful my escape! Why am I not still amongst them? ... These considerations have made this time of hurry and dissipation a happy time to me ...

12 November

My soul much refreshed in communing with a Christian friend, and by a letter from Mr Wesley ...[15]

25 November

This day was set apart by the select band as a day of humiliation, abstinence and prayer, to ask of the Lord a revival of his work in their own souls and those of the society[16] and to intercede for this city in general. The ... hours appointed for prayer were blessed seasons, and a solemn sense of God rested on my heart all the day. I was particularly affected in behalf of my husband and my whole soul importunate with God for him, and found a confident resting in God, assured that he would save his soul ...

22 December

The Lord has given me to see my daughter again with comfort, has preserved her on the road and brought her in safety ... He has made this a comfortable Sabbath to my soul: in conversing about the things of God, my desires were enlarged and my heart filled with sweet expectation of a closer union with my Lord ...

1772

1 January

Arose this morning in some degree awed under a sense of the goodness of God to my soul and body. A view of his gracious dealings with me the past year filled me with astonishment, and yet I am a monument of his grace, preserved as a spark in the ocean, and still through his grace am determined to pursue my way and to follow the Lord my God wherever he shall lead me. And to this end was this day enabled to devote myself anew to him, soul and body, friends and family, husband and children, substance and affairs, all I have and all I am, desiring that he would take all into his hands and deal them out to me as he sees meet; only let me and mine be eternally his ... O come and reign in my heart: proclaim a jubilee there. Let this be the year of release, and let there be no more complaining in all our streets.

18 January

Yesterday dined abroad and came home less solemn than I went out, which brought distress on my soul. This day parted with my brother-in-law, who is gone for America. My heart felt the pain of parting and was distressed with many fears for him, but found a will wholly resigned, giving him up to the care of his and my heavenly father ...[1]

28 January

Have found much heaviness this week past, and much distress in bearing the burden of a dear friend ...[2]

5 February

A variety of trials has kept my mind employed, and temptations suited to them constantly thrown in to disturb and perplex me ...

17 February

Whilst many trials pressed me down, one more heavy than the rest has added to the weight. I felt it before it came – a pressure of spirit and dread of I know not what. I prayed for strength and grace for the time of need … and when the trial came …was … enabled to trust in the Lord and with confidence to cast my burden on him …

16 March
I have had much to do in temporal affairs these few days past, but was enabled to cast my care upon the Lord and to look for all my help from him … My activity and thoughtfulness about temporal things has often been brought against me and charged upon me as covetousness and worldly-mindedness, and all my carefulness brought as proofs against me. I suffered much from this quarter till last night, when news was brought that a chimney belonging to a house of ours where we have six houses joined was on fire and the whole range in danger.[3] I found no disturbance at the news, but a calm, peaceful resting in God, giving up all to him and an entire resignation to his will …[4]

12 May
One of my children[5] being taken ill, I found some sinkings of nature, but an entire resignation of will and giving up all to my God.

17 May
My child very ill, and have found this day many distressing fears and much anguish of spirit even so as to affect my body very much … I find the most tender and distressing feelings of nature such as cannot be described, yet cannot ask the child's life … Nor do I desire to receive my child back into life on any other condition than that the Lord would make him his own child, that he might live to his glory …

22 May
Blessed be my God, my child is recovering. He has been given back to me, as it were, with a promise that he shall be the Lord's … Yesterday at prayer I received a steadfast assurance that he should be restored to me, and was enabled to give the Lord thanks for him. This day I kept as a day of fasting and prayer by agreement with a friend, to ask counsel of God for him in a part-

icular affair.[6] I found ... my heart much drawn out in prayer and importunate with God for my friend, but not able to discern his will in the present affair.

26 May
I have been for some time bearing the burden of another ... I find myself oppressed with his distress and my spirit even borne down by his sufferings, so that I cannot enjoy my own happiness till he is delivered ...[7]

29 May
Parted with my friend and found my heart sorely pained ... I feel my loss in the most sensible manner, which to me is not small: a Christian friend who was as my own soul, with whom I could take sweet counsel and whose advice and reproofs were precious to me but, seeing it is the will of God, I find not one desire in my soul to detain him for my own satisfaction ...

4 June
My body and mind overpowered and my spirits exhausted ... but was this day refreshed by a letter from my friend ...

5 July
... I have been busily employed in preparing for another journey to Waterford, and have had thoughts and attention much taken up about necessary affairs. But the Lord ... knows why he has placed me just where I am. It is not my business to enquire, but to endeavour whatever he gives to do, to do it with all my might ...

13 July
... I have been busily employed all this day packing up to set out on my journey tomorrow morning ...

17 July
Waterford. The Lord brought me here this day in safety, for which I desire to thank him, and found my heart grateful for this mercy and for again seeing my daughter and her family in health and safety ...

23 July
The day after I came to this town brother Christian, the preacher, came also, which I look upon as an instance of the goodness of God to me. I have had some comfortable opportunities of conversing with him, which has been blessed to my soul ... Read a letter from Mr Wesley, which has given me much satisfaction ...[8]

5 August
As I do not desire to transact any affair in life without first asking counsel of my heavenly father and begging his direction and blessing upon it, I have for some time past been asking of the Lord to direct me in the choice of a business and place for my eldest son and requesting that he would point out my way in this matter and, from every circumstance which has attended it, I think the Lord has interposed and directed me. A place offered here. I brought him with me, and have put him to business here. Through the whole I have endeavoured to act agreeable to the will of God and as under his inspection, with much prayer, yet have found much dissipation of mind from some disagreeable circumstances, but the Lord is my helper and my whole trust and dependence is in him ...[9]

13 August
The Lord has dealt graciously with me, has answered my petitions and made my daughter the living mother of a living child ...

16 August
On hearing of much said in praise of my son by his employer, my heart rejoiced in love and thankfulness to my gracious God ... I have been labouring to stir up and press forward one who has rested long without a sense of pardon, having lost his evidence, a leader the most zealous and active of all. My heart was strangely affected towards him and my soul travails in birth for his deliverance. I observed when I first spoke he was offended, but I persisted and the word sunk into his very soul and stirred him up to prayer. The Lord has since given me some opportunities of still pressing him on ...

19 August
The late mercies of my God revive the sense of former ... He has made my joy to abound by setting the soul of the above person at liberty ... My success with him encouraged me to fall upon another for whom I found my heart much drawn out. I see it had a good effect. It drove him to prayer and a determination never to rest till the Lord shall speak peace to his soul ...

21 August
Blessed be my God, he has set this soul also at liberty, and my heart rejoices in his joy ... Spoke very plain and home to the wife of this person, and found the word rested on her heart ... O Lord, give thy blessing and let this soul also be a witness of thy power to save. My son's master being ill and to all appearance in a dangerous way, the Lord does graciously keep me from distressing fears concerning the event, but find a sweet, calm resignation of will and a confident assurance of his care and interposition in my behalf ...

25 August
... At night the Lord spoke peace to the above woman, for which my whole soul is thankful. O, how good a thing it is to act for God! I fear I have hitherto been too backward, but the success which the Lord has given me here has inspired me with courage and resolution to be more active for God than ever I have been. O my Lord ... use me as thou wilt or when thou wilt, only keep me low at thy feet and let all the glory be thine.[10]

27 August
I appointed this as a day of humiliation, fasting and prayer to be kept by these three who were lately converted, that they might remember the Lord's dealings with thankfulness and solemnly devote themselves to him forever. One more and I bore them company, and the Lord did make it a solemn time to us all. As the Lord has been pleased to bless my words to some, I was resolved to speak to another for whom my heart has often been pained, an old conscientious professor without faith, grown stupid under the word, but a letter from Limerick has clipped my

wings. My friend complains of my sharpness and of something that looks like self-importance and self-sufficiency. This letter has distressed me much but perhaps I needed it, though on the strictest search I cannot find that I had any motive but the glory of God and the good of souls in the opposition I made to some of his proceedings in Limerick. However, lest I should give offence to others, I think to stop speaking to any, but turn my diligence on myself where I see much need of it. Though I have been much grieved and borne down by this letter and many reasonings which it has occasioned in my mind, yet I found it much blessed to my soul: it laid me low before the Lord and drove me to close examination and earnest prayer, and my heart was thankful for such a friend, and trust the reproof will be profitable to me ... I cannot but admire one signal act of providence in this letter: it was wrote the 10th of this month and left at my house to be enclosed to me, where it lay forgotten till now.[11] Had it been sent directly, two souls here would to all appearance have been still in unbelief, for I should not have power to speak to them in my present state of mind. O my Lord, let not this or any other trial cause me to sin against thee, but teach me and direct me and lead me whithersoever thou wouldst have me to go.

8 September
These some days past have been days of trial: whilst I laboured under one, a more heavy has come upon me ... My daughter's trials from an unkind husband and wicked incendiaries was till now a secret to me, but how painful is the discovery! My distress has even affected my body so that all who see me observe it. I am terrified at the thought of parting with her, yet I must go. I know not what to do ... I have no resource but prayer: the Lord is my refuge and has the hearts of all in his hand. The tyrant can go no farther than he is permitted. O, may this affliction be sanctified to her; may her disappointments turn her heart to God and cause her to seek that happiness in him which can nowhere else be found ...

9 September
My horses are come and I am preparing for my journey to Limerick. My heart is even rent with different exercises and

yearnings over my child and feel the pain of parting with both my children,[12] but I am enabled to give them up into the care of my God with a degree of confidence …

11 September
Clonmel. Thus far hath the Lord brought me on my way to my own house. I parted my children with a heavy heart, but left them in care of my heavenly Father who will take care of them. In the midst of my trouble, the Lord did refresh my soul by wonderfully plucking a brand out of the fire, a person in Waterford, whose state I have often found pressed on my heart and who I had observed for some time past grow slack in the ways of God and withdraw himself from the people.[13] I often had a desire to speak to him but could not get him to afford me an opportunity. Having some business with him, I went to his house yesterday determined if an opportunity offered to deliver my own soul but, not finding him at home, I left my compliments for him and desired to let him know that I was to leave town the next morning and begged to speak with him before then. The many distresses of mind under which I laboured made the missing him not at all grievous, finding in myself an utter unfitness for this duty and many doubts whether I was called to it or not, and the thoughts of my having already given offence in that way, as mentioned in the letter I received from Limerick, had made me almost determine never to reprove any, but to look more diligently to my own soul. … When the above person came in, he looked condemned, and my heart yearned over him so that I was, contrary to my resolution, drawn out to speak to him in the plainest manner, cutting him to the quick … He acknowledged all: that his heart had departed from God even to the neglect of the means, that he had shunned me lest I should reprove him, and that he was just now on the brink of ruin, being engaged in an affair which he knew would lead him to destruction, yet could not give it up. I did not enquire what this was, but levelled with all my might against it … After a little time, I found him begin to yield, and after I had spent two hours with him in this manner he at length with tears gave it up, and promised to set out afresh and double his diligence. I thought it best to follow the stroke, and therefore appointed the next day as a day of fast-

ing and prayer for him, in which brother Christian and I would bear him company, and appointed particular hours when we were to sequester ourselves from outward things to give ourselves to prayer in his behalf, and promised that my being on the road should not hinder on my part, to all which he agreed and seemed thankful to the Lord for thus stopping him in his career of sin. I did not then know what that particular thing was which he found so hard to give up, but ... was afterward told it was an assignation with a married woman, and were to have their first meeting two hours after the time he was with me. My whole soul was filled with gratitude to God for this very signal interposition ... but still my fears were alarmed lest this abandoned wretch should at the appointed time send for him, and he should not have power to resist ... The uneasiness of my mind would not suffer me to come away this morning till I had seen him. He told me she did send for him, and he refused going and is determined by God's grace to give himself up once more to be the Lord's. I left him under this determination, wondering and thankful for his escape ...

13 September

Blessed be my God who hath brought me again in safety to my own house and given me to meet my family in health, for which I find my heart thankful, and for another signal instance of his gracious interposition in behalf of a backsliding soul. I lay last night at a friend's house within twenty miles of Limerick, and this morning ... at the importunity of my servant, who is a man of a family and in haste home to his harvest, I unwillingly yielded to travel on the Sabbath and in the rain. When I had got a few miles on my way, a genteel-looking man rode after me and passed us by, whom I took for a clergyman going to officiate at some country church. He rode on and we lost sight of him, but in a little time overtook him again, standing under shelter of a hedge from the rain as though he waited for us. He rode up to us, and on asking found he was from Cork and bound for Limerick. As it rained very hard and he delayed in company, I was pained to see him in danger of being wet to the skin and perhaps by that means in danger of his life. I had a great desire to take him into the chair to shelter him from the rain, but feared overloading my horse, and there was not a mail pillion or any convenience for carrying my portmanteau, which was tied behind the chair. I could not account for the uneasiness I had for him, nor for his delaying in company, and often wondered that he did not ride off and hasten out of the rain but, coming to an inn where we stopped a little, I immediately got a man to carry the portmanteau on his horse, and gave him a seat in the chair as it still rained incessantly. I endeavoured to turn the discourse on religious matters, and found he had a head well-informed, which made me eager to search his heart. But how was I surprised when I found that he was a backslider from God after being in the society six years, and had now been a year out of it, seeking happiness where it cannot be found and, as he acknowledged, unhappy and sure of eternal damnation if he continued in his present state. I now saw the providence of God in suffering me to travel on the Sabbath and in the rain, in not giving him power to quit the company of the chair, in so soon meeting with one to carry the portmanteau and in every little circumstance of our meeting. I ... spoke to him as the Lord enabled me till his heart was broken, and got a promise from him that he would immediately leave his sins and set out anew to seek the salvation of his soul. O, may the Lord help him to do so ...[14]

17 September
Many things unite to depress my spirit, already much bowed down: the cause of God, the state of some particular souls, the affliction of my daughter, and many temporal things of a distressing nature ... But in all the Lord is my refuge and I do lay my cause before him ...[15]

21 September
... In the case of my daughter, where I besought the Lord to interpose and where no second means could do, he has graciously answered according to my request, has calmed the tyrant's rage and by that means eased me of much grief of heart ... O, how good a thing it is to trust in the Lord! ...

14 October

My trials continue and affect me exceedingly, being levelled at the tenderest part. The Lord my God does graciously keep me from sin ... I desire that his whole will may be done in me, but I often fear that the feelings of nature are too strong ...

26 October

The afflictions are grievous and often press down my soul with their weight, yet I find they are profitable to me ... I see my great deficiency and the need I have of an increase of every grace, yet I think the Lord has made me passive in his hands, desiring that all his will may be done in me, and O, that I may suffer it with patience and humble resignation ...

9 November

This day was set apart by the select band to humble ourselves before the Lord and implore his blessing and a revival of his work in our own souls and the souls of others ...[16]

29 November

The enemy has sorely harassed my mind this week concerning my son who is in Waterford, distressing me with dreams and fears of evil, but blessed be my God for a comfortable letter this day from him ... And still ... my earnest desire is that his will may be sanctified to me and mine, and made a means of turning my children's hearts to seek happiness in God alone.

3 December

The person mentioned the 13th of September last has been often brought to my mind in prayer. On enquiry, I find he is still entangled by the world and has not set out again to seek the salvation of his soul ... I ... could not think myself clear till I had delivered my own soul, so at the desire of a few friends I wrote him the following letter.[17] O, may it have the desired effect – at least it will leave him without excuse.

Sir, It may appear strange to you to receive a letter from a person with whom you have had but a few hours' acquaintance, but be assured it comes from a friendly hand with (shall I say) my last efforts for the salvation of your soul. When I

consider every little circumstance which attended our seemingly accidental meeting, I am rather led to think it was entirely providential: the Lord, who can and frequently does
use base and foolish instruments, after having tried many
great and powerful ones with you, at last threw you into my
hands. The knowledge I then received of your state and the
openness and freedom with which you declared it has made
me some way interested in your soul's welfare ... You are not
happy: I know you are not. Your most social pleasures are
embittered with keen remorse, your sweetest enjoyments are
disturbed with painful reflections, and your own conscience
tells you that the curse of God is in your basket and in your
store ... But look up; it is not too late. The Lord is now willing
to receive you. Take the prodigal's resolution now; arise and
go to your father, venture on his mercy. O, for the Lord's
sake, delay not. Come now; resolve this moment. He waits to
receive you with arms of love and will not upbraid you for all
that is past. O, let there be joy in heaven over you, let the
Lord himself rejoice over the lost sheep, over the purchase of
his own blood[18] ... But what shall I say if you are yet undeter-
mined, halting between two opinions? ... If this be the case,
be assured that God will certainly enter into judgement with
you for so many slights to his offered mercy. And how will
you be able to appear, how answer him to one of a thousand?
How will you answer the solemn promise you made me the
13th of last September when the Lord touched your heart,
gave you a feeling sense of your state and some earnest desires to return? I say, remember the promise you then made
me in the presence of God, that you would leave your sins,
would give yourself to prayer and, as soon as you should go
back to Cork, would unite again with the people to seek the
salvation of your soul. I demand the performance: the Lord
was present and heard and demands it, and will in the day of
judgement, before angels, men and devils, require it at your
hands. ... Don't think I have said too much. Your own conscience shall witness for me to the truth of all, but receive it in
love and let it have its desired effect. Perhaps it may be the
last admonition the Lord may see fit to grant you. Pray over

it, and be thankful to God for it and, if your heart be not so far hardened as to take offence at what I have said, I entreat a few lines from you, which if you are kind enough to indulge me with, Mr Collins will enclose it to me. I am, with sincere desires for your soul's welfare, your affectionate friend, EB.

7 December

This day the select bands in Limerick and Cork united in fasting and prayer to beseech the Lord that he would revive his work in these places and in our own souls. I found much of the power of God this day, and my heart much drawn out for the above person whom we particularly laid before the Lord ...

1773

1 January

This day was set apart by the whole society as a day of fasting and prayer to humble ourselves before the Lord for our unprofitableness and shortcomings the year past, to acknowledge his goodness and long forbearance, to thank him for past and present mercies and to make a solemn dedication of ourselves to him on this first day of the new year. In all this I found my heart sincere with God, though Satan strove to hinder by many painful representations to my mind ... O, that my diligence might increase with the new year ... But every year I purpose this, and yet at the end I find myself as deficient as ever. O my dear Jesus ... let me ever feel my need of thee and ever find my all in thee.

27 January

The present posture of my temporal affairs, together with a contrariety of dispositions and many disappointments, makes numberless trials for me so that I am almost continually exercised in mind ... Yesterday, on some new difficulty arising, I laid all my case before the Lord ... My soul longed to be with him and methought the time was near, which brought much comfort to my heart and power to plead for my husband and children, and a comfortable hope that my request should be granted.

10 February

Yesterday received an account from America of the death of my brother-in-law.[1] In the midst of grief, I found a secret satisfaction of soul at his escape from the world, the flesh and the devil. Since his leaving this kingdom, I have had many fears for him lest anything should draw him aside from God, but now they are all over and my soul rejoices over him. O, when shall my turn come? ...

17 March

... It is now twenty-four years since the Lord sent his messenger into the streets and lanes of this city and inclined my heart to receive his truths[2] ... The sense of these mercies has rested on my heart this day, and found the Lord present in prayer and an entire devotion of all I have and am to him.

12 April

Yesterday was appointed by the select band as a day of abstinence and prayer to entreat the Lord for a blessing on Mr Wesley's coming again amongst us.[3] I found much heaviness of spirit … but this day was comforted by a letter from Mr Wesley …[4]

30 April

The Lord has made my heart glad and thankful in behalf of a friend who was once an enemy to holiness of heart, but is now not only convinced, but made a happy partaker of this blessing …[5]

5 May

Blessed be my God, he did this day make my heart thankful for the coming of his faithful messenger, John Wesley, to this city. O, may it not be in vain! …[6]

12 May

This day Mr Wesley left us[7] … I found his coming here has been made a blessing to my soul, and this day found earnest desires and resolutions to be more given up to God …

18 May

Blessed be my God, yesterday and this day have been good days to me. The prosperity of other souls fills mine with gladness and thankfulness. A person in my band, weary of her inbred sin and groaning for deliverance, came to me yesterday under much trouble of soul and whilst we prayed together she was delivered and went away happy … This day her child died and she rejoices in the will of God, being enabled to give him up freely. My soul rejoices in her joy, and this day, on reviewing my covenant made with the Lord my God twenty-nine years ago in my youth, I was filled with wonder at the gracious dealing of God with me[8] …

> Now I am thine, forever thine,
> Nor shall my purpose move.

Thy hands have loosed my bands of pain,
And bound me with thy love.[9]

7 June
This has been a time of much trial and dissipation. My son and daughter[10] have come from Waterford on a visit to us. I found my heart thankful to my God for again affording me a sight of my children, but the kindness of our friends has kept us in a continual round of visits, so that my mind has been very much disturbed from that calm, peaceful resting in God which I enjoyed before they came ... yet through the whole my heart does cleave to the Lord Jesus and is determined to be eternally his ...

18 June
This last week has been a time of trial, outward affliction and inward distresses, yet through all the Lord has wonderfully supported me ... Parted with my son again, giving him up to the care of my God. O, of how short duration are all earthly enjoyments! ...

29 July
Yesterday parted with my daughter. My heart sunk and felt the pain but, looking immediately to Jesus, I found such sweet, solid resting in him ... as fully recompensed my loss, and was enabled to give my child up into the care of my God with a firm confidence in his protective care over her. This day was kept as a day of fasting and prayer by the whole society ...

9 August
The Lord has made this a blessed day to my soul ... My mind has been often burdened with uneasy and painful fears concerning my son who is in Waterford lest he should, by the cunning craft of Satan, be drawn into sin. I do, indeed, feel thankfulness and gratitude to my God for the good accounts I receive from my friends concerning him yet, knowing the carnal mind and what the heart is unchanged by grace, and ... the many follies youth is subject to, ... my heart is even rent with fears and dread concerning him ... I was this day particularly distressed from this quarter and retiring to prayer I laid my case before the Lord

... and was enabled to give him up into the Lord's hands ... being steadfastly assured that what I have so committed to his care he will faithfully keep. O ... my Redeemer, my gracious covenant God ... thou knowest my distress lest my child should be drawn into the snares of the devil, and thou knowest his death would be far more tolerable ... He has been early given up to thee and thou, Lord, knowest that my constant request has been that he might not be spared to me only on condition that he should be thine. And now, O Lord my God, I insist on my agreement: I now give him up by a solemn surrender into thy own hands. I demand thy aid, thy care and inspection over him, wholly committing his soul into thy hands, being steadfastly assured that what I have now committed to thy charge thou, my God, wilt faithfully keep, and at thy hands will I require the soul of my child ...[11]

15 August

Received satisfactory accounts from my children for which I find my heart thankful ... I have been much borne down these some days past from many disappointments in temporal things which, like Job's messengers, have come at the heels of each other.[12] Indeed, the Lord has for months past wonderfully supported me by taking the burden of these things off my spirit, but new ones arising and a prospect of more does at times lay such a load of distress on me as I am scarce able to support under. O Lord, my trials are known to thee and to thee only ... O, help me to suffer thy will, whatever it may be.

25 August

New disappointments make the former the heavier ... O thou who art the strength of the weak and the support of the feeble, and whose aid I have ever experienced nigh in the time of need, stand by thy most helpless creature. Remember me now thou art in thy kingdom and let not the floods overwhelm me, but help me in patience to possess my soul and to stand fast, believing in thee.[13]

10 September

This week the enemy thrust sore at me by hindering my speaking for God when I had it in my power but, being condemned in my conscience, I at length broke through, took the person in private, we talked and prayed together and the Lord did help her to believe that he had cleansed her heart from sin, and did enable her to rejoice in his full salvation …

2 October
I kept yesterday as a day of abstinence and prayer by agreement with a friend in Cork and a friend in England … I found my friends present in spirit at the hours appointed and surely the Lord our God was present with us …

14 October
… This day was set apart to fast and pray and implore the Lord for seasonable weather …

28 October
This is a trying time, but my God does make his will sweet. A poor creature whom I took in has brought a fever into my family. He is recovering, and my maidservant is down …

15 November
Blessed be God, my servant is recovering and the Lord has yet preserved the rest of my family …

4 December
This has been a time of dissipation and distress, outward trials and inward temptations, which has brought on me much heaviness of soul. I am now preparing for a journey to Waterford, and find in myself such perfect weakness and feebleness of soul as sinks my spirits and brings many discouraging fears upon me …

22 December
Thus far[14] hath the Lord brought me unhurt through many dangers, and when my carriage broke on the road he did wonderfully preserve me and my child so that we received no damage and, though this has been a very uncomfortable journey, full of dis-

appointments, yet ... through the whole the Lord my God did preserve my mind ... calm, peaceful and resigned ... and gave me the comfort of meeting my children here in health and peace.

1774

17 January

I am here as out of my native element, shut out from the means and people of God. There has no preacher come here since I came, nor have I had many opportunities of conversing with the people but, blessed be my God, he has caused me to rejoice in behalf of some whose souls are very dear to me[1] ... I asked of him that he would rebuke the storm and give my daughter peace and comfort, and he has done it in a wonderful manner, turned the lion into a lamb and frustrated the counsel of the wicked. I asked of him that he would take my son into his own care, that he would preserve him from sin and folly and would give him sense and discretion to conduct himself to the satisfaction of all, and the Lord my God has granted me this also and has given me much comfort after much distress[2] ... The 11th I kept as a day of fasting and prayer, with a thankful remembrance of that day four years when my husband fell from his horse and the Lord preserved his life and restored him to me as from the dead.[3] ...

6 February

A preacher came yesterday to town so that I had an opportunity of hearing this day. I found my heart thankful for the word and the conversation of the people ...

17 February

Blessed be my good and gracious God, he does multiply his mercies to me and mine: he has ... delivered my daughter and made her the joyful mother of a living child ...

8 March

This has been a time of hurry and uneasiness ... the infant being taken sick but is now better. Through all, the Lord does keep my soul in peace, stayed upon him ...

17 March

My soul has been very happy these two days in conversing with two persons whose souls are on the stretch after holiness of heart. Whilst I endeavoured to press them forward, the Lord did water my own soul. It is now twenty-five years this day since I first heard the Methodist preaching.[4] The Lord brought it to my mind and I set this day apart to fast and pray, to humble myself because of my great unprofitableness and to thank my God for his sparing, preserving, long-suffering grace ...

19 March
I kept this day in fasting and prayer with the above two persons, and the Lord made it a happy day to us all. My God has graciously given me my errand here and am now preparing for my return.

22 March
Another signal instance of the care and protection of my good and gracious Lord over the most unworthy of all his creatures: I set out this morning for Limerick and when I had got about a mile and half on my way my horse and chair was overturned in a slough, but my child and I remained unhurt. The chair was broke by the fall so that I was obliged to walk back to Waterford. Through this accident the Lord preserved my mind calm and peaceful, without any dissatisfaction, even to the servant who was the cause or impatience at the disappointment. I could only look at the goodness of God towards me in preserving us so that even the beast did not receive the least hurt, and my heart is filled with thanksgiving and gratitude to my God for his mercy.

28 March
Blessed forever be my God who has again brought me home to my friends and family in health and safety ...

30 March
I have been much borne down since I came home: Satan has been labouring to sow discord amongst the people of God ... My spirit is grieved and my soul distressed on account of this and, seeing what advantage the enemy hath gained, I am under many fears lest my spirit also should catch the infection ...[5]

3 April

My mind is much distressed for others and for the cause of God and, being much taken up about these matters, have found a want of that attention which I should have to my own state so that this solemn season of our Lord's resurrection has come upon me, as it were, unaware[6] ...

17 April

My spirit has been much borne down by the affliction of a dear friend, and also by the advantage that Satan has gained over some of the people of God. The distress I have felt on account of this and dissatisfaction at those who have been the authors has brought heaviness on my own soul ... Yesterday my husband received a hurt but was wonderfully preserved from the total loss of his eye: Lord, I see thy hand and thy care in everything ...

19 May

I have been these few days in the country, engaged in an act of friendship for others, but in serving them have neglected my-self: my mind has been dissipated, and have come home in much heaviness of soul and dissatisfaction with myself. The day before I returned I wrenched my instep, which I look upon as from the Lord, reproving me for my sloth and calling me back to recollection and diligence ...

22 May

Of how short duration is all earthly comforts and how small a space is there between joy and grief! The frequent accounts which I have had from Waterford concerning my son have been so satisfactory and comforting as have been continual cause of thankfulness to God on his behalf, but this day received an ac-count of his being in a fever. Nature feels the stroke in the ten-derest part, but do find my soul wholly resigned to the will of my God.

29 May

This has been a trying week: from the delay of letters I have suf-fered much pain of mind, not knowing but my son was dead ... But this day I received an account of his being better, for which I desire to render thanks and praise to my good, my gracious God, and beseech thee, O my Lord, that the life which thou has spared may be forever devoted to thy service …

20 June

This day … has been set apart by the select band to supplicate the throne of grace for a revival of his work in our own souls and the souls of the people … Yesterday my soul was exceedingly blessed in conversing with the preacher[7] and pressing him forward to perfect love. We both felt the power of God and his willingness to give all that he had promised in his word, and this morning the savour of his grace remains on my heart …

23 June

O, how shall I thank the giver of all my mercies who has brought me again to this era, the anniversary of my espousals to himself![8] … Indeed, I feel myself as necessitous now, as weak, as ignorant, as helpless as the first moment I set out in the ways of God, but I know the Lord is my God, my father and my friend and, after twenty-five years' experience of his love and faithfulness, it would be impious to distrust his future care … My friend's soul prospers; the Lord does bless our communion and in my poor little weak endeavours to help him the Lord does help and bless my own soul …

1 July

… My friend is happy in the perfect love of God. Whilst we conversed and prayed together, the Lord did hear and answer and take full possession of his heart. My soul was much blessed and shares in his happiness and rejoices in his joy.

3 July

This Sabbath … the Lord … did manifest himself to my soul … and in the evening did give me to see my son and son-in-law and grandchild from Waterford. I found my heart thankful to my God for bringing them in safety and for once more indulging me with a sight of them …

10 July

... I do find on the strictest scrutiny that ... my heart is given to God and can only be satisfied with himself ... I love my husband, children and friends with the tenderest affection, but they do not detain me here. My heart and my treasure is above, and my soul longs for the full enjoyment. My friend is happy and confident in what the Lord has done for him, and my soul shares in his joy and is thankful for him even as for myself.

20 July

This day parted with my son, son-in-law and grandchild. My heart felt the pain of parting in the tenderest part, but with perfect resignation and thankfulness to my God for the favour, committing them to his care and protection ...

11 August

Ill in body and much sunk in spirit, but my confidence is steadfast and my soul has been much refreshed by a letter from my friend who is this week in the country. The manifestations of God's love have been very great to his soul, and my whole heart is thankful for him and shares in his happiness ...

22 August

How wonderfully do the mercies of my God surround me continually: my youngest son received a hurt a few days ago on the pan of his knee. ... Looking to the Lord, I sent up a sigh of distress and immediately received a steadfast assurance that it should do well, and accordingly in two days the pain and lameness was all gone ...

1 September

... I have been for some time past asking of the Lord that he would direct and assist concerning the disposal of my youngest son whom my husband would have bred a scholar, which I was very averse to as I have an entire dislike to the law from the dishonesty of its professors, and would not have him thrust into the church except he was called of God to it. These considerations made me willing he should rather be put to business than bred a scholar. I submitted the matter to the Lord, entreating his interposition and assistance and, whilst I looked for the answer, his father suddenly determined to send him to Kingswood School, which I would not oppose lest I should take my own will and frustrate the Lord's intentions concerning him.[9] I believe the thing is of God ... and trust he will take this matter into his own hand and conduct it as he sees fit.

9 September

Having received an account of the death of one of my grandchildren, I found my will perfectly resigned, only an earnest desire that this visitation might be sanctified to the parents. I have been entreating of the Lord that he would either forward or frustrate the above affair concerning my son as he may see best for the child and his own glory, and believe he will. I feel in myself a want of that earnestness and fervour which I should have, my mind too attentive to the little things of time and sense and a want of patience with my children. Lord ... save me from myself.

13 September

Parted with a dear friend whose conversation has been helpful to me and with whom my soul has been much blessed, but the Lord enabled me to give him up with perfect resignation to his will and has brought another with whom I have been labouring for some time past into the liberty of his children ...[10]

28 September

Received a satisfactory letter from Mr Wesley in answer to one wrote to him concerning my son[11] ... When I read the letter and found the way open for the child, I found my heart filled with thankfulness ...

4 October

Busily employed preparing my son for his journey ... Had a satisfactory letter from my friend. His soul prospers and the Lord does prosper his labours, and my heart is thankful for him.

26 October

This day my husband and son set out for Waterford from whence he is to send the child to Bristol. At parting, my spirits sunk exceedingly and, in spite of all my fortitude, nature gave way. Retiring to prayer, I committed them both into the hands of my God with an entire dependence on his care and protection over them ...[12]

17 November
The Lord my God ... does afford me satisfactory accounts from my husband and children. My son has sailed and I am still enabled to trust in the Lord for his future care and protection of him ... Yet nature feels the separation: I have felt much heaviness of soul for some time past and my spirit much depressed ...

28 November
... Received good accounts from my husband and children in Waterford and of the safe arrival of my son in Bristol ...

5 December
... Whilst others suffer under the afflicting hand of God, I am spared, me and mine preserved: yesterday morning one not far from my house died suddenly. A monument of mercy – in one week convinced, converted and taken to glory! My soul was filled with thankfulness to God on his behalf, and a deep sense of his unbounded goodness to me, having received good accounts from my children and my husband restored to me safe after his journey ...

22 December
I this day see how good a thing it is to drop a word for God. About three or four months ago I met a young lady accidentally on a lonesome walk. I then spoke a few words which reached her heart, and this day she came to me on purpose to give me such another opportunity. I spoke to her as the Lord enabled me, and found her open of heart and thankful. I found it hard to pray with her but could not resist. Lord, make me more simple of heart, and grant instruction to this poor, bewildered soul. Point out her way, direct her heart and save her from a cursed conformity to the world.

29 December

This day has been set apart by the select band to thank the Lord for his mercy and goodness the year past, and to devote ourselves anew to his service ... Blessed be my God, he has made this a comfortable season. O, may I be thankful![13]

1775

8 January
My spirit much depressed from some grievous trials which have even shook my animal frame but, blessed be my God, through all I am enabled even by these trials to see his work on my heart more clearly, and find my spirit patient and submissive, free from anger or the least desire of revenge on the abandoned villain who has robbed me of my substance and shot my servant, under which he now lies languishing. The fear of his death is more to me than all my loss, but have a degree of confidence in the Lord that he will restore him. O Lord, thy will be done ...

12 January
My spirit has been much depressed by the sudden death of a relation, a young creature in the bloom of youth and beauty and aspiring hopes, as a flower opening its leaves to the sun and cropped in an instant ... It was to me an improving sight, though my heart is sensibly affected for her tender parents. During her illness I was much drawn out in prayer for her and have reason to hope she died happy, but have been condemned for some omissions on my part ...

16 January
Satan has been very busy endeavouring to distress my mind by placing before me the many losses I sustain and disadvantages I lie under by being religious, but ... found a sweet resignation of soul and giving up of all I have and am into the hands of my Lord, choosing him, with every loss that may attend, as my only portion ... His favour is dearer to me than life or every advantage in life and, as to my children, I have cast them on his care. I desire not riches, grandeur or popularity or the favour of this world for them. I desire his grace as their best portion, his friendship as their inheritance and whatever portion of this world he is pleased to allot them, I am content – only let them have his blessing with it, that he would ... save them eternally that I might meet them at his own right hand in glory.

5 February

My spirit has been much grieved and even bowed down because of the cause of God and the slackness of others, and whilst I laboured under this another trial has come upon me. My heart is touched in a tender part[1] ... My trust is in the Lord, and into his hands I commit my cause ...

10 February

My spirit is much borne down and distressed: the sufferings of my child from an unkind husband bear heavier on me than my own ... But the Lord has promised it shall be well ... and, though nature feels and suffers, yet my soul rests confidently on him.

16 February

Trials seldom come alone. Whilst I laboured under many of my own and others, another has made the former still more heavy: the sins of some and the sufferings of others and the cause of God wounded by its professors has so pained my heart as even to affect my body and make me weary of life.[2] O my God, maintain thy own cause, encourage and support thy poor, feeble followers, and let not the enemy of souls triumph over thy cause and people.

27 March

I have been prevented from writing[3] by a complaint in my eyes. I have found much heaviness of soul for some time past with many trials, but the most grievous of all is what I find in myself: a proneness to a listless supineness of spirit ...

5 April

My heart is even loaded with distress: a dear Christian friend and preacher of the gospel, being delirious in a fever, got out of bed in the absence of his nurse, leaped out of a window and by that means put an end to his life[4] ... Why has God suffered this? Surely his ways are in the deep ...

21 April

... The Lord does graciously support me and enables me to ...

give my children into his care with a degree of confidence, yet I cannot help the feelings of nature, my daughter being near the time of her travail and I so circumstanced that I cannot be with her. My heart feels sore pangs at times, but am confident that what is best the Lord will do ...

10 May
Found my spirit revived and my heart thankful for being again permitted to see that dear special messenger of Jesus, Mr John Wesley,[5] yet have cause to be ashamed of myself because of the small progress I have made since I first saw him, notwithstanding the many blessed opportunities I have been favoured with ... O my Lord ... quicken my soul and make me to run in the ways of thy commandments.

17 May
Much indisposed in body and mind ... This day parted with Mr Wesley.[6] My heart felt the pain of parting yet found much thankfulness for the blessed opportunities put into my hands for many years past ...[7]

1776

[undated] January[1]

I have already suffered what I still suffer, and the prospect of what is still before me has so affected my animal spirits and constitution as to render me less able to endure, but the Lord my God can and will help me, will perfect his strength in my weakness and give me the victory at last. The constant agitation of my mind and infirmities of my body occasioned my desisting from this exercise for some months past but, as the Lord my God has again graciously brought me to the beginning of another year, I again return to set to my seal that he is true, and that it is the full purpose of my heart to cleave to him all the days of my life and, though he slay me, yet to trust in him and do, with a dependence on divine grace, determine that neither persecution nor famine nor nakedness nor peril nor sword nor height nor depth nor any other creature shall ever be able to separate me from the love of God in Christ Jesus my Lord …

8 January

More trials still, heavy and grievous, to be borne … I am ready to say, this is more than I can bear, but if I must bear it O, strengthen me by thy spirit's might, make me patient to suffer and strong to endure, and submissive under thy correcting hand …

11 January

A return of this day has brought to my mind the mercies and goodness of God to me when this day six years he restored my husband to me on the high road as from the dead[2] … I found this day my heart thankful, but distressed to find that the very object of this mercy had no feeling sense of it. O Lord, when wilt thou lay to thy hand and turn his heart to thyself? …

25 January

Found my heart thankful for satisfactory letters from both my sons. The Lord does graciously mizzle sweet things with the bitter that I may not be depressed above measure …

6 February
Trials come so fast ... on the heels of each other that my spirit is
kept down and much depressed. My daughter in Waterford
being to all human appearance in a declining state of health, the
most gloomy representations are made to my mind. I find it
hard to give her up and harder still to resign her in an unconverted state ... Indeed, the unchanged state of my husband and
children is a continual weight upon my heart. I have a degree of
dependence on the Lord that he will save them all but am often
discouraged through delay ... But I will still trust in the Lord for
this and for strength and grace to suffer all his will.

15 February
I have been for some days afflicted with indisposition of body
and acute pain which has often occasioned me to call myself to
account ... O my blessed Lord, who thyself suffered in and from
the flesh, help my infirmities and strengthen my soul and, after
all thou has done for me, suffer not a Laodicean spirit to steal
upon me.[3]

10 March
The Lord has been pleased to grant me a comfortable sight of my
son from Waterford and to receive a good account of him from
his master ... At parting, I committed him into the care of my
heavenly Father and find a degree of confidence in him that he
will protect him.

17 March
Blessed be my God, he did make this a comfortable Sabbath to
my soul. It is twenty-seven years this day since I first heard the
gospel from the special messengers of Christ sent out into the
streets and lanes of the city and into the highways and hedges.[4]
The remembrance of this brought much thankfulness into my
heart ... Yet found much grief of heart for my husband. Indeed,
my soul is often distressed for him and discouraged in praying
for him, seeing no fruit of my prayers after so many years, but I
will yet trust in the Lord for my husband and children and stay
my soul on his mercy and faithfulness ...

24 March
The Lord has afforded me comfortable accounts from my children, blessed forever be my God ...

29 March
... This day, meeting with some unreasonable behaviour in my servant, I found much dissatisfaction and agitation of mind and spoke a few words unadvisedly, which grieved my spirit and brought much distress on my soul ...

8 April
Yesterday being the anniversary of our Lord's ascension[5] ... I found an awful sense of the solemn season rest upon my mind, but not with that degree of love and gratitude which I would desire ...

11 May
How shall I describe the feelings of my heart? I have lost what I ever esteemed the greatest treasure on earth – a dear, faithful, bosom friend, a sympathising companion[6] ... called away suddenly, in less than an hour removed into glory. How happy for her that she was always ready! O my God, let not the admonition be given in vain ... Give me in the simplicity of my heart to enjoy that sweet union and communion with thyself, that close intimate friendship in thy love that neither death nor hell can ever destroy.

22 May
The Lord does make everything work together for my good. Even the loss of my dear friend has proved a blessing to my soul by quickening my spirit and causing me to cleave to the Lord my God more entirely as my only friend ... The burden of my husband and children still out of Christ lies heavy on my heart ... but my trust is in the Lord, and am determined to depend on him though I see no answer of my prayers.

26 May
Whit Sunday: the Lord ... brought to my mind the blessings I received as on this day[7] ... and in looking back on my own past

life, notwithstanding my great unprofitableness, I found thankfulness of heart that I had so early set out to seek the Lord and had spent so many years in his service, and a full determination by his grace ... to live and die in his service ...

23 June
... I find cause to reproach myself for not recollecting this day timely: it is an instance of my heedlessness and negligence.[8] O Lord, forgive my trespass and ... impress on my heart a lasting sense of thy favours ...

1 July
... I spent this day in the country and found my thoughts so busied about the scenes which surrounded me that I could not command them or keep them stayed upon God. O my gracious Lord, thou seest in all things how poor and deficient I am ... but ... in thee I have all and abound, in thee my wants are richly supplied, thy mercy and faithfulness are both engaged on my behalf ... O, blessed, blessed forever be my rock! Blessed, blessed be God for Jesus Christ!

> Long as I live I'll bless thy name,
> My king, my God of love;
> My work and joy shall be the same
> In the bright realms above.[9]

17 August
Have been so taken up with company this fortnight past as to have no time for this exercise. My daughter from Waterford with her husband and children having come to visit us, I have been entirely taken up with company abroad and at home so that my spirit has been even wearied with it. I found a degree of thankfulness for a satisfactory sight of my child and her children, but in general much heaviness of soul and dissipation of spirit and dissatisfaction with myself. At their parting I found myself much affected, but ... found a desire to return from all outward things and commune with God in the secret of my heart ...

1 September
Trials come fast upon me and find that I am not strong to bear them … I cry to the Lord but he seems not to regard my prayer, yet will I trust in him, for from him alone must my help come …

27 September
A new trial has bore very heavy on me but, blessed be my God, I have found some good effects from it. O, that everything I meet with might tend to wean my heart more from the world and unite it still closer to my God! …

22 October
Blessed be my God, he does enable me to stay my soul upon himself … Indeed, the sense I have of my emptiness and unfaithfulness depresses my spirits exceedingly, and the word preached by Mr Bradburn does search my heart and point out my defects, and for this I find my heart thankful …[10]

17 November
The Lord does search my heart by Mr Bradburn's preaching and conversation, and for this and for his messenger I find my whole soul thankful, and find an earnest desire to be all that my God would have me to be …

20 November
My heart is even broke on account of a dear friend under temptations. I feel his sufferings even as my own, my soul agonises in prayer for him and cannot, must not, will not cease till the answer comes down … O, let it not be said to thy dishonour that, whilst he proclaims liberty in thy name to all around, his own chains should evidence against the great truth … Lord, I ask, believing thou wilt grant, and I rest upon thy word and will trust in thee for the accomplishment …[11]

23 November
By accounts from my daughter, her trials are returned again upon her[12] and my fears and distress are as much as I am able to support under and has this day brought a return of my bodily complaint on me, but I am in the hands of the Lord and he does

wonderfully support me in my affliction ... I would desire to go and comfort my child, yet I would not take my own will. Some hindrances lie in the way, which if the Lord is pleased to remove I shall look upon it as his will that I should go. If not, he himself can supply my place ...

26 November
My accounts from my daughter are more favourable, and for this I feel my heart all thankfulness ... My friend has had a deliverance for some days from his temptation, but it has returned upon him again ... I feel his distress even as my own ...

13 December
This day ... appointed as a day of public fasting and prayer by order of government ...[13] O, blessed be God for this day. I have reason to be thankful for it on more accounts than one: it is thirty-one years this day since I was married to my husband. It came to my mind at prayer and brought such a recollection of the numberless mercies of my God during that space to my mind as filled my whole soul with love and thankfulness and praise, particularly the exceeding goodness of God in so long preserving and still continuing to me my dear companion, with all the thousands of blessings, mercies, favours and particular deliverances I have experienced since we came together ... And, as thou hast united us in the closest bonds of love here, O gracious Father, let us not be separated to all eternity, but remember my dear partner and children for good, speak in power and in mercy to their hearts and O, let thy all-powerful grace subdue them to thyself, that we may all appear before thee with joy in the great day. And O, remember my friend under temptation and if thou art not pleased to remove the trial, gracious Lord, sanctify the chastisement and let thy grace be sufficient for him.

25 December
I did not find so deep an impression of this solemn season on my heart as I should or would desire to have ... My soul was deeply humbled under a sense of this on my going to the sacrament, and earnestly desirous to live more to the glory of God. Was overcome with drowsiness at the evening preaching but at the love feast the Lord did refresh my soul: all glory be to him!

1777

1 January

I found a sense of the goodness of God this day in so graciously bringing me to the beginning of another year, and a thankful recollection of past mercies, both spiritual and temporal but found, indeed, much shame and sorrow for my great deficiencies and non-improvement of his grace and for my present slackness and remissness. I see what need I have to double my diligence. I desire to do so and determine to do so every day, yet at night find cause to reproach myself that this day has passed as heedlessly as the former: thus am I continually resolving and as continually failing ...

7 January

Heard an excellent discourse from Mr Bradburn on 'Take unto you the whole armour of God.'[1] It searched my heart, as indeed most of his sermons do, and the exhortation to the bands came still closer ... The present deadness of my soul fills me with distress, yet find much thankfulness for that pure word which discovers my deficiencies ...

11 January

Set this day apart for abstinence and prayer under a thankful remembrance of the goodness of my God in the restoration of my husband on this day in the year '70, and his graciously sparing him to me ever since and giving me again to see the return of this day with thankfulness[2] ...

18 January

... Yesterday ... my friend being determined on a matter which I thought not right and not being able to dissuade him from it, I laid it before the Lord, beseeching him to interpose and direct in this matter and not to suffer him to speak or act inconsistent with his character or the glory of God, and the Lord did answer my request and changed my friend's mind ...[3]

21 January

Yesterday parted with my dear friend which affected me very

much, even so as to affect my body, yet on the closest examination could not find one desire to detain him contrary to the will of my God ...

3 February
Have been put out of my method by the coming of some friends to me from the country, which has kept me more in company than I would choose or than I find profitable ...

10 February
Have been much distressed on account of not hearing from my children for some time ...

12 February
... My soul was much comforted yesterday whilst speaking to a person under convictions, and my heart earnest with God for her ... This day one under trouble of soul came to me. I spoke to her as I was able, and hope it was not in vain ... Being still disappointed in letters from my children, my mind suffers the most painful anxiety and grievous forebodings ...

13 February
... I was in trouble, having received no letters from my children for some time past, and as the time was prolonged my distress increased till my spirit was borne down with fears and forebodings, and these certified to me by the most uneasy dreams ... Last night at secret prayer I ... lift my heart to the Lord in behalf of my children, beseeching him to help me to bear any tidings I might receive with patience and submission to his will, when immediately I received the most confident assurance that all was well with them and that I should receive good accounts from them the next day ... I called my husband, who was going to sleep (and had also been distressed with fears), desiring him to be comforted for that I now knew all was well with our children. I rose this morning ... fully assured that all was well ... At prayer I had sweet, near access and much liberty, and afterward received a letter that all was well ...

18 February
Another instance of the care and goodness of my God: the clothes of one of my grandchildren taking fire, he narrowly escaped being burned to death, yet was not much hurt. When I read the account my heart glowed with gratitude and love ...

1 March
... This day a person came to me in deep distress of soul. My heart sympathised in her trouble, I spoke to her and prayed with her, and her burden was taken off and her soul set at liberty and she went away rejoicing in the Lord ...

8 March
All glory to my God, the above person is happy and has been so from that hour. My spirit rejoiced in her joy and my heart encouraged to speak for God. O, my good, my kind, my tender Father, if any talent be committed to me, instruct me how to use it ... and let every power of my soul be on the stretch to do thy will.

18 March
Yesterday was a good day. The Lord brought to my mind much of his mercy and faithfulness since I first heard his pure gospel, which was twenty-eight years yesterday ...[4] Coming home at night I wrenched my ankle, which accident has confined me ...

22 March
Though I am confined by reason of the hurt I received in my ankle, the Lord does afford me blessed opportunities of conversing with his people which I should not otherwise have, and of pressing some forward who have lately set themselves to seek the Lord[5] ... My friend's soul prospers and another is made happy, which has much refreshed my spirit ...

3 April
... Yesterday morning my spirit was much depressed under a view of the many trials with which I am surrounded and, going to read the Bible according to my usual custom ... I looked up to my Father, reminding him of my troubles and beseeching him

now to direct me to a portion of his word that might be a suitable support to me, and opening the book these words first presented: 'These things are good and profitable.'[6] ... Went to the preaching for the first time since I hurt my ankle and found my heart thankful ...

8 April
My spirit much grieved for the sins and indiscretions of others ...

20 April
Since my being able to go abroad, I have not found my soul so happy. I now look back with regret on my confinement when the constant visits of my religious friends afforded me constant opportunities of religious conversation and of pressing some forward after God. This is always a profitable exercise to me ...

4 May
... O my God, why do I live only to suffer, and that in the tenderest part? I am ready to say my distress is now more than I am able to bear ... Sustain me, gracious Lord, in this most needful time of trouble. Give me patience, give me resignation to thy will, give me light to see thy will and make my heart obedient to it[7] ...

14 May
I know not what to say: I am all a heap of confusion, my spirit is borne down and dejected under a load of distress. O gracious Lord, thou knowest what I suffer by the sins of others ... O, help, help, for thou alone art able and O, suffer me to intercede for the sinner. Gracious Jesus, pluck that soul as a brand from the burning ... and O, let even this work together for good!

17 May
... Words cannot describe the rendings of my heart, but thou, O my God, knowest what I suffer. Let thy will be done but O, save the sinner! Let thy mercy pursue and overtake that soul, and be thou glorified in his salvation. This which should be a memorable day has been but a dull Whitsunday to me ... yet the Lord

did comfort my heart at night. One under trouble of soul came to me, I for a time forgot my own sorrows and laboured to press her forward and whilst we prayed she was enabled to believe and holds her confidence ...

28 May
This has been a time of trouble and sore distress, outward afflictions and inward conflicts. My spirit is bowed down and my mind confused ...

3 June
This morning my husband set out for Dublin, which in my present situation is an addition to my distress ...

7 June
Some aggravating circumstances appear to increase my present trouble. My spirit is much bowed down and my mind encumbered and bewildered, not knowing what to do. O my Lord, direct me ... Received a letter from my husband with an account of his safe arrival in Dublin, for which I thank my good God.

15 June
The Lord has restored my husband safe, blessed be his name ... I carry about a disordered body and mind: O, what a double cross is this! Lord, help me to bear it patiently and improve it profitably.

26 June
More trouble still ... I know not what to do, my mind is full of perplexity and many fears ...

6 July
More distress still ... My heart is torn with sorrow and my spirit sunk under a load of distress, trouble upon trouble and grief upon grief ... Lord, it is the time of need. I want thy aid, thy counsel, thy assistance, for without thee I can do nothing ...

15 August
... Received an account yesterday from Waterford of the arrival of my son from Kingswood who, on account of the ill-treatment

he received, was provoked to run away from the school, took his passage in a ship and has arrived in Waterford[8] ... O my Lord, what shall I do? ...

21 August
... My sorrows come against me as a troop. Received an account from Waterford of my daughter being dangerously ill, in a fever ... O Lord, surely this is a time of need! ...

27 August
Blessed be my God for all his favours: my daughter still lives and has had a favourable change ...

3 September
Received my son home after his elope from Kingswood, a poor, starved, dejected figure. The sight so affected me that I thought my heart would break ... O my God, make me contented with thy will, keep me from murmuring at any of thy dispensations and make me passive as clay in thy hand. My daughter's amendment continues, blessed be my God.

14 September
Still my gracious God affords me favourable accounts from my daughter ...

10 October
... This day I lost a dear, faithful, praying, sympathising friend, taken away by a sudden death, without one moment's warning[9] ... O, how happy for her that her work was done, and how sweet, how comfortable was her death, without pain or conflict! Whilst I grieve for my loss, I ... rejoice for her happy escape, and in so happy a manner ... and I found a secret wish in my heart to follow in the same manner, which I was obliged to suppress lest I should offend ...

14 October
Having received a letter from a friend informing me of the sufferings of my daughter in Waterford, I found my heart sorely burdened with sorrow and distress, even as to affect my body.

But what can I do? I laid it all before my God and, interceding for my suffering child, I left my cause in the hands of him who only can deliver ...[10]

8 November
... This day my husband was called away to Dublin. I gave him up into the hands of the Lord and trust he will preserve him.

21 November
I have had many distressing thoughts on the usage my son received at Kingswood, which has been increased by provoking letters from his masters but ... find my mind perfectly free from prejudice or resentment towards them, and for this I desire to thank my God and for conducting him, my child, home in safety but above all for giving him a serious spirit and an earnest desire to save his soul ... O my God, I thank thee for all, and for good accounts from my husband.

28 November
More provocation from the masters at Kingswood, but ... the Lord does comfort my soul and makes me thankful for the disappointment by giving me to see the boy deeply serious, determined to seek the Lord with his whole heart. This has made me willing to forget all the trouble and sorrow I have had ... and gives me hopes that the Lord will visit the souls of my other children also ...

7 December
The Lord has graciously restored me my husband in safety, blessed be his name. ...

13 December
Blessed be my God, he has in some degree revived my soul and this day gave me much liberty in praying for my husband and children and a sweet confidence that the Lord my God would save them all ... O gracious Lord, let not my unfaithfulness prevent thy blessing to my children, but let thy full, unmerited grace be magnified towards them and me, that we may praise thee together in thy kingdom to all eternity.

1778

1 January

… O my God, I thank thee with all my heart for all thy number-less mercies, both spiritual and temporal, for life and health and friends, for the life and health of my family, for food to eat and raiment to put on, for a comfortable habitation and for the con-veniencies of life … and for the continuance of all, year after year. But above all, I thank thee for thyself, for thy people, for thy pure gospel, for the means of grace and for the comfortable hope of eternal glory. Lord, I am surrounded with thy mercies, my heart is filled with a sense of thy goodness …

22 February

Another instance of the goodness and long forbearance of my God: he visited me with sickness[1] to chastise me for my unfaith-fulness but O, how tender, how mixed with love are all his re-proofs! …

1 March

The sense of my unworthiness and unfitness for the work has often for some time past made me think of giving up my class, not that I might ease myself of the burden, but that they might be profited by another. I met them this day for the first time since my illness. I went to the class with a heavy heart, under a deep sense of my unfitness, but no sooner had I sat down amongst them than my burden was taken away, my spirit loosed and my heart enlarged towards them, so that I loved them as my dear children. It then appeared to me that I was just where my God would have me to be … The Lord did make it a happy meeting to us all. Observing my son H[enry] for some time past growing slack in the service of God, my spirit has been much grieved for him … and looking up to the Lord on his behalf, im-mediately I received such a steadfast assurance that he should be saved as banished all my fears and comforted my soul …

17 March

The Lord brought the return of this day to my mind with thank-fulness yet with sorrow and shame, considering his great and abundant mercy, his continued care and protection and my own base ingratitude and unprofitableness under all his favours[2] ... May I never forget that love which ... after ten thousand revolts has brought me to this hour, supplying me with a very needful help: food to eat and raiment to put on, a comfortable habitation, fire to warm, a bed to rest on, servants to attend and friends to comfort, my children to be a blessing and my husband a support; and with these mercies has also magnified his grace towards me in spiritual mercies, has given me my being in a land where his name is known, and in this gracious gospel day has opened my heart to receive his grace, has given his word as a light to my path, his messengers to instruct, his people to assist, his spirit to confirm, his rod to drive and his staff to support, and above all his blessed Son to die for my sin and rise again for my justification; and has with all these given me in some degree a grateful heart, sensible of all his great and manifold favours ... I am astonished at thy goodness and can only give in return what is already thine: a poor, unfaithful heart ...

2 April
... Being about to fix our son, Thomas, in business, I have for some time past found my mind much taken up with thoughts concerning it ... but, blessed be my good God, he does enable me to give it all up to him, desiring that he would either forward or frustrate it as he should see best ... And why should I not depend upon him? Surely I find it good so to do, and since my son, Henry, has begun to serve the Lord, I find my heart much encouraged to depend upon him for the rest of my children and my husband also ...

13 April
... My heart was sore pained this day on finding that my son, Henry, had quit the society ...

4 May
This day the Lord filled my heart with joy and thankfulness on again seeing his faithful servant John Wesley. His word was blessed to my soul and my heart was all praise ...[3]

11 May
This day parted with Mr Wesley: may the almighty Lord be his safeguard and defence and bless him with abundant success in his labours. I found his word exceeding profitable and my soul much blessed by this visit ...[4]

29 May
This day my husband and son, Thomas, set off for Dublin to buy shop goods. I gave them up into the care of my heavenly Father, having confidence in him that he will keep them and prosper their way, and restore them safe to me again.

20 June
Received my husband and son home again ... I feel many fears cast into my mind lest my heart should be drawn away from God by caring too much for my children ... Save me, I beseech thee, from every evil bias, interpose in my behalf and let not lawful things become unlawful to me.

5 July
Have been busily employed about my son's shop[5] so as to have but very few intervals of retirement. I find my heart thankful for this kind dispensation. O my God, let it not prove a snare to me ... The Lord gave me the comfort of seeing my daughter from Waterford this day. I found my heart filled with thankfulness at seeing my children once more all together with comfort ...

12 July
This day parted with my daughter. Gracious Father, let thy loving kindness follow and protect her and hers, conduct her safe and let her and hers be thine, and let me meet her again at thy right hand.

1 August
Busily employed in the world so as to have scarce a moment to myself. I feel thankfulness for having it to do, but find many fears lest it should draw or detain my heart from God ...

5 September
Busily employed day and night assisting my son in his business
and, blessed be my God, he does give me a thankful heart for
having it to do and for a measure of health to enable me to do it
… Being much fatigued from the labour of the week and thereby
hindered from the public means of grace, I found the return of
this Sabbath sweet …

13 September
Much fatigued in body but my soul at rest, stayed upon my God …

1 November
Another instance of the long-suffering and patience of my God:
… in my illness,[6] the Lord did make it an humbling time … and
did preserve my mind patient, passive and resigned through the
whole. But since I began to recover I find less power to exert my
mind after God, but rather a sinking of my spirits which leaves
me powerless …

12 November
… I have been inconstant, unwatchful, unfaithful, have looked
too much at the trials of life which have been sent for my profit,
have suffered unbelieving fears and anxious cares to take place
in my mind when I should be simply believing in Jesus and casting all my care on him. O my patient, long-suffering Father,
without thee I can do nothing …[7]

5 December
My spirit is for the most part bowed down under a deep sense of
my great unfaithfulness … and this day found a hasty spirit in
reproving one of my children, which has been a cause of much
sorrow to me since.[8]

25 December
Surely this has been a day of much labour of mind: a solemn
sense of this happy season rested on my mind in the morning,
but found it hard to keep it up all the day … and I came from the
Lord's table ashamed and unsatisfied. When I came home I
found my eldest son laid on the bed sick with every symptom of

a fever, which seems to increase ... O gracious Father ... sanctify this visitation to him, make it profitable to his soul and let it be a means of bringing him near to thyself.

27 December
Blessed be my God, my child is better. O, how manifold are all thy mercies to me! ...

1779

6 January
This morning in bed before day, I found my heart deeply affected under a sense of my base ingratitude and unfaithfulness to my God. I had power to cry to him and to lay my wants before him and implore his grace … and after I arose had much comfort and sweet encouragement in prayer. Found power to plead for my husband, children and sister and received comfortable hopes for them all …

12 January
The changing the tickets[1] was a solemn time to me: I was deeply convinced of my unfaithfulness … and on receiving my ticket it was as if the Lord had said to me: 'Now I will try thee once more.' And my heart accepted the favour with thankfulness, and determined by his grace to use more diligence and prayer for the future …

16 January
Was much blessed at the love feast: the Lord was with us and gave much freedom …

18 February
I know not how to describe the present state of my soul … I know the Lord is my God and am enabled to draw near to him as his child, yet I … have not the close, intimate communion, the sweet, sequestration of spirit, the delightful fellowship with the Father and the Son, the soul-reviving testimony of his spirit that my heart is cleansed from sin … O thou gracious author of light and life, shine upon my darkness and bid there be light … Remove the spirit of slumber and cause the sun of righteousness to arise on my soul …

5 March
Have been convinced of much neglect in the duty of self-examination and have endeavoured to resume it, but have not found it as easy as usual. O my God, pardon my neglect and assist my feeble endeavours, I beseech thee …

10 March

On examining my heart, I find it my chief desire to be wholly given up to my God in comparison of which all other enjoyments are but as dung and dross, yet with this I find much feebleness of soul, slackness and heaviness in duties, backwardness and dryness in prayer and an unsteadiness of mind, so that I cannot stay my thoughts upon God ... O save me, revive thy work in my soul and cause me again to bear fruit to thy glory.[2]

Notes

INTRODUCTION

1. Bennis Family genealogy in the Archives of the Religious Society of Friends, Dublin.
2. Ernest H. Bennis, *Some Reminiscences of Limerick Friends*, 1930, manuscript in the same Archives.
3. Charles H. Crookshank, *Memorable Women of Irish Methodism*, London, 1882, p 21
4. Charles H. Crookshank, *History of Methodism in Ireland*, Volume I, Belfast, 1885, p 47
5. Matthew 11: 28
6. Elizabeth Bennis, *Journal*; Crookshank, *Memorable Women*, p 27
7. James Boswell, *Life of Johnson*, 31 July 1763
8. *The Letters of John Wesley*, edited by John Telford, in eight volumes, London, 1931
9. Letters from Wesley to Elizabeth Bennis, 27 July 1770, 24 July 1769, 18 September 1769, 13 June 1770, 15 May 1771, 20 July 1771, 28 October 1771, 3 December 1771, John Wesley, *Christian Correspondence*, Dublin, 1842.
10. Letter from Wesley to Robert Carr Brackenbury, 15 September 1790
11. Letters from Wesley to Elizabeth Bennis, 30 May 1769, 24 July 1769, 27 July 1770, 29 July 1771, 16 December 1772, 21 December 1776
12. Finn's *Leinster Journal*, 12 November 1768, from Matthew Butler's *Waterford Family Papers*, National Library 9495 Book 10 p 15
13. Ibid, 12 March 1768
14. Ibid, 9 November 1768 and Faulkner's *Dublin Journal*, 8 November 1768
15. Crookshank, *Memorable Women*, p 28. *Christian Correspondence*, p156
16. Unpublished Bennis correspondence.
17. Registry of Deeds, Dublin ref 236/158/153278
18. John Wesley, *Journal*, 1762
19. Ibid, 8 June 1765
20. Registry of Deeds, Dublin ref 191/323/128271
21. *Limerick Chronicle*, 1 July 1771
22. George Geary Bennis, *Biographies Contemporains*, Paris 1854. English translation of the Bennis entries held in the Archives of the Religious Society of Friends, Dublin.
23. Letter from Wesley to Elizabeth Bennis, 10 September 1773
24. Letter quoted in *The Letters of John Wesley*, Volume 6
25. Letter from Wesley to Elizabeth Bennis, 1 December 1773
26. Registry of Deeds, Dublin refs 231/90/149285, 349/164/ 233373, 282/523/186515, 298/8/186269, 302/342/200332, 334/644/266846, 358/305/240624. *Limerick Chronicle*, 12 April 1779
27. Gary Martin Best, *Continuity and Change: A History of Kingswood*

School 1748-1998, Bath, 1998
28. Registry of Deeds, Dublin ref 358/305/240624
29. *Memorable Women*, p 29

FAITH, FAMILY AND ENDEAVOUR

1. Elizabeth Bennis, Journal, 16 October 1765. Robert Swindells arrived in Ireland with John Wesley in March 1748. 'A man of deep piety, great zeal and remarkable benevolence', he was also, according to Crookshank, 'a fine, handsome fellow'. C. H. Crookshank, *History of Methodism in Ireland*, I, 1885, pp 36, 52-3.

2. On Methodist association with the poor, see David Hempton and Myrtle Hill, *Evangelical Protestantism in Ulster society, 1740-1890*, London, 1992, p 8. In fact, according to Hempton and Hill, Wesleyan preaching was less directed towards the poor in Ireland than in England. Nevertheless, Crookshank cites a number of instances in which potential female members or their relatives were alarmed by the social implications of conversion. Agnes Smyth, for instance, 'resented the association with a despised people', and feared that 'I shall be for ever called a Swaddler' if she attended one of their meetings. *History*, I, p 293.

3. Journal, 16 October 1765.

4. See, among many other such references, ibid, 24 May 1767.

5. John Wesley preached in the open air for the first time on 2 April 1739 at Bristol: 'at four o'clock', he recorded, 'I submitted to be more vile and proclaimed in the highways the glad tidings of salvation, speaking ... to about three thousand people.' Roy Hattersley, *John Wesley: a brand from the burning*, 2002, p 148. On prejudice against Methodism, see John Walsh, 'Methodism and the mob in the eighteenth century', G. J. Cuming and Derek Baker eds, *Popular belief and practice*, Cambridge, 1972, pp 213-227. A particularly severe instance of persecution, noted by Elizabeth in the journal, occurred in Cork in 1749. A number of members were injured, and one woman was reportedly 'almost murdered' by the mob. *History*, I, p 61.

6. Hattersley, p 151. The first quotation is from a letter to Wesley's brother, Charles, the second from one to his friend, James Hervey. The term 'connexion' denotes the network of societies and believers in 'connexion' with Wesley and with each other.

7. Wesleyan Methodism was taken to North America during the 1760s by Irish emigrants. Among the pioneers were Barbara Heck and Philip Embury, both originally members of the Limerick Palatine community. The movement was introduced to the West Indies in 1760 by an Antiguan landowner, Nathaniel Gilbert. The society which he established was led after his death by two local women. Missionaries later travelled to some of the other islands, and by the time of Wesley's death membership in the West Indies numbered 6,570. John A. Vickers ed, *A*

dictionary of Methodism in Britain and Ireland, Epworth Press, 2000

8. *Dictionary* and Hattersley, p. 315. These figures include membership figures for both Ireland and Great Britain. Irish members in 1767 totalled 2,801, and in 1791 14,198. David Hempton, 'Methodism in Irish society, 1770-1830', *Transactions of the Royal Historical Society,* 5th series, 26, 1986, pp 117-42, table 1, p 140.

9. Wesleyan Methodism did not separate from the Established Church until after Wesley's death, and he himself was adamant in his attachment to Anglicanism. Nevertheless, innovations such as field preaching, the employment of lay preachers and the particularly vexed issue of ordination made such an outcome inevitable.

10. John Wesley, *Journal,* 17 August 1747. However, he added, 'on that very account they must be watched over with the more care, being equally susceptible of good and ill impressions.'

11. *History,* I, p 22.

12. Olwen Hufton, *The prospect before her: a history of women in Western Europe, 1500-1800,* 1995, p 357.

13. C. H. Crookshank, *Memorable women of Irish Methodism in the last century,* London, 1882; David Hempton and Myrtle Hill, 'Women and Protestant minorities in eighteenth-century Ireland', in Margaret MacCurtain and Mary O'Dowd eds, *Women in early modern Ireland,* 1991, pp 197-211, p 196 and passim; David Hempton, *Methodism and politics in British society, 1750-1850,* London, 1984, p 13; Hempton and Hill, *Evangelical Protestantism in Ulster society,* p 12. For discussion of the reasons for Methodism's success, and specifically of its appeal to women, see Hufton, pp 315-316; Mary O'Dowd, *A history of women in Ireland, 1500-1800,* London, 2005, pp 189-192; Hempton and Hill, 'Women and Protestant minorities in eighteenth-century Ireland', pp 197-211; Hempton, 'Methodism in Irish society', pp 119-125, 128-133; Rosemary Raughter, 'Mothers in Israel: women, family and community in early Irish Methodism', Alan Hayes and Diane Urquhart eds, *Irish women's history,* Dublin, 2004, pp 29-42, pp 30-31.

14. Hempton and Hill, *Evangelical Protestantism in Ulster society,* p 12.

15. *Memorable women,* p 135.

16. John Wesley, *Christian correspondence: a collection of letters written by the late Rev John Wesley, and several Methodist preachers in connexion with him, to the late Mrs Eliza Bennis, with her answers,* Dublin, 1842. Originals of a number of these letters are held in the archives of St George's United Methodist Church, Philadelphia and one (John Wesley, Ashby, to Elizabeth Bennis, 27 July 1770) in the archives of Willamette University, Oregon, USA.

17. Agnes Woodley to President Smith [of Willamette University], Portland, Oregon, 14 October 1947. Ms Woodley states that Mrs Bennis's 'daughter, who must have been an old lady at the time, gave it to my grandfather, Reverend Bartholomew Weed.' There is no record of either of Elizabeth's daughters having emigrated to North America:

the original donor may have been her daughter-in-law, Thomas's wife, Ann.

18. The Record of Members of St George's Church, Philadelphia, 1793-1879 lists Thomas and Ann Bennis as members, 16 January 1795. According to the Register of Births and Baptisms, 1785-1816 and of Marriages, 1789-1817, Thomas and Ann had previously been members in New York. St George's Church Archives. In 1800 Thomas Bennis's household in Philadelphia consisted of Thomas himself, two males under ten, a female aged 16-25, another aged 26-44 and a third, aged over 45. The two latter were presumably Ann, Thomas's wife, and his mother, Elizabeth. Information supplied by Barbara Parshley. There is no mention of Elizabeth in any of the surviving records of St George's Church.

19. On women and writing at this period, see O'Dowd, pp 225-229. While Mary Leadbeater's diary covered a period of more than forty years, she was, unlike Elizabeth, a professional author, who drew on her journal for her published works.

20. Notable examples included Dorothea Johnson, Alice Cambridge, Theodosia Blachford and Angel Anna Slack: see *Memorable women*, pp 53-62, 142-147, 180-189, 200. Dorothea Johnson, converted in 1757, began a journal in 1771, which she kept intermittently until her death in 1817. Alice Cambridge left a number of autobiographical 'papers', which described her moment of conversion, the development of her understanding of her faith and the value of female fellowship. In 1780 Theodosia Blachford drew up some 'recollections of every year since 1747, when I was three years old' (and her daughter, Mary Tighe, began a journal at the age of fourteen in 1787 and maintained it until 1802), and Angel Anna Slack's journal 1787-1796 is at once a record of her spiritual state and of her usefulness as a promoter of Methodism in her own area of county Leitrim. See Dorothea Johnson, *Memoirs*, ed Rev. Adam Averell, Cavan, 1818; John James McGregor ed, *Memoir of Miss A Cambridge ... compiled from her papers and the communications of friends*, Dublin 1832; for Blachford and Tighe journals, see mss 3575 and 4810, Wicklow Papers, NLI; on Angel Anna Slack's ms journal, O'Dowd, pp 189-192.

21. Journal, 23 June 1749.

22. The fullest account of Elizabeth's youth and family background, including reference to her father's death, is in ibid, 16 October 1765. For her father's appearance in a dream, see ibid, 11 February 1755. Elizabeth had one sister, Alice, of whom she was evidently fond, but who did not share her religious views: see ibid, 30 June 1749, 20 November 1769 and 6 January 1779.

23. Elizabeth's writings included poetry as well as prose: see ibid, 26 February 1766 and 20 December 1771. Other verses by her are reproduced in a manuscript collection of writings by members of the Bennis family: they include a poem 'given with a tablet to a friend ... from

whom she had received a pack of scripture cards' and another 'given in a blank book to a friend'. Copies supplied by Barbara Parshley.

24. On reading see ibid, 26 October 1765, 11 September 1754, 6 April 1770. Other authors mentioned include Edward Young, Johann Arndt, Macarius of Egypt and Bishop Beveridge. Ibid, 22 February 1751, 21 February 1752, 8 August 1753, 25 December 1768.

25. At least six children were born to Elizabeth and Mitchell between 1750 and the birth, in 1765, of Elizabeth's last child, Elizabeth. The journal also reports the deaths of six children during this period. Some births, therefore, must have gone unrecorded. See note 1, 1750 for more information on this point.

26. By the mid-eighteenth century Limerick was the third largest town in Ireland (after Dublin and Cork), with a population of about 20,000. J. L. McCracken, 'The social structure and social life, 1714-60', T. W. Moody and W. E. Vaughan eds, *A new history of Ireland*, vol IV, pp 31-56, p 31. For a short account of the state of Limerick in 1750 and subsequent urban development, see Eamon O'Flaherty, 'Three towns: Limerick since 1691', Howard B. Clarke ed, *Irish cities*, Cork, 1995, pp 177-190.

27. For references to trials and opposition at this period, see Journal, 30 June, 5 July, 3, 13, 17, 20 August, 30 Sept, 10, 18 October, 3, 10, 20 November 1749.

28. On 'invectives' see ibid, 3 August 1749. The person concerned is not identified in this entry. However, Elizabeth's mother-in-law is mentioned as a trouble-maker on 13 August 1749.

29. Ibid, 30 June 1749. Elizabeth's concern for her husband's soul is a recurring topic throughout the journal.

30. Ibid, 29 December 1751.

31. Ibid, 23 May 1763. On the distinction between the 'almost' and the 'altogether' Christian, see John Wesley, 'The almost Christian', *Forty-four sermons*, Epworth Press, 1944, pp 11-19

32. Journal, 16 October 1765. See also entry for 23 May 1763, upon which the later account is based.

33. Ibid, 16 October 1765.

34. Ibid.

35. John Wesley, 'The new birth', *Sermons*, pp 514-526, p 523.

36. Journal, 21 June 1755.

37. Ibid, 21 January 1777.

38. Ibid, 15 January 1766.

39. See ibid, 12-21 August 1753 on Mrs Beauchamp's death. On Elizabeth's assumption of leadership, see ibid, 27 August 1753, and on the preacher's refusal to appoint another leader, ibid, 17 September 1753.

40. Ibid, 11 February 1754.

41. David Hempton, 'Methodism in Irish society, 1770-1830', pp 120-121. Classes were groups of about twelve individuals, divided according to age and sex, which met weekly under the direction of a leader for

hymn-singing, exhortation, personal testimony and a collection. Bands were smaller groups of about six or seven people, which met weekly for worship, prayer and personal testimony. With the decline of the bands, the class meeting became the basic unit of Methodist organisation, and remained so well into the twentieth century. *Dictionary* and Dudley Levistone Cooney, *The Methodists in Ireland: a short history*, Dublin, 2001, pp 163-164.

42. Ibid, 16 October 1765.

43. Ibid, 16 October 1765.

44. Ibid, 22 November 1765.

45. Ibid, 12-21 August 1753, 31 January 1764, 11 May 1776, 10 October 1777.

46. Elizabeth Bennis, Limerick, to Thomas Walsh, 20 January 1757, LVI, *Christian correspondence*.

47. Samuel Bradburn, Dublin, to Elizabeth Bennis, 14 June 1777 and Elizabeth Bennis, Limerick, to Samuel Bradburn, 22 June 1777, LXXXVI and LXXXVII, *Christian correspondence*.

48. Journal, 17 June 1771. Wesley argued that believers could become 'perfect in love', although this did not exclude the possibility of un-recognised 'sinful' tempers and sin through ignorance. His doctrine, set out in his *Plain account of Christian perfection* (1766), was opposed by, among others, Calvinists, who believed that the saved individual nec-essarily remained a sinner. *Dictionary*.

49. The friend in question was probably John Dillon. For the progress and eventual resolution of this episode, see Journal, 2, 6, 17 June, 3, 5, 13, 16, 17, 21, 22, 29 July, 3, 6, 7, 20, 23, 25 August 1763.

50. Ibid, 13 August 1752.

51. John Wesley, *Journal*, 12 June 1756.

52. Journal, 10 June 1756.

53. Ibid, 28 June 1758.

54. Ibid, 2 July 1758.

55. Ibid, 23 May 1763.

56. Elizabeth Bennis, Limerick, to John Wesley, 2 August 1763 and John Wesley, Pembroke, to Elizabeth Bennis, 23 August 1763, I and II, *Christian correspondence*.

57. Journal, 25 June 1769; Elizabeth Bennis, Limerick, to John Wesley, 13 July 1769, XI, *Christian correspondence*.

58. *History*, I, p 299.

59. John Wesley, Whitehaven, to Elizabeth Bennis, 12 April 1770, XV, *Christian correspondence*.

60. Elizabeth Bennis, Waterford, to John Wesley, 20 May 1770, XVI, ibid.

61. Elizabeth Bennis, Limerick, to John Wesley, 15 October 1771, XXIV, ibid. The preacher who had just arrived was William Collins. The for-mer preacher was Jonathan Hern.

62. On the latitude enjoyed by women in early Methodism, see Hempton and Hill, 'Women and Protestant minorities in eighteenth-century Ireland', pp 198-202.

63. *Memoir of Miss Alice Cambridge*, p. 39.

64. John Wesley, Manchester, to Elizabeth Bennis, 29 March 1766, IV, *Christian correspondence*.

65. John McGregor, Limerick, to Elizabeth Bennis, 1 September 1790, CXIII, ibid.

66. Elizabeth Bennis, Limerick, to John Wesley, 17 March 1772, XXVIII, ibid.

67. Journal, 22 and 26 May 1772.

68. Elizabeth Bennis, Limerick, to John Wesley, 26 May 1772, ms correspondence, St George's Church Archives, Philadelphia.

69. Elizabeth Bennis, Limerick, to John Wesley, 18 October 1772, XXXIV, *Christian correspondence*.

70. John Wesley, Colchester, to Elizabeth Bennis, 3 November 1772, XXXV, ibid.

71. Elizabeth Bennis, Limerick, to John Wesley, 1 December 1772, XXXVI, ibid.

72. John Wesley, Shoreham, to Elizabeth Bennis, 16 December 1772, ms correspondence, St George's Church Archives, Philadelphia.

73. Elizabeth Bennis to John Wesley, 25 August 1773, ms correspondence, St George's Church Archives, Philadelphia.

74. Journal, 22 November 1769.

75. Ibid, 5 December 1769. On this occasion, however, her intervention was ineffective, and she 'was grieved to find I could do him no good'.

76. Ibid, 13 December 1769.

77. Ibid, 19 December 1769.

78. Elizabeth Bennis, Waterford, to John Wesley, 20 May 1770, XVI, *Christian correspondence*.

79. 'How is this with respect to Waterford? They would, and they would not. I sent two preachers to that circuit – why did they not keep them? Let me hear more from you on this matter.' John Wesley, Yarm, to Elizabeth Bennis, 13 June 1770, XVII, ibid.

80. Elizabeth Bennis, Limerick, to John Wesley, 8 July 1770, XVIII, ibid.

81. John Wesley, Ashby, to Elizabeth Bennis, 27 July 1770, XIX, ibid.

82. John Wesley, Limerick, to Elizabeth Bennis, 15 May 1771, XXI, ibid.

83. See Journal, 16, 19, 21, 25 and 27 August 1772.

84. Elizabeth Bennis, Waterford, to John Wesley, 8 August 1772, XXXII, *Christian correspondence*.

85. However, she also exerted her authority in other centres of Methodism, notably in Clonmel. See, for instance, Elizabeth Bennis, Limerick, to John Wesley, 8 July 1770, XVIII, *Christian correspondence*: 'Sister Ann S- is lately married to brother L- of Clonmel. Brother Bourke and I made up this match, and I think it is the Lord's doing: she is as usual all alive to God, and I trust will be a means of saving his soul. Brother Bourke, at my request, has taken Clonmel into the circuit ... I have to request your forgiveness for my officiousness. If you disapprove, it can be re-altered.'

86. John Stretton, Carbonear, to Elizabeth Bennis, 29 October 1770, LXXXVIII, *Christian correspondence.*

87. For details of Stretton's career, see Sandra Beardsall, '"I love to tell the story"; women in Outport Newfoundland Methodism', *Canadian woman studies*, vol 17, 1, pp 26-30 and Hans Rollmann, 'The origins of Methodism in Newfoundland', www.mun.ca/rels/hrollmann/meth/texts/ptohomd.html

88. *History*, I, p 169. Stretton also had connections with Limerick: John Wesley met his parents there during one of his visits to the city. John Wesley, London, to John Stretton, 25 February 1785, Wesley, *Correspondence.*

89. John Stretton, Carbonear, to Elizabeth Bennis, 29 October 1770, LXXXVIII, *Christian correspondence.*

90. See John Stretton, Harbour Grace, to Elizabeth Bennis, 14 November 1773, XCI, ibid; John Stretton, Harbour Grace, to Elizabeth Bennis, 4 November 1774, XCII, ibid; John Stretton, Harbour Grace, to Elizabeth Bennis, 14 November 1775, XCIII, ibid; John Stretton, Harbour Grace, to Elizabeth Bennis, 2 December 1778, XCIX, ibid.

91. John Stretton, Harbour Grace, to Elizabeth Bennis, 8 November 1776, XCIV, ibid.

92. John Stretton, Harbour Grace, to Elizabeth Bennis, 29 June 1785, CI, ibid. Elizabeth's representations were evidently persuasive: in Stretton's next letter he acknowledged the arrival of a preacher [John McGeary] sent by Wesley, but feared he might not stay long. In his next letter he reported that McGeary, having married unwisely and given offence to many, had been of no use and had now returned to England. John Stretton, Harbour Grace, to Elizabeth Bennis, 15 November 1785, CI, ibid; John Stretton, Harbour Grace, to Elizabeth Bennis, 18 November 1788, CII, ibid.

93. Elizabeth Bennis, Limerick, to John Stretton, 22 March 1777, XCV, ibid.

94. Elizabeth Bennis, Limerick, to John Stretton, XCVII, ibid. In his last surviving letter to Elizabeth, Stretton reported a revival in the Harbour Grace area. 'Many were converted ... and ... I have gathered near sixty young persons, and many little children that have serious impressions on their minds ... Surely He who has begun this great, this glorious work in the dreary wilderness, will carry it on, until this dark region is illuminated with Gospel light, knowledge and love.' John Stretton, Harbour Grace, to Elizabeth Bennis, 29 November 1791, CV, *Christian correspondence.* Stretton remained in Newfoundland until his death in 1810, when he was buried 'with songs of Christian triumph'. *Encyclopedia of Newfoundland and Labrador.* Within eighty years of Stretton's mission, 'Methodists would form 20 per cent of the entire Newfoundland population, soaring to a 30 per cent high in the 1920s'. Beardsall, p 26.

95. Journal, 6 January 1768.

96. See, for instance, ibid, 1 August 1778, when Elizabeth found herself 'busily employed in the world so as to have scarce a moment to myself. I feel thankfulness for having it to do, but find many fears lest it should draw or detain my heart from God.'

97. Ibid, 16 October 1765: 'Then I said, I will now ask to have my idols taken out of my heart, but whilst I sought them they were gone, taken away in a moment, and their place so filled with God that there was no room for anything besides ... I sought for my husband and children in my heart (that is, I examined whether my heart was in any degree so bound up in them as to separate any part of it from God), but they were given up to God, and my heart so filled with his love that I was constrained to cry out, "Lord Jesus, thou art the only object of my soul. Thou has taken possession of my heart, and there is no room for any beside thyself".'

98. Ibid, 13 August 1749.

99. Ibid, 8 July 1770.

100. Ibid, 26 August 1763.

101. On hostility to Elizabeth's conversion, see journal, 30 June, 3 August, 30 September, 10 October and 3 November 1749; on her stays in the country, see ibid, 5 July and 20 August 1749.

102. See ibid, 3 and 13 August and 20 November 1749. On subsequent episodes of this kind, see 3 June 1751, 15 March and 5 and 20 July 1756, 8 and 21 January and 4 October 1757. There are no similar references after this date, and the Mrs Bennis whose burial is recorded in the registers of St Mary's Cathedral on 12 September 1761 may be Elizabeth's mother-in-law. Information supplied by Barbara Parshley.

103. Ibid, 18 October and 10 November 1749.

104. However, in 1766, in consequence of a 'wrong' against her and 'oppositions' from an unspecified quarter – probably her husband – Elizabeth was temporarily 'debarred the company and conversation of my Christian friends'. See ibid, 14 October, 2, 10, 14 November 1766. The ecstatic entry of 30 November 1766 suggests that she was once more free to associate with her friends. More usually, however, Mitchell's antagonism seems to have been verbal, as on New Year's Day 1758, when Elizabeth reports him 'railing at and abusing the truths and people of God': ibid, 1 January 1758.

105. Ibid, 1 April 1751.

106. Ibid, 28 January 1770.

107. Ibid, 5 October 1751.

108. Ibid, 7, 10, 13 October, 19, 20, 23 November 1751.

109. Ibid, 24 March 1752.

110. Ibid, 27 March 1752.

111. Ibid, 31 May and 4 June 1752.

112. Ibid, 10, 11, 13, 16, 19 June and 22 July 1752.

113. Ibid, 1 January 1753.

114. On Mitchell's confinement, see ibid, 29 June and 31 July 1756. On

Elizabeth's opinion of her husband's judgement, see ibid, 14 January 1758. At this period – indeed, until the 1870s – civil debtors might be imprisoned following legal process. The place of detention in such a case depended on the court involved: for instance, the sheriffs' courts and manor courts had their own prisons, while those proceeded against in the court of King's Bench would be consigned to the Four Courts Marshalsea. The arrangement reached here, whereby Mitchell apparently passed a period of detention in his own house, was not usual. Information supplied by Professor Nial Osborough.

115. Ibid, 8 and 24 July 1770.

116. Ibid, 10 August 1770.

117. Ibid, 8 and 22 July 1770.

118. Ibid, 15 March 1766.

119. Ibid, 17 May 1772.

120. Ibid, 7 November 1756.

121. Ibid, 8 April 1760.

122. Ibid, 30 April 1760. Elizabeth does not specify whether the child who died was the one inoculated. For details of other children's deaths, see note 1, 1750. The system of inoculation used at this period was not vaccination, developed by Dr Edward Jenner in 1796, but variolation. Originally developed in Asia and introduced into Great Britain in 1721 by Lady Mary Wortley Montague, variolation involved infecting the individual with a mild form of smallpox. The process carried a risk: between one and two per cent of those variolated died, although this must be set against a death rate of about thirty per cent for those who contracted smallpox naturally. Following successful experiments on prisoners and foundling children, members of the royal family submitted to inoculation, and the practice spread rapidly thereafter. www.nlm.nih.gov/exhibition/smallpox/ index.html

123. Ibid, 1, 4, 6, 12, 16, 24 May and 1 June 1760.

124. The first entry following this long silence is that for 23 May 1763, and records the events of the previous day, when Elizabeth recovered her sense of her justification. This was the ultimate result of the encouragement provided by Wesley's preaching during his 1762 visit.

125. Ibid, 26 September 1768.

126. Ibid, 4, 17 October and 25 November 1768.

127. Ibid, 25 November 1768.

128. Ibid, 10 February 1775.

129. Ibid, 5 August 1772.

130. Ibid, 1 September 1774.

131. Ibid, 1, 28 September and 17 November 1774. However, it was to Mitchell (but addressed to Mrs Elizabeth Bennis) that Wesley wrote to confirm Henry's admission to Kingswood. John Wesley, Bristol, to Mitchell Bennis, 13 September 1774, Drew University Methodist Collection, www.atla.com/digitalresources/

132. Journal, 15 August, 3 September, 21 and 28 November 1777.

133. See ibid, 12 and 30 September and 3 November 1769 for Elizabeth's wish to see her daughter. On Elizabeth's visits to Waterford, see entries 11 November 1769 – 9 January 1770; 31 March – 3 June 1769; 25 April – 8 July 1771; 17 July – 9 September 1772; 22 December 1773 – 22 March 1774.

134. On concern for Thomas, see ibid, 16 and 21 August, 29 November 1772, 7 and 18 June, 9 August 1773, 22 and 29 May, 3 and 20 July 1774, 10 March 1776. On Thomas's business and Elizabeth's involvement in it, see ibid, 2 April, 29 May, 5 July, 5 September 1778.

135. Ibid, 6 February 1776.

136. Ibid, 28 November 1777.

137. Ibid, 1 March and 13 April 1778.

138. On Thomas, Henry and Eleanor see Levistone Cooney, Introduction, passim. On Henry's Quakerism, see Bennis Genealogy, R65/20, Society of Friends Historical Library, Dublin

139. On Elizabeth Finney (nee Bennis) see Levistone Cooney, Introduction, p 14. Elizabeth's published correspondence includes two letters from Rev JF who, although unidentified, was clearly Rev John Finney, Elizabeth's husband. Judging from his epistolary style – which recalls Jane Austen's Mr Collins rather than one of John Wesley's 'sons in the gospel' – it might be inferred that John Finney was not the type of clergyman of whom his mother-in-law would have wholeheartedly approved. See Rev JF, Cove, to Elizabeth Bennis, 7 April 1783 and Rev JF, Cove, to Elizabeth Bennis, 12 May 1783, CVII and CIX, *Christian correspondence*.

140. However, see Levistone Cooney, Introduction, pp 22-23, on Elizabeth as possible cause of the calamity mentioned by some of her mother's correspondents.

141. John Stretton, Harbour Grace, to Elizabeth Bennis, 18 December 1790, CIV, *Christian correspondence*.

142. This impression is supported by a fragment of an elegy written by Elizabeth Finney, in which she mourns 'the mother and the friend'. The subject, who 'instructed still to tread the narrow way, That leads to mansions of unclouded day', may have been her mother, the older Elizabeth, or another, unidentified, mentor. In either case, the content does indicate that at the time of writing Elizabeth Finney was engaged on her own quest for spiritual fulfilment. The collection also includes poems by Elizabeth Bennis and by Henry Bennis. Photocopy ms provided by Barbara Parshley.

143. 'You have had the comfort … of seeing your husband die in the Lord – that tender and affectionate partner of forty-three years, for whose eternal happiness you sent up so many prayers.' John McGregor, Limerick, to Elizabeth Bennis, 1 September 1790, CXIII, *Christian correspondence*. On Elizabeth's 'strong and confident hopes', see Journal, 12 April 1766.

144. Elizabeth Bennis, Limerick, to John Wesley, 11 November 1773, XLIV, *Christian correspondence*.

145. Journal, 11 March, 29 May and 5 September 1778. However, a succession of entries indicates a crisis in the family's affairs during 1777: see ibid, 27 April, 4, 14, 17, 28 May, 3, 7, 9, 15, 26 June, 6 July and 5 August 1777.

146. See Dudley Levistone Cooney, Introduction, pp 18-21, on Mitchell's business difficulties and the collapse of the family enterprises after his death. For Stretton's letter, see John Stretton, Harbour Grace, to Elizabeth Bennis, 18 November 1788, CIII, *Christian correspondence*. A long break in Elizabeth's correspondence with Stretton between 1779 and 1785, however, hints at some upheaval in her life even before Mitchell's death.

147. Elizabeth's removal from Limerick to Waterford and her continuing 'complicated troubles' are noted in Richard Condy, Limerick, to Elizabeth Bennis, 27 March 1790, John McGregor, Limerick, to Elizabeth Bennis, 1 September 1790 and John Stretton, Harbour Grace, to Elizabeth Bennis, 18 December 1790,CXIV, CXIII and CIV, *Christian correspondence*.

148. John McGregor, writing in 1790, asked her to convey 'my sincere love to the Waterford preachers and people'. John McGregor, Limerick, to Elizabeth Bennis, 1 September 1790, CXIII, *Christian correspondence*.

149. Walter Griffith, Dublin, to Elizabeth Bennis, 9 February 1792, CXVI, *Christian correspondence*. In the same letter, Griffith urged gratitude to God 'for having kept you so long from sinking beneath the weight of various afflictions'.

150. Record of Members of St George's Church, Philadelphia, 1793-1879, St George's Church Archives.

151. *History*, I, p. 45.

152. 'O Lord … give me a holy boldness in thy cause, that I may never be ashamed of thy cross, but may thereby be crucified to the world, and the world crucified to me.' Journal, 24 October 1756.

153. However, on the relegation of women to supportive roles within Methodism, see Hempton and Hill, 'Women and Protestant minorities', p 203.

154. On evangelical women as agents of social change, see Jane Rendall, *The origins of modern feminism: women in Britain, France and the United States, 1780-1860*, Chicago, 1985, pp 73-101.

155. Journal, 23 June 1749.

156. See, for instance, Elizabeth's account of the period following her conversion in ibid, 16 October 1765.

157. Ibid, 18 October 1763.

158. Ibid, 1 January 1767.

159. Ibid, 10 March 1779.

160. No volumes of the journal for the period after 1779 have come to light, and no letters from Elizabeth after November 1791 have been preserved.

161. Journal, 17 March 1773.

162. Elizabeth Bennis, Waterford, to Mr Joseph Cr--, 26 November 1791, CXVIII, *Christian correspondence*. The recipient, 'a well-meaning Papist', had written to Elizabeth to urge the claims of the Catholic church as 'the true church of Christ'. Mr Joseph Cr--, Carrick, to Elizabeth Bennis, 23 November 1791, CXVII, *Christian correspondence*.

THE JOURNAL 1749-1779

1749

1. Elizabeth's first encounter with Methodism occurred on 17 March 1749, when she witnessed the arrival in Limerick of Robert Swindells, the first Methodism preacher to visit the city, and later went to hear him preach. For an account of this event, see entry for 16 October 1765. Methodism developed from an evangelical group known as the 'Holy Club', established in 1729 at Oxford by the brothers John and Charles Wesley and others. The name refers to the 'regular method of study and behaviour' which it advocated.

A number of Methodist preachers came to Ireland during the 1740s, and John Wesley himself arrived in 1747 on the first of twenty-one visits to the country. At the time of his final tour in 1789, there were more than 14,000 Irish Methodists.

John Wesley (1703-91) was born in Epworth, Lincolnshire. His father was a clergyman, but his mother, Susanna, was by far the stronger influence. A formidably intelligent, strong-minded woman, she guided her son's spiritual development and remained his intellectual mentor until her death in 1742. Following a disastrous mission to Georgia in 1738, John returned to London, where he underwent a conversion experience and went on to establish an itinerant ministry and to create a network of societies covering the British Isles and extending in his lifetime to North America. A tireless traveller, evangelist and controversialist, he was also the author of approximately 500 titles. He died at his London headquarters in City Road on 2 March 1791. John Vickers ed, *A Dictionary of Methodism in Britain and Ireland*, Epworth Press, 2000.

2. John Haughton (fl 1746-1755) worked with John Wesley in Yorkshire in 1746 and in 1755 was one of the 'chief local preachers'. Much of his ministry was in Ireland. He was eventually ordained into the Anglican priesthood and served as rector of Kilrea, County Londonderry. See Methodist Archives and Research Centre Biographical Index, www.rylibweb.man.ac.uk.

3. Elizabeth is describing the experience of justification, in Wesleyan theology an essential stage in the progression towards 'sanctification' or 'perfect love'. As explained by Wesley, 'justification is pardon, the forgiveness of sins. It is that act of God the Father, whereby, for the sake of the propitiation made by the blood of His Son, He "showeth forth His righteousness" (or mercy) "by the remission of the sins that are past".' Once justified, all the believer's past sins 'are blotted out ... God will not

inflict on that sinner what he deserved to suffer, because the Son of His love hath suffered for him.' John Wesley, 'Justification by faith', *Sermons on several occasions*, Epworth Press, 1944, pp 49-61, pp 53-54.

4. Elizabeth's husband, Mitchell Bennis (1720-1788) did not share her commitment to Methodism, and this is only the first of many prayers for his conversion throughout the period covered by the journal. However, he did, reportedly 'die in the Lord'. See John McGregor, Limerick to Elizabeth Bennis, 1 September 1790, letter CXIII, John Wesley, *Christian correspondence: a collection of letters written by the late Rev John Wesley, and several Methodist preachers in connection with him, to the late Mrs Eliza Bennis, with her answers*, Dublin, 1842. Elizabeth's sister Alice Patten, makes only three appearances in the journal, and seems not to have become a Methodist: see also entries for 20 November 1769 and 6 January 1779.

5. Possibly John Haughton.

6. The earliest of Elizabeth's correspondence to have survived dates from 1755: see Thomas Walsh, Dublin to Elizabeth Bennis, 13 December 1755, LV, *Christian correspondence*. Original in St George's United Methodist Church Archives, Philadelphia.

7. Methodists were strongly discouraged from idle or trivial conversation. See John Wesley, 'The law established through faith', *Sermons*, pp 395-406, p 405. Wesley's directions to his followers to observe 'strictness of life' also included 'making it a rule, to abstain from fashionable diversions, from reading plays, romances, or books of humour, from singing innocent songs, or talking in a merry, gay, diverting manner.' John Wesley, *Advice to the people called Methodists*, 1745.

8. This is the first of numerous cryptic references to hostility to her religious opinions which Elizabeth encountered within her own family. The entry for 13 August 1749 suggests that the chief opponent now and for some years to come was her mother-in-law and aunt, Elinor Bennis.

9. Charles Wesley visited Cork in 1748 and John Wesley in 1749. In 1749-50 Methodists there were the target of a number of attacks instigated by a ballad-seller, Nicholas Butler. The civil authorities took the view that the violence had been prompted by the Methodist preachers. John Wesley recorded receiving word from Cork that 'twenty eight depositions were laid before the Grand Jury there, but they threw them all out, and at the same time made that memorable presentment ... We find and present Charles Wesley [and others] to be a person of ill fame, a vagabond, and a common disturber of His Majesty's peace, and we pray he may be transported.' John Wesley, *Journal*, 19 August 1749, www.godrules.net/library/wesley/ One of those also mentioned in the depositions was Robert Swindells. For an account of these riots, see C. H. Crookshank, *History of Methodism in Ireland*, I, pp 51-52, 58-62.

10. 'A good name is better than precious ointment; and the day of death than the day of one's birth.' Ecclesiastes 7:1. Quotations are from the King James or Authorised Version of the Bible. First published in 1611, this is the version with which Elizabeth was familiar.

1750

1. Elizabeth's childbearing history, as recorded in the journal, is incomplete: at the time of this baby's birth, recorded on 20 April 1750, she already had one child, Eleanor, baptised on 14 December 1748. She records further live births on 1 February 1752, 2 July 1753 (probably a son), 9 November 1755 (a daughter), 19 September 1758, 4 November 1759 and 14 March 1765 (her younger daughter, Elizabeth). In addition, of course, some of the illnesses mentioned may have been miscarriages. She also records the deaths of a number of children: one on 14 May 1752 (perhaps the baby mentioned on 1 February), and another (a daughter) on 23 April 1753. On 6 November 1756 a son died of smallpox, followed on 12 November by his sister. A baby (born on 19 September 1758) died on 7 October 1758, and another child died of smallpox on 30 April 1760. The difficulty is that, while eight live births and six deaths are recorded, Elizabeth actually had four surviving children: Eleanor, Thomas, Henry and Elizabeth. It must be assumed, therefore, that some births went unrecorded.

2. See entry for 1 September 1749.

3. 'Fear thou not: for I am with thee: be not dismayed; for I am thy God: I will strengthen thee; yea, I will help thee; yea, I will uphold thee with the right hand of my righteousness. Behold, all they that were incensed against thee shall be ashamed and confounded: they shall be as nothing; and they that strive with thee shall perish.' Isaiah 41:10-11. At the Lent Assizes in Cork, 'all the preachers then in Ireland ... went ... in a body to the Courthouse, accompanied by several respectable inhabitants of the city ... At length [the Judge] called for the evidence, and Butler entered the witness box. On his saying in reply to the first question, what is your calling, that he was a ballad-singer ... his lordship turned to the preachers and said, "Gentlemen, there is no evidence against you, you may retire".' The dismissal of the case against the preachers proved, as Wesley put it, that 'there is law even for Methodists'. *History*, I, p 62 and Wesley, *Journal*, 14 April 1750.

4. See entry for 23 June 1749.

5. 'The morning preaching', as well as band and class meetings, probably took place in the room which the Methodist society had by now secured in 'the remains of an old abbey [St Francis's Abbey] ... fitted up for a place of worship.' *History*, I, p 50. This is an example of the onerous and time-consuming schedule of commitments to which Methodists were subject, with meetings held throughout the week (2 July was a Thursday) as well as on Sundays. The heavy demands made on members put into context Elizabeth's frequent complaints of 'drowsiness' during meetings and at prayer.

6. Bands, introduced into Methodism in its early days, were groups of about six or seven individuals, who met weekly for worship, prayer and personal testimony. The band meeting has been described as 'the Methodist confessional and court of discipline in action, for the pursuit

of holiness. It is in no sense a meeting for public worship. Admission is by ticket of membership only, granted to those who reliably satisfy the strict conditions. Men and women, married and single, meet separately. The confessional and penitential discipline is administered in a little company, upon all by all ... Membership of the band was not dependent upon attainment to holiness, or assurance. The simple condition is that of an entire earnestness to attain, cost what it may.' John Lawson, 'Our discipline', *A history of the Methodist church in Great Britain*, London, 1965, p 191. The spiritual discipline imposed on band members, and detailed by Wesley in the *Rules of the band societies* (1738) and *Directions given to the band societies* (1744), was stringent enough to discourage all but the most committed, and even before Wesley's death the system was in decline. Classes, introduced by Wesley in 1742, initially as a means of fundraising, were slightly larger groups of about twelve individuals, also divided according to age and sex, which met weekly under the direction of a leader. Meetings included hymn-singing, exhortation, personal testimony and a collection. With the decline of the bands, the class meeting became the basic unit of Methodist organisation, and remained so well into the twentieth century. *Dictionary* and Dudley Levistone Cooney, *The Methodists in Ireland: a short history*, Dublin 2001, pp 163-164.

7. On Sundays Elizabeth would probably have attended the service of morning prayer at St Mary's Cathedral, situated just a few yards from her home in Bow Lane, as well as gatherings of the Methodist society. In addition to their own meetings, Methodists were expected to be diligent in attendance at their local Anglican place of worship, and in particular at the sacrament of Holy Communion. On the Methodist attitude to frequent Communion, see Hattersley, pp 202-203 and Levistone Cooney, Introduction, p 13.

8. Before becoming a member of a band, members were required to answer the following questions: 'Do you desire to be told of all your faults, and that plain and home? ... Do you desire we should tell you whatsoever we think, whatsoever we fear, whatsoever we hear, concerning you? Do you desire that, in doing this, we should come as close as possible, that we should cut to the quick, and search your heart to the bottom?' John Wesley, *Rules of the band societies*, drawn up 25 December 1738, www.godrules.net/library/wesley/

1751

1. Edward Young, 'The complaint, or night thoughts on life, death and immortality'. This was the most popular work of Edward Young (1683-1765), poet, dramatist and Anglican minister. This long poem in nine parts, or 'nights', was inspired by the deaths of the author's wife, stepdaughter and son-in-law, and is concerned with the quest for Christian consolation in the face of bereavement.

2. 'As the hart panteth after the water brooks, so panteth my soul after thee, O God.' Psalm 42:1.

3. From Isaac Watts, 'Kind is the speech of Christ our Lord'. The lines should read: 'What mighty wonders love performs, And puts a comeliness on worms.' Watts and John and Charles Wesley are the authors most frequently quoted by Elizabeth. Isaac Watts (1674-1748) was an Independent minister, writer and poet. He is credited with the authorship of over 750 hymns, many of them still in use today.

Hymn-singing was a crucial feature of Methodist worship, an expression of faith and communality and an effective means of providing religious instruction and disseminating Wesleyan theology. Both John and Charles Wesley produced many hymns – Charles was particularly prolific, and is credited with the authorship of at least 6,500, possibly as many as 10,000. John Wesley's first hymn-book, *A collection of psalms and hymns*, was published in 1737, and this was followed by a number of other volumes, and finally by *The collection of hymns for the use of the people called Methodists*, published in 1780, and intended to supersede all earlier collections. *Dictionary*.

4. The means of grace were defined by Wesley as 'outward signs, words, or actions, ordained of God, and appointed for this end, to be the ordinary channels whereby He might convey to men, preventing, justifying, or sanctifying grace … The chief of these means are prayer, whether in secret or with the great congregation; searching the Scriptures … and receiving the Lord's supper.' 'The means of grace', *Sermons*, pp 134-152, pp 136-7.

5. As Methodism expanded, a system of 'United Societies' emerged, consisting of local societies, or Methodist congregations, which were in turn organised into circuits or rounds. One or more itinerant, fulltime preachers were appointed to each circuit, and were expected to visit each society in turn. The society was divided into classes, each of which was under the direction of a class leader. Levistone Cooney, *The Methodists in Ireland*, p 131, and *Dictionary*.

6. The weather for June 1751 was described as 'fair and warm', with 'a great drought'. John Rutty, *A chronological history of the weather and seasons, and of the prevailing diseases in Dublin*, 1770, p 162.

7. The text is from Hebrews: 2: 3. The preacher on 11 June may have been George Whitefield: see entry for 13 June.

8. George Whitefield (1714-1770). Ordained into the Anglican priesthood 1736, he began field preaching in 1739 and encouraged John and Charles Wesley to do likewise. Over the next thirty years he travelled widely, making seven visits to America as well as Scotland and Ireland. An exceptionally eloquent and persuasive preacher, his oratory attracted many thousands to Methodism, and throughout his life he, rather than John Wesley, personified the movement in the public mind. His Calvinistic views created a breach with the Wesleys and a split within Methodism, but when he died in 1770 John Wesley preached his memo-

rial sermon. Whitefield arrived in Dublin on 24 May 1751 and after about ten days there embarked on a tour of the provinces: 'everywhere there seemed to be a stirring among the dry bones, and the trembling lamps of God's people were supplied with fresh oil ... At Limerick he preached seven times to large and affected audiences, and the Lord vouchsafed His special presence.' *History*, I, pp 82-83. The text from which Whitefield preached on this occasion was: 'Behold, I stand at the door, and knock: if any man hear my voice, and open the door, I will come in to him, and will sup with him, and he with me.' Revelations 3:20.

9. John 1:29.

10. See entry for 23 June 1749.

11. Samuel Larwood (d 1755), an Englishman, was engaged on the Irish itinerancy from 1748, and attended the first Irish Conference, held at Limerick in 1752. He left the Methodist Connexion shortly afterwards and set up his own mission in Southwark. Nevertheless, when he died in 1755, Wesley officiated at his funeral. John Wesley, *Journal*; Biographical index.

12. Mark 8:36.

13. 'Let your speech be always with grace, seasoned with salt, that ye may know how ye ought to answer every man.' Colossians 4:6.

14. Matthew 19:24 and Mark 10:25.

15. One of Elizabeth's favourite similes, from an episode described in Judges 6:36-40.

16. Elizabeth is probably referring to a smallpox epidemic: see entry for 14 October 1751.

17. A night-time service, continuing until after midnight. The practice, initiated by members in imitation of the early church, was encouraged by Wesley. Initially held on the Friday night nearest the full moon, in time such services came to be held on New Year's Eve, as in the Moravian tradition. *Dictionary*.

18. The love feast was a simple communal meal of 'a little plain cake and water', with hymn-singing and personal testimony, held quarterly. Only band-members were permitted to attend. The practice of holding love feasts was maintained from Methodism's earliest days to the end of the nineteenth century, when it began to wane. *Dictionary*.

19. The 'outward trials' may refer to business difficulties: Mitchell Bennis owned property in Limerick, as well as engaging in his hardware and saddlery business. For further details of his business and property holdings, see Levistone Cooney, Introduction, pp 14-20. The reference to the danger to her husband's health is mysterious, as is the hint that Elizabeth herself was in some way responsible for his plight. However, she may be referring to a lawsuit ongoing at this time: see entry for 31 May 1752.

20. Probably St Mary's Cathedral.

21. The meeting of the 'public bands' may be the type of gathering re-

ferred to by Wesley in his *Plain account of the people called Methodists* (1748), when he 'desired all the men-bands to meet me together every Wednesday evening, and the women on Sunday, that they might receive such particular instructions and exhortations as, from time to time, might appear to be most needful for them.'

22. This is one of several occasions on which Elizabeth compares herself to Martha, the woman 'cumbered about much serving ... careful and troubled about many things', in contrast to her sister Mary, who, by abandoning domestic tasks to attend to Jesus' word, 'hath chosen that good part'. Luke 10:38-42. See also entries for 26 March 1753 and for 29 February 1755.

23. Exodus 20:8. This is the fourth of the ten commandments given by God to Moses.

1752

1. Johann Arndt (1555-1621), German Lutheran theologian and author. His *True Christianity* (1605) was translated into several languages, became a spiritual classic and was among the works represented in John Wesley's *Christian Library*. Stressing the mystical union between Christ and the individual believer, Arndt described true Christianity as 'the exhibition of a true, loving faith, active in genuine godliness and the fruits of righteousness'. *The Christian Library*, published by John Wesley in fifty volumes, 1749-55, included extracts from works by the Early Fathers, and from Anglican, Catholic and Puritan authors.

2. 29 March 1752 was Easter Sunday.

3. The text is from Isaiah 42:11.

4. A hallowed place, from the Hebrew meaning 'house of God'.

5. Thomas Williams, a Welshman, came to Dublin in 1747 as the first Methodist preacher to work in Ireland. As the preacher in charge of the Limerick society after Robert Swindells introduced Methodism to the city in 1749, he presided over an impressive but temporary growth in membership. He remained in Ireland until 1752, when he withdrew from the Methodist Connexion on account of his Calvinistic views. Crookshank describes him as being subject to 'rashness and folly ... a man of attractive appearance, pleasing manner, and good address, with great zeal and enterprise, and most acceptable as a preacher, but ambitious, impatient of control, unstable in his religious views, and sadly lacking in high moral principle.' Biographical index; *History*, I, p 14.

6. The issue of predestination, derived from Calvinist theology, was one which caused much dispute within early Methodism. Wesley himself rejected predestination, insisting on the universal availability of grace, while other evangelicals, notably George Whitefield and the Countess of Huntingdon, adhered to the Calvinist notion of a predestined 'elect'. The argument in this instance may have been provoked by Thomas Williams's recent defection.

7. Unidentified. See also entries for 23 and 25 May 1752.

8. James Wild was received as a preacher in 1752, but 'did not continue long in the itinerancy'. *History*, I, p. 92.

9. In his journal Wesley recorded 'the particulars of the late riot' in Dublin, which was directed against the recently-opened Methodist chapel – the first in Ireland – at Whitefriar Street: 'some weeks ago, a large mob assembled one evening, broke many of the windows, and had just broke into the house, when a guard of soldiers came. The chief rioters were apprehended and tried. But ten or eleven of the jurymen, being papists, frightened the twelfth, so that he did not contradict, when they brought in their fellows, "not guilty".' Wesley, *Journal*, 20 July 1752. See also *History*, I, pp 89-90.

10. As the mention of 'my former engagements' suggests, this was not the first occasion on which Elizabeth had entered into a written covenant with God. See the entry for 16 October 1765. John Wesley advocated the practice of making a covenant with God, using forms drawn up by the Puritan writers, Joseph and Richard Alleine. The covenant service came to be held on the first Sunday of the year as a communal affirmation of individual commitment. *Dictionary*.

11. Wesley landed at Dublin on 17 July 1752. He reached Limerick on Thursday, 13 August, and spent the following two days in conference with his preachers there. Conference is the supreme legislative body of Methodism, and this Conference of 1752 was the first to be held in Ireland. Limerick was also the venue in 1758 and 1760. Otherwise, Irish Conferences during Wesley's lifetime were held in Dublin. Wesley, *Journal*; *Dictionary*; Levistone Cooney, *Methodists in Ireland*.

12. During his stay in Limerick, Wesley 'spake with each of the members of the society; many of whom, I now found, were "rooted and grounded in love" and "zealous of good works".' He left Limerick on Friday, 21 August 1752. Wesley, *Journal*.

13. John Edwards (1714-85) was converted by George Whitefield in Ireland in 1747. He became a lay preacher and later an itinerant and had ministries in Limerick as well as in Dublin and later in England. His Calvinist views led him to withdraw from the Connexion in 1753. *Dictionary*.

14. In May 1751 Parliament passed the 'Act for regulating the commencement of the year and for correcting the calendar now in use'. This replaced the Old Style (Julian) calendar with the New Style (Gregorian) calendar in use in mainland Europe since the sixteenth century. Under this legislation, the Julian calendar ceased on 2 September 1752, and the following day was dated 14 September.

15. 'Now all these things happened unto them for ensamples: and they are written for our admonition, upon whom the ends of the world are come. Wherefore let him that thinketh he standeth take heed lest he fall. There hath no temptation taken you but such as is common to man: but God is faithful, who will not suffer you to be tempted above that ye are able; but will with the temptation also make a way to escape, that ye may be able to bear it.' 1 Corinthians 10:11-13.

16. The 'disturbance between some in my band and a teacher in the church' may have had some relation to the dispute currently raging within the Dublin society between those who subscribed to Wesley's Arminian views and those of Calvinistic opinions. *History*, I, pp 95-96.

17. Galatians 4:18. Elizabeth's quotation is slightly inaccurate: the sentence actually reads, 'but it is good to be zealously affected always in a good thing.'

18. See note 21, 1751.

19. This is a reference to the parable of the ten virgins in Matthew 25:1-13.

1753

1. Elizabeth is perhaps referring to the recent breakaway of some members with Calvinistic views from the Dublin society. See *History*, I, pp 95-6.

2. From Isaac Watts, 'Great God, indulge my humble claim', Hymn 577, *Methodist hymnal*, 1889 edition. The first line should read: 'With fainting heart, and lifted hands ....'

3. See entry for 16 October 1765, in which Elizabeth describes her first encounter with Methodism.

4. Macarius of Egypt (c 300-c 390), monk and hermit. He was among the authors represented in the *Christian Library*. In fact, the fifty homilies ascribed to him may be the work of another author.

5. Subsequently identified (see entry for 18 August 1753) as Mrs Beauchamp. On 12 June 1756, while visiting Limerick, John Wesley recorded an account of Ann Beauchamp's death received from 'one of our sisters'. The 'sister' in question was certainly Elizabeth, since the details which he quotes are for the most part identical to those given here. See Wesley, *Journal*. In 1758, when visiting Limerick, Wesley was the guest of a Mr Beauchamp, and a Robert Beauchamp was listed in 1769 as a clothier at Thomond Gate. *History*, I, p. 131 and *Ferrar's Limerick Directory*, 1769.

6. Sanctification is the process of achieving 'Christian perfection', not, in Wesleyan theology, through merit, but through the Holy Spirit. According to John Wesley, while some believers might find 'Christian perfection' or 'perfect love' in life, others might experience it only at the moment of death.

7. In taking over leadership of her band, Elizabeth was assuming a position of leadership within the local society. See John Wesley, *Rules of the band societies*, 1738, and *Directions for the band societies*, 1744, for the demands made on members.

8. Following about a month of intermittent illness, on 26 November John Wesley was advised by his doctor that his only chance of recovery was a regime of 'country air, with rest, asses' milk and riding daily.' So convinced was Wesley himself of his impending death that he composed his own epitaph: 'Here lieth the body of John Wesley, a brand plucked out of the burning, who died of a consumption in the fifty-first

year of his age, not leaving, after his debts are paid, ten pounds behind him: praying, God be merciful to me, an unprofitable servant.' Wesley, *Journal*.

9. On Wednesday, 28 November, Wesley noted in his journal: 'About noon … a thought came into my mind to make an experiment. So I ordered some stone brimstone to be powdered, mixed with the white of an egg, and spread on brown paper, which I applied to my side. The pain ceased in five minutes, the fever in half an hour, and from this hour I began to recover. The next day I was able to ride …' Wesley, *Journal*.

1754

1. Band members were exhorted 'to read the Scriptures and meditate therein at every vacant hour'. Wesley, *Directions given to the band societies*.

2. From John Wesley, 'O God, what offering shall I give'. Hymn 431, *Methodist hymnal*, 1889 edition.

3. Good Friday fell on 12 April, and Easter Sunday on 14 April 1754.

4. A reference to the parable of the talents, Matthew 25:14-30.

5. Cornelius Bastable, entered the itinerant ministry 1745, died 1777. Bastable was described by Wesley as 'an uncommon monument of the power of grace … For so weak a head, and so bad a temper as he once had, I do not know among all our preachers.' *Methodist ministers and probationers who have died in the work*, http://rylibweb.man.ac.uk/data1/dg/methodist/ministers/ and *History*, I, p 171.

6. This day of public intercession was probably in celebration of the Williamite victory at the Battle of the Boyne, which took place on 12 July (1 July old style) 1690; also perhaps of the Battle of Aughrim, which occurred on 12 July 1691, after which the Jacobite forces were driven back to Limerick.

7. 1 Thessalonians 5:17.

8. This period is described as 'mostly fair, and sometimes hot'. Rutty, *Chronological history*, p 179.

9. No further information is available on Angel Mounsel. He may be one of the Maunsells, a prominent Limerick family. Richard Maunsell (died 1770) was Mayor of Limerick 1734-35, and became MP for the city in 1741. Ferrar, *History of Limerick*, 1788, pp 285, 293.

10. This appears to be a reference to the affair first mentioned on 22 July 1754. See also 25 and 31 July and 1, 2, 5, 19 August.

11. Thomas a Kempis (c 1380-1471, Augustinian monk, mystic and devotional author. His best-known work, *De imitatione Christi (The imitation of Christ)*, was among the spiritual classics which profoundly influenced John Wesley as a young man.

12. There are no entries between 21 October, when Elizabeth records a 'disordered body', and 4 December 1754.

1755

1. The first of the two Willamette volumes of the manuscript journal ends here. The second volume opens on the following day, 4 February 1755.

2. Revelations 2:5 reads: 'Remember therefore from whence thou art fallen, and repent, and do the first works; or else I will come unto thee quickly, and will remove thy candlestick out of his place, unless thou repent.'

3. See entry for 23 June 1749. In celebrating this event on 4 July, Elizabeth is making allowance for the 1752 adjustment of the calendar.

4. Thomas Walsh (1730-59), born County Limerick and brought up as a Catholic. Converted to Methodism in 1749, he began to preach in 1750. He proved himself a gifted orator in both Irish and English, was the target of mob violence on several occasions, and his powers of persuasion, courage and scholarship won John Wesley's special esteem. He worked in England 1752-58, but his health was irreparably damaged by overwork and ill-treatment, and he died of consumption in Dublin in 1758. He and Elizabeth joined the Methodist Society in Limerick at about the same time, and Walsh was one of her early correspondents. Biographical index and *Dictionary*; for correspondence between Walsh and Elizabeth, see letters LV, LVI, LVII and LVIII, *Christian correspondence*.

5. 'On the nineteenth of September, a fire broke out in St Francis's Abbey, which consumed above eighty thatched houses. A collection of three hundred pounds was made for the sufferers.' Ferrar, *History of Limerick*, 1788, p 128. From 1749 to the opening of the Meeting House in 1763, the Methodist society rented the old church in St Francis's Abbey. Ibid, pp 199-200.

6. 'You are ... neither to buy nor sell anything at all on the Lord's day.' Wesley, *Directions given to the band-societies*.

7. This was the earthquake which destroyed Lisbon on 1 November, and which was followed by a tsunami.

8. The Lisbon earthquake occurred on the morning of All Saints' Day, 1755 and resulted in between 60,000 and 100,000 deaths. The impact was felt throughout Europe and North Africa, and as far afield as Martinique and Barbados, as well as on the coast of southern England and the south and west coasts of Ireland. News of the catastrophe prompted Wesley to write 'Serious thoughts on the earthquake at Lisbon'. In a sermon on 'the cause and cure of earthquakes', published in 1750, he had set out to show that 'of all the judgements which the righteous God inflicts on sinners here, the most dreadful and destructive is an earthquake.' Wesley, *Journal*, 26 November 1755 and 'The cause and cure of earthquakes', *Works*, www.godrules.net/library/wesley/wesley.htm

9. See Thomas Walsh to Elizabeth Bennis, Dublin, 13 December 1755, ms correspondence, St George's Church Archives, and as letter LV in

Christian correspondence. Walsh writes that 'tho' I did not see you since your happy deliverance, I have not forgot you. I believe God has re-veal'd his Son in your heart … Yet, still you feel a want of many things. There is sin, emptiness in your soul.' He ends by sending 'my love to your band', and requesting her prayers and a letter from her.

1756
1. 'His heart is as firm as a stone; yea, as hard as a piece of the nether millstone.' Job 41: 24.
2. Probably a misquotation of Jeremiah 10: 25. 'Pour out thy fury upon the heathen that know thee not, and upon the families that call not on thy name.'
3. This daughter was presumably the child born on 9 November 1755.
4. Unidentified.
5. Wesley arrived in Limerick on the evening of Monday, 7 June 1756. Wesley, *Journal*.
6. Wesley left Limerick on Wednesday, 23 June.
7. See entry for 23 June 1749.
8. Mitchell's confinement was to last for a month, and the sum involved (£600) was substantial. See also entries for 30 June, and 31 July 1756. The arrangement whereby he was confined to his own house, rather than in prison, was unusual. Professor Nial Osborough to the editor, 1 August 2006.
9. 'My other trouble' presumably refers to Mitchell's indebtedness.
10. 'A brand plucked from the burning' was the phrase used by John Wesley in the epitaph which he composed for himself when he believed himself to be dying in 1753. The source is Zechariah 3:2, which actually reads, 'Is not this a brand plucked out of the fire?' A similar phrase oc-curs in Amos 4:11. In Wesley's case, the phrase had a double meaning, referring to his supposedly miraculous escape from a house fire in childhood, as well as to his salvation by faith.
11. Methodism's greatest appeal was to members of the Protestant, es-pecially the Anglican, community. While there were converts from Catholicism, they were, as Hempton remarks, 'more notable for the fuss made of them than for their quantity.' David Hempton, 'Methodism in Irish society, 1770-1830', p 125.
12. This dream clearly relates to the Wesleyan mission to regenerate Anglicanism.
13. 'And I will put enmity between thee and the woman, and between thy seed and her seed; it shall bruise thy head, and thou shalt bruise his heel.' Genesis 3:15.
14. There is no record in the registers of St Mary's Cathedral of the burial of this son, or of his baby sister who died a few days later.
15. This was the child born just a year earlier, on 9 November 1755. The surviving child was Eleanor, then aged about eight.
16. 1756 had seen Wesley's first visit to Ireland for four years. He spent

more than four months in the country, travelling for the first time to
Ulster, where he preached to large congregations. The year also saw a
growth in numbers in the Limerick region: during his visit to the city,
Wesley made contact with the Palatine community at Ballingrane, 'and
was much impressed with the plain, artless, and serious disposition' of
its members, many of whom subsequently adopted Methodism.
History, I, pp 107-117.

1757

1. Elizabeth is referring to her desire to attain the state of sanctification
or 'Christian perfection', with which she was much preoccupied at this
period. On 20 January she wrote to Thomas Walsh to enquire whether,
given that 'my heart is evil ... my will perverse, my affections cold and
dead and my faith ... weak ... may I expect or look for an entire, instantaneous change of heart, without first experiencing a growth in grace?'
Elizabeth Bennis, Limerick to Thomas Walsh, 20 January 1757, LVI,
Christian correspondence. See also entries for 23 May 1763 and 16 October
1765 for a further accounts of this period.
2. John Wesley condemned theatrical entertainments as contrary to
piety and seriousness, but 'particularly hurtful to a trading city' in fos-
tering 'drinking and debauchery ... indolence, effeminacy and idleness'
and discouraging industry and 'close application to business'. John
Wesley, London, to the Mayor and Corporation of Bristol, 20 December
1764, *Letters*.
3. Elizabeth was pregnant at this time: see entry for 24 May.
4. Thomas Olivers (1725-99) became an itinerant preacher in 1753, and
served in the itinerant ministry in England, Scotland and Ireland. A
poet, polemicist and hymn-writer, he supported Wesley in his opposition to Calvinism. Biographical index and *Dictionary*. Olivers was stationed on the Limerick circuit in early 1757, 'where God was pleased to
own his labours much, many soldiers as well as others being converted.'
History, I, p 118.
5. The public national fast was probably for success in the Seven Years'
War (1756-63), which had broken out in the previous year between
Britain and Prussia on the one hand, and France and Austria on the other.
6. There is no entry between this date and 24 May, when Elizabeth
records the birth of a 'living child'.
7 See entries for 1 August 1752 and 16 October 1765 on covenanting
with God.
8. See entry for 23 June 1749, and note 3, 1755 on change in the calendar.
9. George Whitefield paid his third, and final, visit to Ireland in July
1757. He preached in Dublin before travelling into the provinces.
'Everywhere', he wrote, 'the glorious Emmanuel so smiles upon my
feeble efforts, that it is hard to get off. At Portarlington, Athlone,
Limerick, and in this place [Cork], the word has run, and been glorified.' *History*, I, pp 119-121.

10. The war was currently raging in India, where a British army under Clive had defeated the French in the course of the year, and in Europe. A few weeks before this entry Frederick the Great of Prussia had defeated a French and Austrian army in Saxony.

1758

1. Thomas Walsh (see note 4, 1755). Walsh was already very ill: John Wesley, meeting him in Limerick in June 1758, described him as 'just alive.' Walsh died later in 1758. See Thomas Walsh to Elizabeth Bennis, London, 5 November 1757, LVIII, *Christian correspondence* and Wesley, *Journal*, 17 June 1758.

2. Wesley arrived at Dublin at the end of March 1758, reaching Limerick on Friday, 16 June. On Wednesday, 21 June Conference opened, attended by fourteen preachers. On Sunday 25 June he preached 'about six ... in the island in a square, green enclosure, which was formerly Oliver Cromwell's camp'. The congregation was such as 'I have not seen ... since we left London.' He preached again on Sunday, 2 July to 'thousands of hearers' and again on the evening of Wednesday, 5 July. Wesley, *Journal*.

3. Wesley defined the duties of the leader of a class as being '(1) To see each person in his [sic] class once a week at least, in order to enquire how their souls prosper; to advise, reprove, comfort or exhort, as occasion may require; to receive what they are willing to give toward the relief of the poor. (2) To meet the Minister and the Stewards of the society once a week, in order to inform the Minister of any that are sick, or of any that walk disorderly, and will not be reproved; to pay to the Stewards what they have received of their several classes in the week preceding; and to show their account of what each person has contributed.' John Wesley, *Nature, design and general rules of the united societies* ... 1 May 1743, www.godrules.net/library/Wesley/ 274wesley_h7.htm

4. While in Dublin a few weeks before, Wesley had exhorted the society there 'to follow the example of their English brethren, by jointly renewing their covenant with God.' Wesley, *Journal*, 7 April 1758. This was evidently such a service.

5. Wesley's departure from Limerick was delayed by a short illness. He left Limerick for Charleville on Friday, 7 July. Wesley, *Journal*.

6. Given the presence of a garrison at Limerick, such occurrences cannot have been uncommon. John Wesley's visit to Limerick in 1762 coincided with a similar event, as he recorded. 'Numberless crowds ran together about this time, to see the execution of the poor deserter. And I believe some of them retained serious impressions for near four-and-twenty hours! But it was not so with the soldiers: although they walked one by one, close to the bleeding, mangled carcase, most of them were as merry within six hours, as if they had only seen a puppet-show.' Wesley, *Journal*, 7 June 1762.

7. There are no entries between 10 October and 1 November 1758.

1759

1. The fast was probably for success in the ongoing war.

2. John Trembath was one of John Wesley's early preachers, having entered the itinerancy in 1743. He was notable for 'zeal, enterprise and popularity, but also ... instability of character and lack of moral principle.' He retired from preaching in around 1753 to become a farmer, but subsequently became a local preacher for a time. He died at Cork around 1793. *History*, I, pp 15, 109-110, 121-122.

3. This is a reference to the parable of the rich man and 'a certain beggar named Lazarus, which was laid at his gate ... desiring to be fed with the crumbs which fell from the rich man's table.' In death, however, the rich man was condemned to the torments of hell, while Lazarus 'was carried by the angels into Abraham's bosom'. Luke 16: 19-31.

4. At the time of Elizabeth's conversion in 1749, she and Mitchell were living in Bow Lane. This may have been a move to a new house, or simply a renovation of their existing home.

5. 1759 saw a number of British victories over the French. They included the Battle of Minden and the capture of Quebec, as well as naval victories at the battles of Lagos and Quiberon Bay.

1760

1. The inhabitants of Laodicea were reproached, in Revelations 3:14-17, for being 'lukewarm, and neither cold nor hot'.

2. Inoculation against smallpox was introduced into the British Isles by Lady Mary Wortley Montague, who had observed the practice in Turkey. This method involved deliberate infection with a mild form of the disease and, despite opposition by some physicians and clergymen, rapidly became popular. In 1750, for instance, Bishop Synge reported that his friend, Mr Waller of Kilmore in County Roscommon, had had his children inoculated. (Bishop Edward Synge, Elphin, to Alicia Synge, 5 June 1750, Marie-Louise Legg, *The Synge letters*, 1996) However, between one and two per cent of those so infected did die. In 1796 Dr Edward Jenner developed a vaccine using cowpox fluid, which had the effect of giving immunity against smallpox.

3. The previous entry was on 17 April.

4. Following the report of Elizabeth's child's death on 30 April and reiterated expressions of spiritual emptiness, the journal falls silent. There are no more entries for 1760, none for 1761 and only a single entry for 1762.

1762

1. Elizabeth had not written in her journal for more than eighteen months.

2. There is no indication of what this may have been, but the entry for 23 May 1763 suggests that Elizabeth, while remaining within the society, had undergone a period of spiritual despair. See also entry for 16 October 1765, in which she refers to being in a 'state of deadness' at about this time.

3. This is a reference to the parable of the prodigal son: Luke 15:11-32.

1763

1. The journal resumes following a fifteen-month silence on 23 May 1763. In her unusually long entry for this date, Elizabeth described her spiritual struggles over the preceding six years and her experience of the previous day, Whitsunday, which initiated a new stage in her religious life. Elizabeth drew on this entry and on others at this time for her written testimony of 16 October 1765.

2. Among the 'many' converted at this time were members of the local Palatine community. In 1756 John Wesley had visited the Palatine settlement at Ballingrane. During the same tour, he preached at Newmarket to 'an earnest congregation of poor people' and to some of the local gentry. See Wesley, *Journal*, 16 June 1756 and *History*, I, p 110. George Whitefield's 1757 tour had also resulted in many conversions at Limerick and elsewhere. *History*, I, p 121.

3. See entries for January and 2 February 1757 for this period and Thomas Olivers's role.

4. Wesley was in Limerick from 29 May to 14 June 1762. On Tuesday, 8 June he 'visited the classes, and wondered to find no witness of the great salvation'. The following evening, however, 'a cry went up on every side; and the lively believers seemed all on fire to be "cleansed from all unrighteousness".' Wesley, *Journal*.

5. 'Therefore I say unto you, what things soever ye desire, when ye pray, believe that ye receive them, and ye shall have them.' Mark 11:24.

6. 'For with the heart man believeth unto righteousness; and with the mouth confession is made unto salvation.' Romans 10:10.

7. This presumably refers to the long period between mid-1760 and mid-1763 when Elizabeth made only one entry in her journal.

8. Whitsunday is the seventh Sunday after Easter. The feast commemorates the coming of the Holy Ghost to the Apostles, which took place on the Jewish festival of Pentecost. Described in Acts 2:1-4.

9. For the story of 'blind Bartimaeus', a beggar, healed by Jesus on his final journey to Jerusalem, see Mark 10:46-52. The 'leper by the poolside' is probably a reference to John 5:2-9, which describes the healing of an 'impotent' (rather than a leper) by the pool of Bethesda.

10. Bread and wine, representing the body and blood of Christ.

11. A reference to Jesus' statement that 'it is easier for a camel to go through the eye of a needle, than for a rich man to enter into the kingdom of God.' Matthew 19:24. See also Mark 10:25.

12. See entry for 23 June 1749.

13. John Dillon had become a Methodist while stationed as a soldier in Cork. Shortly afterwards he was transferred to Limerick, where he took an active part in the society. In 1765 he became an itinerant preacher, visiting Waterford and Cork. He moved to the north in 1767 and then to Dublin, where he died on 11 May 1769 following a long illness. See entry for 16 May 1770 for news of his death. One of Elizabeth's correspondents from at least 1764, he may have been the 'Christian friend' so frequently mentioned during this period, and whose 'frequent visits' gave rise to gossip. See entries for 29 July and 20 August 1763.

14. The select bands were made up of believers whose profession of faith had been tested and proved by consistent Christian living and by clear growth in grace. Members probably accounted for no more than one in ten of the overall band membership.

The preacher in Limerick at this point was John Johnson: on his arrival on 10 July, 'God was pleased to favour him greatly by giving him to see the prosperity of the cause in the city ... Brother Dillon assisted him much, and God crowned his labours also in the conversion of many.' *History*, I, p 172.

15. Hebrew, meaning 'the stone of help'. 1 Samuel 7:12.

16. The previous entry was dated 12 August.

17. Mark 10:21.

18. Elizabeth's first surviving letter to John Wesley is dated 2 August 1763. In this she relates having 'sunk into a dead formal state' since her first conversion. Wesley's preaching on his last visit to Limerick had encouraged her to new fervour, and finally, on 2 June, 'at prayer I found in a moment my idols taken away, and my will wholly subjected to the will of God'. However, she continued to feel 'heaviness of soul' and 'deadness in prayer' and questioned whether she had indeed attained sanctification. In his reply, received by her on 11 September, Wesley reassured her that 'pure love' was not incompatible with being 'in heaviness', 'wanderings' and 'deficiencies'. Elizabeth Bennis, Limerick to John Wesley, 2 August 1763 and John Wesley, Pembroke to Elizabeth Bennis, 23 August 1763, I and II, *Christian correspondence*.

19. John Johnson (1725-1803), an English-born convert from Catholicism to the Church of England. Converted to Methodism by Whitefield and became an itinerant preacher in 1758. He travelled in Ireland for the next decade, eventually settling in Lisburn where he acted as a local preacher for many years. In 1784 he married Dorothea King (fl 1756-1795), a leading member of the Dublin society. She worked with him in Lisburn, was praised by John Wesley for her influence there, and was one of the 'memorable women' of early Methodism memorialised by Crookshank. Biographical index.

20. Psalm 42:1.

21. See entry for 28 February 1764 in which John Dillon makes a similar proposal.

1764

1. Elizabeth is referring to the form of service for admission to the select band.

2. The departing friend may be John Dillon, who certainly left Limerick at about this time. See John Dillon, Dublin, to Elizabeth Bennis, July 1764, LXVII, *Christian correspondence*. 22 April was Easter Day.

3. This 'trial' seems to involve some misdemeanour on the part of a servant or employee: see entry for 19 May 1764.

4. Elizabeth made no entries between 30 June and 22 July 1764, evidently because of illness.

5. There are no entries between 31 July and 10 August, due to illness. This was presumably the 'severe affliction of body' to which John Dillon referred in a letter written a few weeks later. John Dillon, Dublin to Elizabeth Bennis, 15 September 1764, LXVIII, *Christian correspondence*.

6. Class tickets were distributed quarterly as tokens of membership of the society. Possession of a ticket was necessary for admission to society meetings, love feasts and the covenant service. Separate band tickets were also issued, distinguished from the class tickets by the addition of a letter 'B'. *Dictionary*.

7. John Johnson was in Limerick during the third quarter of 1764. *History*, I, p 178.

8. The entry for 9 October 1764 is the final one in the Willamette volume of the journal. The Philadelphia volume opens with an entry for the following day, 10 October.

9. There was evidently some diminution in zeal in the Limerick society at this point. On his departure in October 1764 following a three-month stay, John Johnson reported finding congregations as large as formerly, 'but he did not see as much fruit'. Thomas Taylor, arriving in Limerick in early 1765, found 'the people ... languid and lifeless'. *History*, I, pp 178, 181-182.

10. This is the final entry for 1764. From November until early January, Elizabeth was incapacitated by 'a tedious and dangerous illness of body'. She was also about five months pregnant, giving birth to her last child in March 1765.

1765

1. The previous entry was dated 23 November 1764.

2. Identified later in this entry as Mrs Moore. There is no mention of the death of such a person in the records of St Mary's Cathedral, Limerick at this period. Noreen Ellerker, archivist, to the editor, 30 June 2006.

3. There are no entries between 23 February and 14 March. During this interval, Elizabeth's last child, a daughter, also named Elizabeth, was born.

4. John Wesley arrived at Limerick on Saturday, 8 June 1765, and found the new preaching house there 'the best of any in the kingdom; being neat ... elegant, yet not gaudy'. On the following day he preached at the Mardyke, in 'violent' heat, to a large crowd, and during the following

week examined the society. He preached again at the Mardyke on Wednesday, 12 June, 'to, I think, the largest congregation which I ever saw in Limerick'. On the following days, heavy rain forced him to speak in the meeting-house. He left Limerick for Cork on Monday, 17 June. Wesley, *Journal* and Robert Haire, *Wesley's one-and-twenty visits to Ireland*, pp 81-82.

5. The friend to whom Elizabeth wrote was perhaps John Dillon, with whom she was in correspondence at this time. See John Dillon, Dublin to Elizabeth Bennis, 1 June 1765, LXIX, *Christian correspondence*. Other correspondents in 1764-65 included William Penington and Thomas Taylor, as well as John Wesley himself.

6. There are two pages missing in the manuscript journal at this point. The entries resume at the end of July 1765.

7. This 'Christian man from Holland' is described in *Christian correspondence* as 'a gentleman from Holland, who was on business in this city'. The original ms version of Elizabeth's letter describes him in more detail as 'the master of a Dutch vessel which then lay waiting for a cargo. He was a godly man and had a deep work of grace wrought on his heart. The Lord did often bless us together and gave me much light in speaking to him.' Elizabeth Bennis, Limerick to John Wesley, 11 March 1766, III, *Christian correspondence*; Elizabeth Bennis to John Wesley, 11 March 1766, ms correspondence, St George's Church Archives.

88 From Charles Wesley, 'Christ from whom all blessings flow', hymn 518, *Methodist Hymnal*. The full verse reads: 'Love, like death, hath all destroyed, Rendered all distinctions void, Names, and sects, and parties fall. Thou, O Christ, art all in all.'

9. The letter was from John Dillon, as Elizabeth later told John Wesley: 'On the 30 of September last, whilst I was reading a letter I had received from Brother Dillon, I was struck with a sentence in the letter and enabled to believe and found in that moment the testimony of God's spirit, that my heart was cleansed.' Elizabeth Bennis to John Wesley, 11 March 1766, ms correspondence, St George's Church Archives. Elizabeth's published correspondence includes a letter from Dillon, dated 1 June 1765, which concluded: 'Our life is to be a life of faith, tried in the fire; we are called to be good soldiers of Christ … This is not to be done by comfort, but by faith – the Christian's shield … You are not called to reason, but simply to look and cast your burden upon the Lord, who will make all your enemies as chaff.' John Dillon, Dublin to Elizabeth Bennis, 1 June 1765, LXIX, *Christian correspondence*.

10. Elizabeth now believed herself to have achieved the state of sanctification, or perfect holiness, which she had been seeking for so long.

11. This evidently refers to some difficulties within the Limerick society.

12. Joseph Alleine, *An alarm to the unconverted*. Joseph Alleine (1634-68), nonconformist minister and devotional writer, was ejected from his living of Taunton, Somerset in 1662 under the terms of the Act of Uniformity, but continued to preach illegally and was twice impris-

oned. His best-known work, *Alarm to the unconverted*, was published posthumously in 1671, and enjoyed immediate and lasting popularity.

13. Alleine's views on covenanting, along with those of his father-in-law, Richard Alleine, influenced John Wesley, and were instrumental in the introduction of the Methodist covenant service.

14. Elizabeth's father, Isaac Patten, died in 1743. She married her cousin, Mitchell Bennis, on 13 December 1745. *Memorable women*, p 21. See also entry for 13 December 1776.

15. The 'proud Pharisee' is a reference to the parable on spiritual pride in Luke 18:10-14.

16. According to Crookshank, the Patten family were Presbyterians. *Memorable women*, p 21.

17. Robert Swindells (d 1783) arrived in Ireland with John Wesley in March 1748. He returned with Charles Wesley in the autumn of that year, when they visited Cork and other parts of Munster. Swindells stayed on in Ireland after Charles Wesley's departure, reaching Limerick on 17 March 1749. He went on to serve as an itinerant preacher for over forty years. *History*, I, pp 29, 47-48, 366-367 and Biographical index.

18. 'Swaddlers' was a derogatory term for Methodists, reputedly first applied to the preacher John Cennick by a Catholic priest in Dublin in 1746.

19. Swindells preached twice at the Castle Gate on the King's Parade on 17 March 1749. On the following day he preached at the Market House in the Irish Town. *History*, I, pp 47-48.

20. According to Crookshank, Swindells was followed by an 'incensed mob, who followed him through the streets … hallooing and sometimes personally insulting him. *History*, I, p 47. On prejudice against Methodism because of its perceived association with the lower orders, see Raughter, 'Mothers in Israel', p 32.

21. The second preacher to come to Limerick was Thomas Williams: see note 5, 1752.

22. Ephesians 2:8.

23. For Elizabeth's pursuit of 'perfect holiness' at this period, see entries for 25 January and 2 February 1757.

24. Wesley arrived in Limerick on 29 May 1762 and preached on the following day, finding 'no witness of the great salvation'. On the following day, however, 'many of the members seemed all on fire to be cleansed from all iniquity'. *History*, I, pp 164-5.

25. Following his departure from Limerick, Wesley received news from an informant in the city of the revival taking place there: 'There is a glorious work going on at Limerick. Twelve or fourteen have a clear sense of being renewed; several have been justified this week; and on Sunday night, there was such a cry as I scarce ever heard before; such confession of sins, such pleading with the Lord, and such a spirit of prayer, as if the Lord himself had been visibly present among us.' Wesley, *Journal*, 28 July 1762.

26. 'Then will I sprinkle clean water upon you, and ye shall be clean: from all your filthiness, and from all your idols will I cleanse you.' Ezekiel 36:25.

27. That is, until September or October 1764. See entry for 10 October 1764.

28. That is, until September 1765.

29. John Dillon. See note 9 above.

30. Probably a room or space in her house set aside for meditation and prayer. See also entry for 6 December 1767.

31. Possibly a reference to the criticism of lack of learning sometimes levelled against Methodist preachers, and against which Wesley defended them. 'Will you', he asked, 'condemn a preacher because he has not university learning or has not a university education? What then? He saves those sinners from their sins whom the man of learning and education cannot save.' John Wesley, *Letters*, II, p 148. Nevertheless, Wesley encouraged his preachers to read and study, as well as instructing them by having them accompany him on his travels. According to Lenton, while some preachers had received a classical education and others were self-educated to an impressive degree, 'in general their education was poor'. John H. Lenton, *My sons in the Gospel: an analysis of Wesley's itinerant preachers*, Wesley Historical Society, 2000, p 18.

1766

1. The 'dear, dear Christian friend' may have been John Johnson, who came to Limerick in early 1766 and remained there for two months. *History*, I, p 188.

2. Identified in the margin as 'some select Christian friend'. Probably John Wesley, although John Johnson, John Dillon and John McGregor are also possible candidates. John McGregor was a Scot and a former soldier, who settled in Limerick and was an active and able leader of Methodism there for many years. For his tribute to Elizabeth's role in the society there, see John McGregor, Limerick, to Elizabeth Bennis, 1 September 1790, CXIII, *Christian correspondence*. He was also, with Mitchell Bennis, one of the lessors of the property at Cross Lane, Limerick, which in 1765 became the Methodist meeting house. Levistone Cooney, Introduction, pp 14-15.

3. These problems were seemingly related to her husband's business. See also reference to 'his late losses' on 2 March 1766.

4. On 11 March 1766 Elizabeth wrote to John Wesley to seek clarification on this point: 'Is sin ... some degree of rebellion in the will? And where there is no degree of rebellion in the will, can there be sin? May there not be many imperfections where there is no sin?' In his reply, Wesley reassured her that 'a thousand infirmities are consistent even with the highest degree of holiness, which is no other than pure love, an heart devoted to God.' In the same letter, perhaps in an attempt to discourage her tendency to introspection, he encouraged her to positive

action on the movement's behalf: 'If God has given you this light, he did not intend that you should hide it under a bushel ... It is good to tell the loving kindness of the Lord.' Elizabeth Bennis, Limerick, to John Wesley, 11 March 1766 and John Wesley, Manchester, to Elizabeth Bennis, 29 March 1766, III and IV, *Christian correspondence*; Elizabeth Bennis to John Wesley, 11 March 1766, ms, correspondence, St George's Church Archives.

5. Easter Sunday.

6. The 'dear Christian friend' to whose imminent departure Elizabeth refers was perhaps John Johnson, who left Limerick at about this time.

7. Probably refers to the friend mentioned on 4 and 8 April, but may also have been inspired by John Wesley's letter of 29 March, which would have arrived at about this time. See note 4 above.

8. The 'six troubles' referred to by Elizabeth are probably the deaths of six of her children between 1752 and 1760. See entries for 14 May 1752, 23 April 1753, 6 and 12 November 1756, 7 October 1758 and 30 April 1760.

9. Writing to a friend on 3 February 1769, Elizabeth instructed him: 'Be punctual to the hour of eleven o'clock: count it your privilege to meet then with your friends before the throne of grace, and let our joint petitions go up as incense before the Lord. At this hour we pray earnestly for each other, for our families, for the children of God everywhere, and for the world in general.' See entry for 3 February 1769.

10. This may refer to property at Firrfield which had belonged to Elizabeth and Mitchell's joint grandfather, Thomas Mitchell. Alternatively, it may be the property at Corbally, just outside Limerick, which Mitchell Bennis took over from his unmarried sister-in-law, Elizabeth's sister, Alice Patten. Levistone Cooney, Introduction, p 18 and Levistone Cooney, 'The Bennis Family of Limerick: Huguenots, Methodists, Friends', unpublished paper.

11. 'The very person who should rather cover my defects' is presumably her husband, and this entry seems to refer to an argument between Elizabeth and Mitchell, perhaps on the subject of religion. The entries for 10 and 14 November probably record a continuation of this dispute, which seems to have involved Elizabeth being 'debarred' for a short time from 'the company and conversation of my Christian friends'.

12. Elizabeth was still evidently prevented from attending meetings of the Society.

13. This entry suggests that the crisis was over, and that Elizabeth was once more free to associate with fellow-believers. Certainly, writing to Richard Blackwell a few days before, she was able to report that 'the society here is in a prosperous situation; the select band does meet regularly, and we generally have blessed times together'. Elizabeth Bennis, Limerick, to Richard Blackwell, 27 November 1766, LXIV, *Christian correspondence*.

1767

1. Elizabeth's protestations of 'my own innocence' recall her complaint on 2 November 1766 of being 'taken in a wrong light, misconstrued and misrepresented'. Her oblique reference to a problem which 'love and discretion obliges me to keep concealed' suggests that she and Mitchell were still in disagreement.

2. 'I will rise now, and go about the city in the streets, and in the broad ways I will seek him whom my soul loveth: I sought him, but I found him not. The watchmen that go about the city found me: to whom I said, Saw ye him whom my soul loveth?' Song of Solomon 3: 2-3.

3. In 1769 Elizabeth gave 'opposite Bow Lane' as her address, and John Wesley, writing in 1771, addressed his letter to Mrs Bennis, 'opposite Bow Lane', Limerick. See entry for 3 February 1769 and John Wesley, Dublin to Elizabeth Bennis, 20 July 1771, ms correspondence, St George's Church Archives. The process of preparing the house was to take several months: the actual move did not take place until 30 August 1767.

4. Unidentified.

5. Elizabeth is mistaken in the dating of this entry, which should read 10 (rather than 11) May. John Wesley, who was currently making his eleventh visit to Ireland, had arrived in Limerick on the previous day, Saturday 9 May. On the evening of his arrival he preached in the meeting house, but 'was scandalised at the smallness of the congregation'. This, together perhaps with the 'continued rain', led him to be pessimistic about the future of Methodism in the region: 'I am afraid my glorying touching many of these societies is at an end.' However, he did subsequently attract large congregations at the Old Camp. Haire, p 88 and Wesley, *Journal*.

6. After spending a fortnight in Limerick and the surrounding area, Wesley went on to Shronell in county Tipperary, before moving on to Waterford. Haire, p 88.

7. See entry for 23 June 1749.

8. On 15 July Elizabeth wrote to Wesley that 'your late visit to this city proved a great blessing to my soul ... Yet ... I do not find that measure of life or love which I once enjoyed.' Elizabeth Bennis, Limerick, to John Wesley, 15 July 1767, VII, *Christian correspondence*.

9. The previous entry was dated 5 September 1767.

10. The previous entry was dated 28 October 1767.

11. See entry for 22 November 1765 for a similar arrangement in her former house.

12. See also 19 December 1763 and 1 April 1771, where Elizabeth complains of pains in her head and teeth.

1768

1. The child referred to here is either Thomas or his younger brother, Henry.

2. 'And let us not be weary in well doing: for in due season we shall reap, if we faint not.' Galatians 6: 9.

3. On Bennis property holdings, see Levistone Cooney, Introduction, pp 16-19.

4. The 'particular temporal affair' was evidently the proposed marriage of her daughter Eleanor. See also entries for 4 and 17 October and 25 November 1768.

5. There are no entries between 17 October and 25 November 1768.

6. Eleanor Bennis married Jonas Bull of Waterford on 3 November 1768 in St Mary's Cathedral, Limerick.

7. William Beveridge (1637-1708), bishop of St Asaph. A collected edition of his sermons and other writings was published in 1720, and his 'Thoughts on religion' was included in John Wesley's *Christian library*.

1769

1. Eleanor, following her marriage to Jonas Bull, was moving to Waterford.

2. This individual is subsequently identified (see 16 October 1769) as 'the master of the king's ship'. He is not named in the journal, but may be the Lieutenant Charles Jones to whom Elizabeth wrote several times, and who finally admitted that he no longer felt 'that ardent desire of close communion I formerly did with the children of God.' See Lieutenant Charles Jones, Dublin, to Elizabeth Bennis, 17 December 1770, and Elizabeth Bennis, Limerick, to Lieutenant Charles Jones, 3 January 1771, LXXVI and LXXVII, *Christian correspondence*. On this episode, see also entries for 26, 28 January and 1, 3, 10 and 20 February 1769. For the sequel, see entries for 16 and 20 October 1769.

3. See also entries for 11 November and 1 December 1769.

4. Easter Sunday fell on 26 March 1769.

5. 'Be glad then, ye children of Zion, and rejoice in the Lord your God … I will restore to you the years that the locust hath eaten … And ye shall eat in plenty, and be satisfied, and praise the name of the Lord your God, that hath dealt wondrously with you.' Joel 2: 23-27.

6. Wesley arrived in Limerick on Saturday, 13 May 1769. He preached in 'the Room' there that evening and on the following day, Whitsunday, but 'was much scandalised' at the small attendance. He preached at the Old Camp on that and the two following evenings, but was disappointed to evoke no more than 'a calm, dull attention'. On Friday, 19 May he and the Limerick society observed a day of fasting and prayer, ending with a watch-night service: and it was then, Wesley noted, 'that God touched the hearts of the people, even of those that were "twice dead".' Wesley, *Journal* and Haire, p 97.

7. Wesley left Limerick for Cork on Tuesday, 23 May. Two days later Elizabeth wrote to him that 'I have found my soul much quickened by your late visit, but … I want a present salvation, a heaven within.' Elizabeth Bennis, Limerick, to John Wesley, 25 May 1769, IX, *Christian correspondence*.

8. See John Wesley, Cork, to Elizabeth Bennis, 30 May 1769, ms correspondence, St George's Church Archives. In response to her concerns, Wesley reassured her that even those who felt they had lost 'the pure love of God' might enjoy it again.

9. On Monday, 5 June Wesley revisited Limerick, in response to an urgent request from the members there to give them a further day or two of his time. He remained in the city until 8 June, when he took leave of 'this loving people' to ride on to Waterford. Wesley, *Journal* and Haire, p 98.

10. Elizabeth's 'papers' apparently consisted of three volumes – including possibly her previous or her current journal. She subsequently had misgivings about handing them over, writing to Wesley, 'I have been grievously exercised since I put my papers into your hands when you asked them. I found a satisfaction in gratifying you, but have since been much tempted both to pride and shame. The exercise has often proved a blessing to my soul, and the looking over former experience has frequently borne me up and strengthened my hands, when ready to faint, which makes me still willing to keep them. But indeed they were never intended to be overseen by any but myself, and from their many defects, I do not see how they can be useful to any other.' Elizabeth Bennis, Limerick, to John Wesley, 13 July 1769, XI, *Christian correspondence*. In response, and returning two of 'your written books … the third I must borrow a little longer', Wesley wrote that reading her papers 'makes me love you abundantly better than I did before'. John Wesley, Dublin, to Elizabeth Bennis, 24 July 1769, XII, *Christian correspondence*.

11. This and subsequent references to a 'friend' with whom she engaged in conversation 'about the things of God' may refer to Richard Bourke's stay in Limerick, which had, as Elizabeth told Wesley, 'proved a blessing to my soul, and to his also'. Elizabeth Bennis, Limerick, to John Wesley, 13 July 1769, XI, *Christian correspondence*. 'If you could spare him to us this year', she continued, 'I think it would be productive of good.' Bourke had been stationed preacher in Limerick since mid-1768 and his appointment there was due to terminate in mid-1769. This request for him to be assigned to Limerick for a further year was approved by the annual conference held in Dublin on 19 and 20 July 1769 and, according to Crookshank, 'appears to be the earliest instance on record of the voice of the people being heard in connection with a preaching appointment.' Bourke, who had entered the itinerant ministry in 1765, was described by Wesley as one of his 'truly devoted men'. He died in 1778. *Index of Ministers and Probationers who have died in the work*, http://rylibweb. man.ac.uk and *History*, I, pp 229, 208.

12. In her letter of 13 July Elizabeth confided that 'at present I am exercised inwardly by my enemy, and outwardly by the sickness of two of my children.' Elizabeth Bennis, Limerick, to John Wesley, 13 July 1769, XI, *Christian correspondence*.

13. The stationed preacher at this time, appointed in response to Elizabeth's request to Wesley, was Richard Bourke. He was to be joined in February 1770 by Thomas Taylor. Information provided by Dudley Levistone Cooney.

14. John Wesley, visiting Waterford in 1762, went 'at the desire of Captain Taylor ... to Passage, and preached to many of the townspeople, and as many of the sailors as could attend.' Wesley, *Journal*, 20 June 1762. The text is John 4:29. The full verse reads: 'Come, see a man, which told me all things that ever I did: is not this the Christ?'

15. Hugh Saunderson was an Englishman, who had previously been stationed at Armagh, and seems to have been a rather unsatisfactory recruit. See Haire, pp 95-6. He was now stationed at Waterford where Elizabeth found him 'simple and childlike' (13 November 1769) However, having encountered him again in Limerick the following year, she was to be rather more critical of his behaviour. In a letter written after his departure, she warned him against 'this idol, self', and 'everything that looked like self-confidence, self-esteem, pride, or foppery.' She had evidently other reservations about his conduct, as she continued, 'I had some objections to you in respect of these, when you were here, but having said so much to you then about other things, I was afraid were I to add these, you would think me too severe, but finding since that others take notice of the same, I have been troubled that I did not speak, as I know you will receive it from me in love.' Elizabeth Bennis, Limerick, to Hugh Saunderson, 4 December 1771, LXXII, *Christian correspondence*.

16. Passage East, a small fishing village and ancient port, about ten miles from Waterford.

17. Methodist societies were grouped into circuits or rounds. There were seven in Ireland: Dublin, Waterford, Cork, Limerick, Castlebar, Athlone and the North.

18. This is the second of just three reference in the journal to Elizabeth's sister, Alice Patten. See also entries for 30 June 1749 and 6 January 1779.

19. John Christian was a Waterford man. Currently a class leader, he was appointed an itinerant preacher in 1772, but retired after a few years, 'owing probably to the Calvinism which tinged his religious opinions'. *History*, I, p 238. In her correspondence with him, Elizabeth took issue with him on his differences with Wesley, accusing him of conceit and lack of commitment. Elizabeth Bennis, Limerick, to John Christian, 29 March 1772, LXXIV, *Christian correspondence*. See also Elizabeth Bennis, Limerick, to John Christian, 20 October 1771 and Elizabeth Bennis, Limerick, to John Christian, 22 October 1772, LXXIII and LXXV, *Christian correspondence*.

20. Perhaps Captain Taylor.

21. Possibly John Christian. In 1772 Elizabeth cautioned him that 'as your thoughts in some respects differ from Mr Wesley's, you may be apt to promulge [sic] your own opinions rather than his ... I do not see

how you can find your mind clear to require or accept a travelling station among the Methodists, while you hold any opinions contrary to our professed doctrines, neither can I see how Mr Wesley will be justifiable in sending you forth under such circumstances; and as I must act according to my conscience, I have told him so.' Elizabeth Bennis to John Christian, Limerick, 29 March 1772, LXXIV, *Christian correspondence*.

22. 'Man shall not live by bread alone, but by every word that proceedeth out of the mouth of God.' Matthew 4: 4.

23. See also 1, 13, and 19 December 1769 on fears of an approaching 'trial'.

1770

1. Alice Patten, Elizabeth's sister never married, and Mitchell does not appear to have had any brothers, so 'my brother-in-law' may have been the husband of Mitchell's sister, Frances.

2. Elizabeth was probably reading Mrs Lefevre's *Letters upon sacred subjects*. Mrs Lefevre (c 1723-1756) was a prominent member of John Wesley's congregation at the Foundry in London, described by Charles Wesley in a valedictory tribute as 'darling of every heart that knew thy short-lived excellence', and her *Letters* were published posthumously in 1757. See note 13, Wesley's letters: 1755, http://wesley.nnu.edu/john_wesley/letters/

3. The 'one in this town' whom Elizabeth undertook to meet in spirit at Holy Communion may have been John Stretton, who must at this time have been on the point of emigration. His first letter to her from Newfoundland later in this year reported his 'safe landing' there and expressed gratitude for 'your kindness to me in Waterford, and a thankful remembrance of the Christian admonitions you then pressed on me.' John Stretton, Carbonear, Newfoundland, to Elizabeth Bennis, 29 October 1770, LXXXVIII, *Christian correspondence*. John Stretton (fl 1740-1810) was born in Limerick and was reportedly converted by Elizabeth. In 1770 he emigrated to Newfoundland, settling in Carbonear and later in Harbour Grace. He promoted Methodism in Newfoundland in the face of numerous difficulties for many years, and in 1788 funded the building of the first chapel in Harbour Grace. In later life his mission was disrupted for a time by his fondness for 'strong drink', but he defeated this addiction to resume his leadership role, and following his death his friends bore 'his body … to the grave with songs of Christian triumph'. *Encyclopedia of Newfoundland and Labrador*, http://enl.cuff.com/

4. Writing to Wesley a few days later, Elizabeth reported that 'the people here go on at a poor rate, nor do I think it likely to be otherwise until they have a stationed preacher; they desired me to mention this.' Elizabeth Bennis, Waterford, to John Wesley, 20 May 1770, XVI, *Christian correspondence*.

5. Probably Elizabeth, her youngest child, then aged five.

6. This was the first child of Eleanor and Jonas Bull, and Elizabeth's first grandchild.

7. This was probably John Wesley's letter dated 12 April, which may have been forwarded from Limerick, and in which he enquires about the progress of 'the work of God' there, as well as the state of Elizabeth's own soul. John Wesley, Whitehaven, to Elizabeth Bennis, 12 April 1770, XV, *Christian correspondence*.

8. 'I have got myself bolstered up in bed, to write a last farewell to my dear, dear Sister Bennis ... My last love, my last admonition to the society in Limerick; they have been dear to me; they have my last feeble prayers.' Dillon died four hours after writing this letter. John Dillon, Dublin, to Elizabeth Bennis, May 1770, LXXI, *Christian correspondence*.

9. This individual is subsequently identified (see entry for 20 May 1771) as John Swift, described as 'the happiest soul, though the greatest enthusiast I ever saw'. See also entry for 25 May 1771.

10. This 'matrimonial affair' did result in a marriage: a few weeks later Elizabeth reported that 'Sister Ann S- is lately married to brother L- of Clonmel. Brother Bourke and I made up the match, and I think it is the Lord's doing; she is as usual all alive to God, and I trust will be a means of saving his soul.' Elizabeth Bennis, Limerick, to John Wesley, 8 July 1770, XVIII, *Christian correspondence*. Shortly afterwards, John Wesley expressed the hope that sister L- 'will be made a blessing to the few' in Clonmel. John Wesley, Ashby, to Elizabeth Bennis, 27 July 1770, XIX, *Christian correspondence*.

11. Writing to Wesley a few weeks previously, Elizabeth reported that the select band in Limerick 'meet regular, and a few have been lately added to it; they meet openly and freely, but mostly in a complaining state'. Elizabeth Bennis, Waterford, to John Wesley, 20 May 1770, XVI, *Christian correspondence*.

12. Given subsequent entries for this period (see 8, 11, 22, 25 July and 18, 25 August 1770), it seems probable that the 'one I love' was Elizabeth's husband, and that her misgivings arose from 'an affair which I see will be the ruin of him and his family'.

13. In this letter, Wesley attempted to brush aside Elizabeth's scruples, but also made clear his growing dependence on her judgement, acquiescing with her interventions in the affairs of the societies at Waterford and Clonmel. 'If the preachers on Waterford circuit had punctually adhered to the plan which I fixed, the horse [for the preacher] would have been no burden; but the misfortune is, every dunce is wiser than me: however, at your desire I will send a second preacher into the circuit after Conference; but the preachers must change regularly ... Your alteration of the circuit, so as to take in poor dead Clonmel, I much approve.' John Wesley, Ashby, to Elizabeth Bennis, 7 July 1770, XIX, *Christian correspondence*.

14. See entry for 4 September 1770, in which Elizabeth details losses of £650 and £1,500.

15. 'My youngest child' was Elizabeth. Despite Elizabeth's hopes for an early improvement, this apparently proved to be a serious and protracted illness: see entries for 7, 19, 25 September, 10 November, 17 December 1770.

16. There are no entries between 7 and 19 September 1770.

17. The report of the child's recovery was a postscript to the main entry for 25 September.

18. There are no entries between 10 November and 17 December 1770.

1771

1. See entry for 24 January 1770.

2. These 'trials' evidently involved Elizabeth's husband: see entries for 28 February and for 17 April 1771, which may indicate a resolution of these problems.

3. Wesley arrived in Ireland on 24 March 1771, and reached Waterford on Thursday, 25 April. He preached several times, and on Sunday, 28 April attended the cathedral, where a young man attacked the Methodists as 'grievous wolves'. According to Wesley, however, this simply encouraged many more to come and hear him preach. Also during this visit he 'laboured to calm the minds of some that had separated from their brethren; but it was labour lost'. He left Waterford on Monday, 29 April. Wesley, *Journal*.

4. 'The day you left town', Elizabeth reported to Wesley, 'I met the women's bands; the Lord did wonderfully bless us together, and I find my heart closely united to them.' However, 'last Monday I went to the room, but none of them came.' Elizabeth Bennis, Waterford, to John Wesley, 7 May 1771, XX, *Christian correspondence*. In response, Wesley directed her to intensify her efforts: 'If your sisters miss you any more, there is but one way – you must go or send after them.' John Wesley, Limerick, to Elizabeth Bennis, 15 May 1771, XXI, *Christian correspondence*.

5. This is a variant of Jesus' dismissal of the woman taken in adultery: John 6:11.

6. This may have been Robert Tegart, with whom Elizabeth had become acquainted during her second visit to Waterford the previous year. Tegart was apparently a 'backslider' from Methodism, alternating, as Elizabeth confided to Wesley, 'between conviction and carelessness', and involving himself with undesirable company. Elizabeth Bennis, Waterford, to John Wesley, 7 July 1771, XXII, *Christian correspondence* and John Wesley, Dublin, to Elizabeth Bennis, 20 July 1771, ms correspondence. St George's Church Archives.

7. Wesley took this opportunity of urging Elizabeth on in her labours in Waterford: 'Be not idle, neither give way to voluntary humility. You were not sent to Waterford for nothing, but to "strengthen the things

that remain".' John Wesley, Limerick, to Elizabeth Bennis, 15 May 1771, XXI, *Christian correspondence*.

8. The enthusiasm which gripped believers was sometimes regarded as a precursor or a manifestation of mental instability. William Pargeter, for instance, believed that 'the doctrines of the Methodists have a greater tendency than those of any other sect, to produce the most deplorable effects on the human understanding', and adduced a number of case histories in support of his thesis. John Wesley himself took an interest in the treatment of illness, both physical and mental, suggesting remedies for hysteric disorders, lunacy and 'raging madness', and regarding disease of any kind as a consequence of man's rebellion against God: 'The seeds of weakness and pain, of sickness and death, are now lodged in our inmost substance, whence a thousand disorders continually spring.' Allan Ingram ed, *Patterns of madness in the eighteenth century: a reader*, 1998, pp 98-100, 179-182.

9. The preacher on this occasion may have been John Christian: writing to Wesley a few weeks later, Elizabeth reported that 'Mr Newall paid one visit to the city and Mr Bredin three; in the interim brother Christian acts as usual ... I have heard some object to his opinions, but I think his manner of managing them is such that they do no hurt, to him or the people.' Elizabeth Bennis, Waterford, to John Wesley, 7 July 1771, XXII, *Christian correspondence*. In the subsequent debate on the subject of Christian perfection, reproduced, at some length and apparently verbatim, in the journal, Elizabeth emerges as an able and confident controversialist, countering the preacher's contention that 'we must always be committing sin' with the argument that, while 'we have need of the continual application of [Christ's] blood for our momently defects ... surely the Lord ... does not accuse his children for what they cannot help, or charge that as sin upon them which he knows is their infirmity?' 'For instance', she went on, indicating the six-year old Elizabeth and drawing on her own experience as a parent, 'that little child of mine is guilty of many childish errors which in the strictest sense might be called a breach of that duty due from a child to a parent, but I look upon these as a natural consequence of her childhood. Therefore, they do not alter the case between she and me, and I think the comparison will hold.' Dismissing the preacher's declared concern that 'believers should think to stand in their own righteousness and not in the righteousness of Christ' she pointed out that 'we are speaking of believers in Christ, who look for their all in him, and I never met with any who ever had the least thought of seeking any perfection of grace in themselves, or of finding it out of Christ.' Having dealt with the theological issue, she went on to rebuke her opponent for undermining the confidence of believers, concluding by stating the Wesleyan case and questioning his right, in holding such views, to put himself forward as one of Wesley's preachers: 'Christ is the believer's refuge, and we need not suppose what is not, nor ever will be, because Christ ever liveth to make inter-

cession for us. This is, I think, scripture doctrine, and the doctrine Mr Wesley preaches, and I think it is not honest to be in connection with him and to preach any other, because it is in fact, under the character of a friend, pulling down what he is building up.'

10. See entry for 23 June 1749.

11. Before leaving Waterford, Elizabeth sent Wesley a resume of the situation there, in which she reported on the visits of preachers to the city, the theological views of brother C[hristian] and the condition of Mr T[egart]; also, 'I meet the women's bands regularly, and we generally have a happy hour.' Elizabeth Bennis, Waterford, to John Wesley, 7 July 1771, XXII, *Christian correspondence.*

12. 'Go thy way, sell whatsoever thou hast, and give to the poor, and thou shalt have treasure in heaven: and come, take up the cross and follow me.' Mark 10: 21.

13. See Daniel 3: 8-30.

14. Elizabeth's complaint reflects the growth of Limerick as a centre of politics, business and fashion. By 1771 this process was well under way, epitomised by the development, from the 1750s, of Newtown Pery, the building of a new bridge and the completion in 1767 of the new Custom House. A theatre and an Assembly House opened in 1770.

15. This letter makes clear Wesley's growing dependence on Elizabeth: 'I am in great hopes ... IC will be useful as a travelling preacher; so would JM, if he had courage to break through ... Encourage him. I wish you would lend Mrs Dawson the Appeals ... Be not shy towards brother Collins; he is an upright man. Sister L is already doing good in Clonmel; do you correspond with her?' John Wesley, Rye, to Elizabeth Bennis, XXV, *Christian correspondence.* In a subsequent letter, Wesley urged Elizabeth to encourage brother Collins to greater effort: 'Thrust him out to visit the whole society (not only those that can give him meat and drink), from house to house, according to the plan laid down in the minutes of conference.' John Wesley, Canterbury, to Elizabeth Bennis, 3 December 1771, *XXVII, Christian correspondence.* William Collins entered the itinerancy in 1767 and spent two years in the north of Ireland. He withdrew from the itinerancy in 1770, but re-entered in the following year. From 1773 he worked on English circuits. He died in 1797. Biographical index.

16. A few weeks before, Elizabeth had reported 'an increase of sixteen to the society' during Jonathan Hern's term in the city. However, the society was clearly short of funds, since Hern's wife, 'finding the affairs of the society much embarrassed, refused the usual subsistence, and supported herself and children by working at her trade while here, though she had a young child at the breast ... We are rather cast down', Elizabeth continued, 'by having another married preacher, with a young family, sent to us, before we could recruit our finances; we now owe a heavy debt, and the weekly collections are not equal to the weekly expenses; the bulk of the society are poor, so that the weight lies on a

few.' Elizabeth Bennis, Limerick, to John Wesley, 15 October 1771, XXIV, *Christian correspondence*. Jonathan Hern became an itinerant preacher in 1769. Evidently a man of some education, he served in Ireland until 1780, after which he was appointed to English circuits. In 1791 he was expelled by Conference for drunkenness. Biographical index.

1772

1. This is presumably the brother-in-law whose conversion Elizabeth recorded on 2 May 1770.

2. Perhaps Robert Tegart. On the following day, 29 January, Elizabeth wrote to him to assure him that 'the Lord is willing to pardon all that is past ... Let the sense of such love break your heart, and resolve by his grace to cleave to him while you live.' Elizabeth Bennis, Limerick, to Robert Tegart, 29 January 1772, LXXIX, *Christian correspondence*.

3. These were perhaps the houses adjoining the Market House in Mungret Lane which Mitchell Bennis had acquired in 1761, and which were at that time in a poor state of repair. Levistone Cooney, Introduction, p 18.

4. There are a number of pages missing at this point. The surviving journal resumes in May 1772.

5. Identified in a note in the margin as Henry, Elizabeth's younger son.

6. The 'particular affair' may be a quarrel within the society initiated by the activities of James Deaves. Deaves, who had been stationed preacher at Limerick in 1767-68, was now apparently involved in a dispute with the preachers James Hudson and John Goodwin. Elizabeth's letter of 26 May to John Wesley is largely concerned with this 'discord', and shows her acting as confidante of and advisor to the preachers: 'Indeed, as you say, I fear James D- is mad, but as partners in affliction is some consolation, Mr Goodwin has the satisfaction of seeing that his wrath is not confined to him only ... Both Mr Goodwin and Mr Hudson were grievously distressed after they came here, and seem determined to go home rather than continue in connection with him. As they opened their minds only to me, I advised them to write to you and to give you an exact account of the matter. Indeed, if Mr Hudson had not done so, I must have taken upon me to do it, for their trials affected me very much ... I this week saw a few lines from Mr D- to a friend in Limerick wherein he says he intends to visit his friends here soon ... I rather dread his coming. The Lord has been pleased for some time past to send us the sincere milk of the word, and it would be grievous to have any thing arise which would tend to abate the present fervour of spirit which prevails through the whole.' Elizabeth Bennis, Limerick, to John Wesley, 26 May 1772, ms correspondence, St George's Church Archives. The published version of this letter (Elizabeth Bennis, Limerick, to John Wesley, 26 May 1772, XXX, *Christian correspondence*) omits much detail of this affair.

John Goodwin (1739-1808) was born in Cheshire. Converted as a young man, he entered the itinerant ministry in 1768. He served mainly in England, but also spent time in Dublin. Biographical index. James Hudson was stationed preacher in Limerick 1770-71. Methodist Conference Ireland Minutes, p 11. James Deaves, described as 'a zealous young man', was received into the itinerancy in 1753. Despite his role in the controversy in Limerick, he was still connected with the society in 1777. He later lived in Waterford, where he had a difference of opinion, subsequently settled, with John Wesley about the tenancy of the chapel in Wexford, of which he was evidently a lessee. *History*, I, pp 98, 106, 133-134, 313, 391, 398, 455.

7. Possibly Mr Goodwin, 'whose preaching and deportment has gained him the hearts of all, and his manner of enforcing holiness makes it desirable even to its opposers.' Elizabeth Bennis, Limerick, to John Wesley, 26 May 1772, ms correspondence. St George's Church Archives. Mr Goodwin may also be the friend whose absence Elizabeth regretted in the entry of 29 May.

8. Possibly Wesley's letter of 16 June: 'I believe you are particularly called to be useful to those whom the riches or grandeur of this world keep at a distance from the pure word of God. When you are at Waterford, see that you be not idle there. You should gather up, and meet a band immediately. If you would also meet a class or two, it would be so much the better ... You did well to send me the last enclosure [about James Deaves] ... I have written to Limerick, if JD should go there in the same spirit wherein he has been for some time, to take care that he do not mischief.' John Wesley, Yarm, to Elizabeth Bennis, 16 June 1772, XXXI, *Christian correspondence*.

9. Thomas's master may have been Robert Tegart, to whom he was certainly apprenticed in late 1773: see Elizabeth Bennis, Limerick, to RT, 9 November 1773, LXXXI, *Christian correspondence*. The 'disagreeable circumstances' may have been Tegart's continued backsliding. See Elizabeth Bennis, Limerick, to RT, 22 November 1772, LXXX, *Christian correspondence*.

10. Elizabeth's intensified activity during this visit to Waterford may have been a response to Wesley's encouragement in his letter of 16 June (see note 8 above). At his suggestion, she met a band and a class there: 'We all speak with freedom. I love the people, and I believe they love me. There are three preachers on the circuit, and all have work enough.' Elizabeth Bennis, Waterford, to John Wesley, 8 August 1772, XXXII, *Christian correspondence*.

11. Neither the published nor the unpublished correspondence contains any letter answering this description.

12. Elizabeth's son, Thomas was also remaining in Waterford.

13. Perhaps Robert Tegart. See note 9 above.

14. See entry for 3 December 1772 for sequel to this encounter.

15. Elizabeth's concerns included the condition of Methodism in Limerick. On returning home, she had found the society there 'in a decline and in confusion. The sower of tares [James Deaves] has got amongst them'. Elizabeth Bennis, Limerick, to John Wesley, 18 October 1772, XXXIV, *Christian correspondence*. Wesley's response revealed his confidence in her judgement and leadership abilities: 'Why this want of discipline in Limerick? Whenever this is dropped, all is confusion. See that it be immediately restored. Captain Webb is now in Dublin; invite him to visit Limerick … Speak a little to as many as you can; go among them – to their houses: speak in love and discord will vanish … Whom do you think proper to succeed the present preachers at Limerick and Waterford?' John Wesley, Colchester, to Elizabeth Bennis, 3 November 1772.

Captain Thomas Webb (1725-1796), possibly Irish-born, was a former army officer. Converted in 1765, he became a local preacher, described by John Wesley as 'a man of fire'. He subsequently emigrated to North America, where he played an important part in the introduction of Methodism to the continent, most notably in New York and Philadelphia, where he helped to establish St George's Church. *History* I, p 264, and *Dictionary*.

16. Writing to Wesley on 1 December, Elizabeth reported: 'Our society is once more re-adjusted; we all seem to be in love and in earnest. Captain Webb's visit has proved a blessing: our house was not large enough for the congregations … If we could now have a succession of strange preachers from the neighbouring circuits, perhaps poor Limerick might once more raise its head.' Elizabeth Bennis, Limerick, to John Wesley, 1 December 1772, XXXVI, *Christian correspondence*. Wesley responded favourably: 'The plan you mention is preferable to any which I have heard proposed.' John Wesley, Shoreham, to Elizabeth Bennis, 16 December 1772, ms correspondence, St George's Church Archives.

17. This letter is included in Elizabeth's published correspondence: see Elizabeth Bennis, Limerick, to Mr --, 3 December -, CXII, *Christian correspondence*. The recipient is not identified.

18. Elizabeth is referring to the parables of the prodigal son and of the lost sheep, Luke 15:11-32 and 3-7.

1773

1. See entry for 18 January 1772.

2. See entry for 16 October 1765, in which Elizabeth describes her first encounter with Methodism on 17 March 1749. The 'messenger' was Robert Swindells.

3. Wesley arrived in Dublin on Friday, 26 March. He was in Waterford in late April, where one of his meetings ended in a melee, during which John Christian was injured, and reached Limerick on Wednesday, 5 May. Wesley, *Journal* and Haire, pp 113-114.

4. In this letter Wesley urged Elizabeth on to greater effort on Methodism's behalf: 'I fear you are too idle ... Up and be doing! Do not loiter; see that your talent rust not; rather let it gain ten more, and it will, if you use it.' John Wesley, Dublin, to Elizabeth Bennis, 1 April 1773, XLI, *Christian correspondence*.

5. This 'friend' was possibly Jonathan Hern, who had been stationed in Limerick in 1771, but who had in the interim evidently fallen away from the movement. In a recent letter to him, Elizabeth had expressed her joy that 'God ... has made you a witness of that truth which you have so often and so vehemently contradicted and fought against'. Hern's reply, dated 10 April, included an account of his 'backslidings' and change of heart. Elizabeth Bennis, Limerick, to Jonathan Hern, 27 March 1773, and Jonathan Hern, Cork, to Elizabeth Bennis, 10 April 1773, LXXXII and LXXXIII, *Christian correspondence*.

6. On his arrival in Limerick, Wesley, 'as in time past', found 'a settled serious people, but in danger of sinking into formality.' On 6 May he travelled to Ballingrane and Newmarket, returning to Limerick on the following day. After the morning preaching on Monday, 10 May he met the select society: 'all of these once experienced salvation from sin; some enjoy it still; but the greater part are, more or less, shorn of their strength', though 'not without hope of recovering it.' Wesley, *Journal*.

7. On Wednesday, 12 May, 'I took my leave of this affectionate people, and in the evening preached at Clare.' Wesley, *Journal*.

8. See entry for 16 October 1765. The 'covenant' was the one which Elizabeth took from Joseph Alleine's *Alarm to the unconverted*. This event preceded her conversion to Methodism: she would have been nineteen years old at the time.

9. From Isaac Watts, 'What shall I render to my God', a paraphrase of Psalm 116, part II. *Psalms imitated in the language of the New Testament*, 1719.

10. Thomas and Eleanor.

11. Elizabeth subsequently wrote to RT (Robert Tegart) to protest against his continuing in sin, and to urge him to change his ways, not least because of his influence on 'a youth in the dawn of life, just now susceptible of either good or ill impressions, committed to your care'. The latter is identified in a footnote as Elizabeth's son, Thomas, 'then apprentice to Mr T-.' Elizabeth Bennis, Limerick to RT, 9 November 1773, LXXXI, *Christian correspondence*.

12. The reference is to Job 1: 14-19.

13. Elizabeth wrote to Wesley on this day, firstly to report on the thriving state of the Limerick society, and secondly to ask his guidance regarding the 'disappointments in temporals with which I am now surrounded.' However, these 'disappointments' seem not to have impacted too severely on the Bennis family's prosperity, since later that year Elizabeth expressed thankfulness that 'the Lord has blessed my husband's industry far above our expectations, and has given me both the necessaries and conveniencies of life.' Elizabeth Bennis to John Wesley,

25 August 1773, ms correspondence, St George's Church Archives, and Elizabeth Bennis, Limerick, to John Wesley, 11 November 1773, XLIV, *Christian correspondence.*
14. Elizabeth was now in Waterford.

1774
1. On arriving in Waterford in December 1773, Elizabeth found 'the people ... very dead and do not meet'. In her next letter to Wesley she elaborated on the problems there: 'by the frequent neglect of preaching, and the almost total neglect of discipline, the people are scattered; and of the few that remain, some are grieved, and some offended, with this new method of preaching salvation by works.' Moreover, 'Mr Hawksworth, a Calvinist preacher under Lady Huntingdon, has come here, and preaches regularly at Methodist hours ... Our people, though forbid by the preachers, go almost constantly to hear him.' Elizabeth had spoken to several, 'but with little effect', and visited Hawksworth to remonstrate with him. In response, Wesley urged Elizabeth to greater activity: 'Do you go on; bear up the hands that hang down; by faith and prayer support the tottering knee; reprove, encourage ... Storm the throne of grace, and persevere therein, and mercy will come down.' Elizabeth Bennis, Waterford, to John Wesley, 29 December 1773, XLVI, *Christian correspondence*; Elizabeth Bennis, Waterford, to John Wesley, 10 February 1774, XLVIII, ibid; John Wesley, London, to Elizabeth Bennis, 1 March 1774, XLIX, ibid.
2. On Eleanor's unhappy marriage, see entry for 8 September 1772. On Elizabeth's concerns for Thomas, see entry for 9 August 1773.
3. See entry for 24 January 1770, in which Elizabeth records her husband's accident on his way back to Limerick from Waterford.
4. See entry for 16 October 1765.
5. See also references to this dispute in entries for 3, 10, 17 April 1774. Elizabeth's correspondence with Wesley casts further light on the matter: 'I found, when I came here ... the preacher and people by the ears, divided into parties, and some turned out of the way, for the most trifling matter that can be conceived ... Matters here wear a gloomy aspect ... and in the present situation, much depends on the person who may succeed Mr W.' This dispute was apparently between Mr W and some of 'the young men', whom he had threatened to put out of the society for some unspecified fault. Again, Wesley deputed Elizabeth 'to make peace. 'Go on, and prosper.' Elizabeth Bennis, Limerick, to John Wesley, 12 April 1774, L, *Christian correspondence*; John Wesley, Leeds, to Elizabeth Bennis, 2 May 1774, LI, ibid. The preacher in question was probably Francis Wrigley (1746-1824), who entered the itinerancy in 1769, and who was described in his Conference obituary as a strict enforcer of Methodist discipline. Biographical Index. In a letter to John Wesley, not included in the published correspondence, Elizabeth disclaimed any prejudice against Wrigley before meeting him. However,

'that his own behaviour did afterward prejudice me against him, I do not deny.' Elizabeth Bennis to John Wesley, 30 September 1774, ms correspondence, St George's Church Archive.

6. Easter Day fell on 3 April in 1774.

7. This was probably Jonathan Hern, who was stationed preacher in Limerick 1773-74.

8. See entry for 23 June 1749.

9. The school at Kingswood, near Bristol, was founded by John Wesley in 1748. In 1768 he described it as a boarding establishment for children, who entered between the ages of six and twelve, 'in order to be taught reading, writing, arithmetic, English, French, Latin, Greek, Hebrew, History, Geography, chronology, rhetoric, logic, ethics, geometry, algebra, physics, music.' In addition to this curriculum, 'it is our particular desire that all who are educated here may be brought up in the fear of God, and at the utmost distance as from vice in general, so in particular from idleness and effeminancy.' John Wesley, *A short account of the school in Kingswood,* 1768, pp 1, 3, 7.

Elizabeth was far from being alone in her distrust of lawyers: on this topic, see Toby Barnard, *A new anatomy of Ireland: the Irish Protestants, 1649-1770,* Yale University Press, 2003, pp 121-126.

10. This may refer to the changeover of preachers. Preachers' appointments ran for a year, beginning in July. Jonathan Hern was replaced by Michael McDonald as stationed preacher in Limerick in mid-1774.

11. Writing to Mitchell Bennis, presumably in response to a letter of his, on 13 September 1774, Wesley informed him that 'the price for the schooling, board and everything except clothes of a child at Kingswood is sixteen pounds a year. We have now as many children as I designed to take at once, but I cannot refuse one of yours. Therefore ... I will speak to the Master concerning him, and I apprehend the sooner he is here the better.' John Wesley, Bristol, to Mr Bennis (but addressed to Mrs Elizabeth Bennis), 13 September 1774. Drew University Methodist Collection, www.atla.com / digitalresouces /

12. Replying to Wesley's letter confirming Henry's admission to Kingswood, Elizabeth wrote that her husband, 'as soon as he can settle some affairs which is likely to take up three weeks ... intends going with him to Waterford and shipping him from thence ... The child's heart is so set upon it, that he is even impatient to be gone.' Elizabeth Bennis to John Wesley, 30 September 1774, ms correspondence, St George's Church Archives.

13. A few days earlier, Elizabeth wrote to Wesley to inform him of her son's safe arrival at Kingswood and to report that 'the work of God goes on blessedly here under Mr Snowden and Mr McDonnel ... The Lord is also at work in Waterford, and in most of our country societies.' Elizabeth Bennis, Limerick, to John Wesley, 24 December 1774, LIII, *Christian correspondence.* George Snowden (1737-1812) entered the itinerancy in 1769, and spent the first fifteen years of his ministry in

Ireland. Biographical index. Michael McDonald was currently stationed preacher in Limerick: see note 10 above.

1775

1. Elizabeth mentions a number of 'trials' at this period. However, the
one referred to here may be the news of her daughter's 'sufferings ...
from an unkind husband': see entry for 10 February 1775.
2. This may refer to the activities of Calvinistic preachers belonging to
Lady Huntingdon's Connexion. Elizabeth had encountered one of
them, Mr Hawkesworth, during a visit to Waterford in the previous
year, and had expressed her concern to Wesley about the situation.
History, I, pp 283-4.
3. There are no journal entries between 3 and 27 March 1775.
4. The 'dear Christian friend and preacher of the gospel' was Michael
McDonald, the stationed preacher at Limerick, who, 'having taken ill of
fever, while delirious in the absence of his nurse, jumped out of the
window of his room into the yard at the rere of the preaching house,
and died in half-an-hour.' *History*, I, p 295.
5. John Wesley landed at Dún Laoghaire on 2 April, and on 10 April
began his 'tour through the kingdom', reaching Limerick on
Wednesday, 10 May. On Saturday he preached in the yard of the
Custom House to 'a large congregation of papists and protestants', and
on Wednesday 17 May he 'examined the society at Limerick, containing
now an hundred and one persons, seven less than they were two years
ago', and found the members 'want zeal; they are not fervent in spirit;
therefore, they cannot increase'. Wesley, *Journal*; Haire, p 124.
6. Wesley set off from Limerick for Galway on 17 May 1775. Ibid.
7. The journal for 1775 ends at this point. The following two pages are
missing, perhaps deliberately removed. The first few months of 1775
were particularly difficult ones for Elizabeth: her 'trials' during this period
included robbery with violence, the death of a young relative, her
daughter's unhappy marriage and impending confinement, threats to
her 'earthly advantage', problems in the Methodist society, including
the suicide of 'a dear Christian friend and preacher', and her own ill-
health. Little of her correspondence for this year survives. However,
John Bristol, writing to her towards the end of the year, sympathised
with her in her trials, 'yet', he went on, 'you have not one too many, for
God does all things well, and you may greatly comfort yourself by firmly
believing, that all things shall work together for good to them that love
God.' John Bristol, Bally Moore, to Elizabeth Bennis, 18 October 1775,
LXXXIV, *Christian correspondence*.

1776

1. This entry is undated, either because it was begun on the previous
(missing) page, or because Elizabeth, returning to the journal after an
absence of 'some months', forgot to insert the date.

2. See entry for 24 January 1770.

3. Elizabeth is referring to the criticism of the church at Laodicea by St John the Divine: see note 1, 1760.

4. See entry for 16 October 1765.

5. Easter fell on 7 April 1776.

6. A note in the margin identifies this friend as Mrs Hoesy or Hosey.

7. See entry for 23 May 1763, describing the experience of the previous day, Whitsunday.

8. This is the anniversary of the day in 1749 'when, conversing with the preacher about the state of my soul, the light broke in upon me in a moment and banished all the shades of darkness'. See entry for 16 October 1765.

9. From Isaac Watts, 'Long as I live I'll bless thy name', a paraphrase of psalm 145, part I. *Psalms and hymns*, no 262, www.ccel.org/ccel/watts/psalmshymns

10. Samuel Bradburn (1751-1816), who had joined the itinerant ministry in 1774, was stationed preacher at Limerick in 1776. A friend of Wesley and a powerful preacher, Bradburn pursued a successful ministry in Ireland and England for many years, and served as president of Conference in 1799. *Dictionary* and Biographical index. According to Crookshank, Bradburn on his arrival in Limerick attracted 'amazing congregations'. He preached fifty-seven times during the following month. On 29 September he conducted a watch-night service, 'and preached, prayed, and sang four hours without intermission.' However, his health gave way under this overwork, and he was moved to Dublin in early 1777, where he had 'less to do than in Limerick' and where he was able to recuperate. *History*, I, pp 306, 309. Bradburn is probably the 'dear friend' whose departure is noted on 21 January 1777.

11. The 'dear friend under temptations' may be Bradburn. In the following year he certainly sought and received Elizabeth's opinion on a number of theological points. See Samuel Bradburn, Dublin, to Elizabeth Bennis, 14 June 1777 and Elizabeth Bennis, Limerick, to Samuel Bradburn, 22 June 1777, LXXXVI and LXXXVII, *Christian correspondence*.

12. See entry for 8 September 1772, in which Eleanor's 'trials from an unkind husband' are first revealed.

13. Friday, 13 December, Wesley commented, 'was the national fast ... observed ... throughout the nation, with the utmost solemnity.' Wesley, *Journal*. The rector of Weston Longeville in rural Norfolk similarly noted the event, and the reason for it: 'This day being appointed a fast on our Majesty's arms against the rebel Americans, I went to church this morning and read the prayers appointed for the same.' James Woodforde, *The diary of a country parson, 1758-1802*, ed John Beresford, OUP, 1978, 13 December 1776.

1777

1. The text is Ephesians 6:13.

2. See entry for 24 January 1770.

3. 'My friend' is possibly Bradburn: in a subsequent letter to him, Elizabeth rebuked him for over-scrupulousness and intolerance: 'I hope my dear friend's mind is not puzzled about these matters ... though I should be apt to think it was but justice, for your severity towards those who hold these opinions, which I often thought you carried too far.' Elizabeth Bennis, Limerick, to Samuel Bradburn, 22 June 1777, LXXXVII, *Christian correspondence.*

4. See entry for 16 October 1765.

5. These 'blessed opportunities' presumably included leisure for correspondence: on this day Elizabeth wrote a long letter of comfort and encouragement to John Stretton in Harbour Grace, Newfoundland. Elizabeth Bennis, Limerick, to John Stretton, 22 March 1777, XCV, *Christian correspondence.*

6. 'This is a faithful saying, and these things I will that thou affirm constantly, that they which have believed in God might be careful to maintain good works. These things are good and profitable unto men.' Titus 3: 8.

7. This entry, as well as subsequent ones for 14 and 17 May, seems to indicate some serious wrongdoing or failure on Mitchell Bennis's part, with repercussions extending into June and July 1777.

8. Henry would not have been home since his departure for Kingswood in November 1774: the rules of the school specified that parents should not remove their child, 'no, not a day, till they take him for good and all'. See also entries for 3 September, in which Henry arrives home, 'a poor, starved, dejected figure', and 21 and 28 November, on Elizabeth's correspondence with the 'masters' at Kingswood on the treatment which he had received there. The timetable at Kingswood was certainly spartan: pupils rose at four, began school at seven and finished at five o'clock, before private prayer, supper and the public service, going to bed at eight. There were 'no play-days (the school being taught every day in the year but Sunday), so neither do we allow any time for play on any day. He that plays when he is a child will play when he is a man.' *A short account of the school at Kingswood*, pp 3-4. Wesley himself was well aware of the school's shortcomings, complaining in 1783 that 'at present the school does not in anywise answer the design of the institution, either with regard to religion or learning'. John Wesley, *Remarks on the state of Kingswood School*, 1783.

9. This friend is identified in the margin as Mrs Mason. This may be the 'sister Knight, who lives near Birr... a widow ... and ... a gracious woman', who married 'brother Mason' in 1774. Elizabeth Bennis to John Wesley, 30 September 1774, ms correspondence, St George's Church Archives. There is no reference to the death of Mrs Mason in the records of St Mary's Cathedral. Noreen Ellerker, archivist, to editor, 30 June 2006. Thomas Mason is listed as one of the trustees of the Limerick Methodist society in 1764. Levistone Cooney, Introduction, p 16.

10. This seems to refer to Eleanor's unhappy marriage rather than to her recent illness.

1778

1. There are no entries between 4 January and 22 February 1778.

2. See entry for 16 October 1765.

3. John Wesley had landed at Dublin on 1 April. He reached Limerick on Monday, 4 May, and found that 'poor and rich, protestants and papists, flocked together' to his sermons. After travelling to Newmarket and Ballingrane, he returned to Limerick on 8 May, and on Sunday, 10 May 'examined the society', finding them 'much alive to God' and more 'loving' than he had ever found them before. He preached his final sermon of the visit that afternoon, and left immediately afterwards. John Wesley, *Journal* and Haire, pp 13–136. Henry's defection from Kingswood and Elizabeth's irate correspondence with the authorities there had evidently not marred her relationship with Wesley. Although no letters between them survive after 1776, John Stretton clearly believed her to retain considerable influence with him in later years. John Stretton, Harbour Grace, to Elizabeth Bennis, 29 June 1785, CI, *Christian correspondence.*

4. Elizabeth may have mistaken the date. Wesley himself records that he left Limerick on 10 May 1778.

5. 'My son's shop' may have been the hardware business 'near the Exchange' of which Thomas was recorded proprietor in 1782. Levistone Cooney, Introduction, p 20.

6. There are no entries between 13 September and 1 November 1778.

7. The following page is badly torn. The next entry, which is only partially legible, refers to Elizabeth's first meeting with her class since the illness mentioned on 1 November.

8. Part of the next page is missing, and the remainder of the entry for 5 December and most of that for 22 December is missing.

1779

1. See note 6, 1764.

2. The journal ends at this point.

Index